Praise for *In*

"*Into the Kill Zone* is unlike anything else in print. It is a must-read for anyone interested in the ofttimes violent world of law enforcement."
—Robert D. Keppel, Ph.D., author,
The Riverman and *Signature Killers*

"Written by a former police officer turned criminologist—himself once involved in a fatal shooting—*Into the Kill Zone* offers unique insights into the experiences of officers who have had to make split-second decisions about whether or not to use deadly force in the line of duty. Drawing on scores of firsthand accounts told by police officers, some of them still struggling to deal with the aftermath of shootings in which they have been involved, this gripping book will be of interest to a wide range of readers—from criminologists, social psychologists, and law-enforcement officers to sociolinguists, story analysts, and other human-ists concerned with narrative as a basic sense-making strategy."
—David Herman, professor of English,
North Carolina State University

"*Into the Kill Zone* is one compelling book. It takes the reader inside the hearts and minds of America's police officers as they face danger and grapple with the awesome power they possess to take human life."
—Gil Kerlikowske, chief of police,
Seattle Police Department

"This is a very special book. No one should presume to discuss police violence until they have read it and thought deeply about what it has to teach those of us who have been fortunate enough not to have faced the decision to use deadly force."
—Rodney Stark, professor of sociology,
University of Washington

"Nobody has ever before done what Klinger has accomplished in *Into the Kill Zone*. By presenting the most detailed and private thoughts of officers who have shot citizens, he has made a unique and major con-tribution to the literature on policing."
—James J. Fyfe, Ph.D.,
deputy commissioner of training,
New York Police Department

Into the Kill Zone

David Klinger

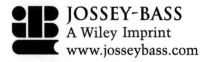 # Into the Kill Zone

A Cop's Eye View of Deadly Force

JOSSEY-BASS
A Wiley Imprint
www.josseybass.com

Published by Jossey-Bass
A Wiley Imprint
989 Market Street, San Francisco, CA 94103-1741   www.josseybass.com

Jossey-Bass books and products are available through most bookstores. To contact Jossey-Bass
directly call our Customer Care Department within the U.S. at 800-956-7739, outside the U.S. at
317-572-3986, or fax 317-572-4002.

Jossey-Bass also publishes its books in a variety of electronic formats. Some content that appears
in print may not be available in electronic books.

Library of Congress Cataloging-in-Publication Data

Klinger, David, date.
  Into the kill zone : a cop's eye view of deadly force / David
Klinger.— 1st ed.
     p. cm.
Includes bibliographical references.
  ISBN-13 978-0-7879-7375-9 (alk. paper)
  ISBN-10 0-7879-7375-0 (alk. paper)
  ISBN-13 978-0-7879-8603-2 (paperback)
  ISBN-10 0-7879-8603-8 (paperback)
  1. Police shootings—United States. 2. Police—United
States—Interviews. I. Title.
  HV8138.K56 2004
  363.2'32—dc22   2003023188

Printed in the United States of America
FIRST EDITION
PB Printing   10 9 8 7 6 5 4 3 2

Contents

For my beloved cousin Barry,
Who never made it back to tell his story.

For my beautiful bride, Sonia,
Whose loving-kindness helped me make peace with my visit.

And for our precious daughter, Carly.
May she never have to go there.

Acknowledgments

This book is the culmination of a journey that began many years ago when, as a young police officer in Los Angeles, I killed a man to save my partner's life. The journey would not have been successful without the help of numerous people over the years, so I take this space to thank them for their assistance.

My initial load of thanks goes to Bobby Hyde, John Spencer, Lyle Prideaux, and John Shaughnessy, my first two sets of training officers at the 77th Street Division of the LAPD. They put up with my naïveté, showed me the ropes, provided worthy counsel about many things, and most important, they gave me the skills to prevail on that warm night in July 1981 and in several other precarious situations during my tenure as a cop. Other senior officers who played key roles in my early police education include Billy Douglass, Steve Gross, Bob Rysdon, Ed Lindsey, and Nick MacArthur. I also had the pleasure of working for some top-notch supervisors: Joe Ramm, Howard Silverstein, Tim Anderson, and Jack Davenport chief among them. I thank all of these men, plus many other members of the LAPD—most notably, Frank Lipus, John Ix, Elmer Pelligrino, Ernie Haleck, and Ken Wiseman—for their kind support and for putting up with my rough edges in the wake of my visit to the kill zone. In a similar vein, thanks are in order to Steve Harris, Chuck Krieble, Ken Koenig, and the rest of the guys and gals I worked with at the Redmond PD as I wrestled with my experiences in the City of Angels.

I am quite grateful that I had many friends outside law enforcement who also provided support and encouragement in my time of need. Special thanks here go to Lauren Hanna, Andrea Merriman, Susan Bergstrom, Laurie Harris, Tommy Bartholomew, Marcel Moore, Greg Crum, Randy Kyte, Al George, Rob Wall, Casey Roberts, Pat and Al Robinson, Tom and Jane Falkenborg, Lu and Kim Gray, Bruce Wotherspoon, Kelly McAllister, the Shaw Family, Kathy Craig, Jeff Towery, Susan McWilliams, Rick Pearl, and Greg Mattingly.

Dick Bennett, Sandy Baxter, Jim Fyfe, and Ron Weiner at American University helped me shift gears from police work to academe. All four were wonderful teachers, friends, mentors, and advisers and have remained a presence in my professional and personal lives. A special thanks to Ron for suggesting the five-step interview process that I used in the study that led to this book. A special thanks to Jim for showing me how to bring an academic eye to the study of deadly force and for his friendship over the years.

George Bridges, Herb Costner, and Judy Howard at the University of Washington played especially large roles in getting me to the final step in my formal education. They taught me how to think like a sociologist, convinced me to broaden my research horizons, and helped me see how to develop the project that led to this book.

Jackie Hagan and Jan Chafetz at the University of Houston helped me turn my ofttimes turgid prose into readable text and thereby allowed me to secure the tenure I needed to undertake the project that resulted in this book. I also thank Nicky Parham and Alan Stoler, two students at U of H, for the assistance they provided as the project moved forward.

At the University of Missouri-St. Louis, I thank Jennifer Bursik for her input early on in the writing process and Richard Wright for his steadfast support throughout. It's always good to have quality people in one's corner. I also thank Laurie Mitchell and Jenna St. Cyr for the great job they did transcribing the hundreds of hours of tapes that I developed during the interviews I conducted.

A double thanks to Jenna for her input regarding the selection of some of the stories that appear in the book and for reading early drafts of material as I produced it. In this connection, I also thank Theresa Wall for reading the stories as I put them together and Cyn Morris, Callie Rennison, and Melody Martin for their suggestions on early drafts.

And last, but certainly not least where crafting this book is concerned, I thank Scott Hoffman, my agent at PMA Literary and Film Management, and Alan Rinzler, my editor at Jossey-Bass, for their diligent work in bringing it to print.

Thanks are also in order for Sam McQuade of the Rochester Institute of Technology and Robert Kaminski of the University of South Carolina. They both worked at the National Institute of Justice at the time I conducted the research that led to this book. I simply could not have conducted the research or written this book without their assistance. In this connection, I am obliged to point out that the research was funded as award number 97-IJ-CX-0029 from the Office of Justice Programs, National Institute of Justice, Department of Justice, and that the points of view in this book do not necessarily represent the official position of the U.S. Department of Justice.

Thanks also to the several men and women who helped me identify the initial group of officers that I interviewed to set the research in motion. Identifying them might compromise the identity of some of the officers I interviewed, so they will remain anonymous. You know who you are and I thank you profusely.

Profuse thanks also to each of the officers who so graciously gave their time and trust to me during the course of the research. This book quite literally could not have been written without you. So thanks from the bottom of my heart.

Finally, I thank my family for their unwavering support over the years: My big sister, Debbie, for being there when I needed her. My little sister, Judy, for never doubting I could do it. My mom, for innumerable acts of generosity and for never letting me know how worried she was until long after I left law enforcement. My dad, for letting me vent when I needed to. And most especially, my wife and daughter.

Sonia has been my partner for nearly two decades, encouraging me every step of the way, putting up with my foibles, and sustaining me through thick and thin. Carly has been the apple of my eye since she came into this world a dozen years ago, bringing joy to my heart every day and always reminding me what's important in life.

I thank you both for everything you've done to make this book possible.

Into the Kill Zone

Introduction

Edward Randolph was twenty-six years old when I killed him. I was twenty-three.

I first laid eyes on him less than a minute before I shot him, so I didn't know his name, how old he was, or anything else about him before I ended his life. I didn't even get a good look at his face before I pulled the trigger, and he died a few minutes after that. I was about fifteen feet away when his heart stopped, watching the paramedics tending to the wounds that I had inflicted moments before. They had all come from a single bullet that slammed into his left side just below his armpit, bored a hole through his left lung, nicked his aorta, and tunneled through his right lung before coming to a stop just under the flesh on the right side of his chest. He died on his back, naked, the paramedics having cut off his clothes to check his body for additional wounds. There were a few scrapes and contusions that he had suffered as my partner, four other officers, and I wrestled from him the butcher's knife that he frantically grasped in his right hand, rolled him onto his stomach, and handcuffed him. And there were a few more that he got when two of the other officers dragged him from the sidewalk where I had shot him to the shadow of a car that was parked

1

nearby. But his only serious injuries came from the bullet that I had pumped into his chest. As I watched the paramedics fighting a losing battle to save him from these wounds, his bladder released its acrid contents, sending an arc of urine toward his head. I knew that people often void their bladders upon death, so when I saw the stream tail off a few seconds later, I knew that Edward Randolph was dead. And that I had killed him.

When I first saw the man I was about to kill, he was standing across the street from me, by himself, seventy-five feet or so away. It was a few minutes after 10:30 P.M. on July 25, 1981, just four months after I had graduated from the Los Angeles Police Academy. My partner, Dennis Azevedo, and I were on the north side of Vernon Avenue, crouched behind a parked car, our pistols trained on a house where just minutes earlier an armed burglar had shot at the home owner.

That was where we'd deployed after responding to a call for assistance from the officers who'd been assigned the call. We'd been directed to meet a sergeant one block west of the house in question, and when we screeched to a halt there, he told us that the shooter was still inside, that other officers had already taken up positions on the east side of the house, and that we needed to secure its west side to keep the gunman from escaping into the night. He also told us that we needed to clear the south side of Vernon Avenue of the dozens of citizens who had gathered to watch yet another midsummer's night drama involving the cops and the crooks on the mean streets of South Central Los Angeles. As Dennis and I ran toward the house along the north side of Vernon, we shouted and motioned for the throng on the south side to clear the area, lest they get shot by the gunman whose escape we sought to prevent. As we ran east, the crowd ran west, and when they hit the first corner, they took a quick left out of the danger zone—all but the man who was about to die, that is. He never took a step.

As soon as the citizens started running, I turned my attention to the house that contained the gunman—I just assumed that all the spectators would flee once they understood the danger in the house across from them—so I didn't notice that one of them hadn't budged as Dennis and I moved along. We stopped in front of the house next to the one that contained the gunman, ducking down on the safe side of a white Cadillac that was parked in the driveway. After a few seconds, I caught a glimpse of a lone figure across the street in the corner of my right eye. I quickly glanced over my right shoulder. That's when I first saw him—just standing there, staring in our direction, with a gym bag hanging from his left shoulder. I yelled for him to leave the area. Then Dennis did. Then we both yelled some more. But the man didn't budge. He just stood there, staring at us.

We didn't know who he was or why he was standing there. Maybe he didn't speak English, I thought, so he couldn't understand what we wanted him to do. Maybe he couldn't hear what we were saying over the din of the police helicopter orbiting overhead. Or maybe he was deaf. All we knew for sure was that whoever he was, he was in grave danger, standing in the open directly across the street from a house that contained a man who had already tried to kill one citizen. Because the man was in danger, Dennis told me he was going to run across the street, get the guy out of there, then come back to join me. He holstered his weapon and took off.

I refocused my attention on the house, fully expecting the gunman to start shooting at Dennis, and getting ready to shoot back. Then, suddenly, about fifteen seconds after Dennis left my side, I heard an angry voice scream over the racket of the orbiting helicopter, "Get your fucking hands off me! Don't tell me what to do!" I immediately peeled my eyes from the house and looked over my right shoulder. There, across the street, stood Dennis and the as-yet-unidentified citizen, no more than two feet apart, facing each other on the sidewalk. Dennis faced west, the citizen east. Their lips were moving, but I couldn't hear what they were saying. A few seconds later, the man turned away and took a couple of steps west down the sidewalk. I thought Dennis had convinced him to get out of harm's way.

But I was wrong.

With Dennis trailing a step behind, the man reached across his chest with his right hand, pulled a large butcher's knife from the bag slung over his left shoulder, and in one fluid motion pivoted back to his right, brought his left hand up to form a two-handed grip on the handle of the knife, and furiously plunged the blade into Dennis's chest.

I simply could not believe what I had seen—and neither could Dennis. He stared at his assailant as the man released his left hand from his right, drew the knife back to chest level, and for a split second stared back at Dennis. As I began to get up from my crouch to run to my partner's aid, the man attacked again.

This time, he drew the knife over his head, and like Anthony Perkins in the shower scene in *Psycho,* he brought it down with blinding speed. As the knife flashed toward him, Dennis stepped back and threw his hands in front of his face, desperately trying to fend off the blow. Somehow he succeeded and took another step back. The assailant took another step toward him, again drew the knife above his own head, and took another hack at Dennis. Dennis somehow managed to block the blow and retreated another step. The madman continued to press his attack as I moved away from the cover of the Cadillac. He hacked at Dennis again and again. And again and again, Dennis threw his hands up to parry the blows as he backpedaled down the sidewalk. Then Dennis tripped and fell flat on his back on the grass strip separating the sidewalk from the street, and the madman immediately moved in to finish him off.

He leaped on top of Dennis, landing with his knees astride my partner's hips, drew the knife above his head with both hands, and brought it crashing down toward Dennis's throat. Miraculously, Dennis managed to reach up and grab both of his attacker's wrists as the blade plunged toward him, stopping it just short of its mark. When I got to my partner's side a moment later, he was locked in a life-or-death struggle, still lying on his back, the assailant still straddling him on his knees, and the knife flickering between them, inches from Dennis's throat.

I immediately dropped to one knee and grabbed the assailant's left wrist with all my might, intending to twist his arm behind him, push him onto his back, and together with Dennis wrest the knife from him. But it didn't work. More quickly and easily than I ever could have imagined was possible, he jerked his arms away from me and effortlessly broke my desperate grip while maintaining his own on the knife. I then heard Dennis shout, "Shoot him!" So I did. Still close enough to reach out and touch him, I picked a spot on the left side of the madman's chest, brought my gun up, and pulled the trigger. As the sound of the gunshot passed into the night, the assailant—in a voice indicating that he realized the jig was up—said, "Oh, shit!" Dennis pushed his arms up, and I reached back in with my left hand and grabbed the madman's right wrist. With Dennis pushing and me pulling, we forced the assailant onto his side, and then to his back. As we did this, the attacker released his left hand from the knife, but he still held it firmly in his right. To increase my leverage, I dropped to my right knee and slammed the attacker's wrist to the turf with my left hand, then pinned it to the ground with my left foot. The assailant continued to fight us, but with my firm grip and full body weight on his wrist, we had the knife under control.

A few seconds later, four of the officers who had been on the east side of the perimeter came charging down the sidewalk toward us. Together, the six of us forced the knife out of the still struggling assailant's right hand, rolled him onto his stomach, and handcuffed him behind his back. Aware of the danger posed by the gunman in the house across the street, two of the other officers grabbed the suspect and quickly dragged him out of the line of fire to a spot behind a car that was parked on the lawn of the house in front of which the shooting went down. Dennis and I, along with a sergeant who had rushed to the scene moments after we cuffed the suspect, ran up onto the porch of the house in front of which the suspect lay, crouched down behind its rock-and-mortar railing, and again trained our guns on the house across the street. Two paramedics appeared and began to work on the man I had just shot, who was now lying no more than twenty feet from me. For the next few minutes, I focused on the house across the street, still expecting the gunman inside to shoot, but intermittently glanced down at the medical drama that was being played out on the grass nearby. It was during the last of these peeks that I saw the urine flow, and I knew that I had just killed a man.

At some point while we were on the porch, I realized that Dennis wasn't bleeding at all. This struck me as odd, inasmuch as I'd seen the blade of a large knife slam into his chest and had watched helplessly as the assailant pressed his follow-up attack while I was running across the street. But Dennis was wearing body armor under his uniform shirt that night, and it saved his life. The blade had torn most of the way through the vest on the initial thrust, but the last few layers of Kevlar stopped it just short of its mark. That Dennis had suffered no cuts as he retreated from his attacker could be chalked up only to Providence, because it was truly miraculous that his hands and arms had not been slashed to ribbons.

The sergeant used a phone in the house on whose porch we were crouched to notify headquarters of the situation, then told us to meet another sergeant who was waiting at our patrol car to escort us back to the police station. We ran to our car, met the other sergeant, and caravanned the four miles back to the station, where the watch commander directed the three of us to the captain's office to wait for the detectives from Robbery-Homicide Division. When they arrived, they interviewed Dennis first, then me. At some point, we learned that SWAT had been called out to deal with the gunman in the house back on Vernon and, consequently, that we would have to wait awhile before we could return to the scene to walk the detectives through what had happened. While we waited, someone informed me that the man I had shot had indeed died, confirming what I had seen from my perch on the porch.

At about 2:30 A.M., after repeated attempts to contact the gunman had yielded no response, the SWAT team entered the house to find it empty. No one ever figured out if the gunman had escaped before Dennis and I arrived on scene or whether he had slipped away during the confusion caused by my shooting, but he was never found.

After SWAT had cleared the house, Dennis and I returned to the scene, reenacted the entire scenario for the investigators, and then returned to the station for more interviews. At some point during this process, one of the detectives told me the name of the man I had killed. I found out later that he was an ex-con from Texas, who had told associates in L.A. that he was tired of being "harassed" by the police and that he would kill the next cop who "bothered" him. The detectives from the shooting team finished up and let me go home at about 10:30 A.M. on July 26, 1981, almost exactly twelve hours after I had killed Edward Randolph.

———

About a year and a half later, I left the LAPD to take a job as a patrol officer with the city of Redmond, Washington, a suburb of Seattle, the city where I had attended college and received my bachelor's in history three years earlier. In the summer of 1984, I quit police work, married a wonderful woman, and moved to Washington, D.C., to attend graduate school. After I received a master's degree in justice from the American University in 1985, my bride and I returned to the Seattle area. I took a year off from graduate school, then started up again at the University of Washington, where I earned a doctorate in sociology. I took a job on the sociology faculty of the University of Houston in 1991, received tenure in 1998, and moved to the University of Missouri-St. Louis a year later.

Over the years, I thought many times about the desperate moments during the summer of 1981 that culminated in Edward Randolph's death. In fact, during the first several years after the shooting, they were never very far from my mind. I had gone into law enforcement to help people, not kill them, and the shock of having taken a life stayed with me for a long time. It was a major reason why I left police work for full-time graduate studies rather than sticking with my initial career plan to pursue advanced degrees on a part-time basis, then move on to a faculty position when my days as a street cop ended. It also animated the course of study that I initially set for myself in graduate school.

From my own experience, discussions with numerous other officers who had also shot people, and reading law enforcement publications, I was keenly aware that police shootings can have a dramatic impact on officers who pull the trigger. Officers who are involved in shootings can experience a variety of short- and long-term reactions, such as recurrent thoughts about the incident, a sense of numbness, nausea, sadness, crying, and trouble sleeping. Indeed the existence of such responses has led mental health professionals to identify them as symptoms of a type of post-traumatic stress response, commonly called *post-shooting trauma* in law enforcement circles.[1]

A closely related issue that also interested me was officers' reactions during shooting events themselves. It was common knowledge in the law enforcement community that during shootings officers can experience a variety of unusual reactions, such as a sense of disbelief that the incident is happening, intrusive thoughts about irrelevant matters, and sensory distortions such as a narrowing of the visual field, decreased auditory acuity, and altered perceptions of time.[2] At the time that I left police work in 1984, however, no thorough research on officers' reactions during and after shootings had been conducted, so what was known about these topics was quite limited.

I had intended to devote my academic career to developing a deeper understanding of how shootings affect officers who pull the trigger, but during grad school, I became interested in different aspects of policing, so I put deadly force on the back burner. A few years ago, however, my interest in the consequences of shooting people heated back up because very little sound research on the personal impact of shootings had been conducted since I left police work. So with the help of a grant from the United States Department of Justice, I started to interview police officers who, like me, had been involved in shootings. By the time I completed my research, I had interviewed eighty officers from nineteen different police departments spread across four states.

During each interview, I asked the officers about their lives before they became involved in law enforcement, their experiences during academy and field training, instances in which they believed they had cause to shoot someone but held their fire, situations in which they did shoot people, and what took place in the aftermath of these shootings.

The fact that I was a former officer who had been there increased the officers' willingness to talk candidly about their experiences, as did the fact that under the terms of my grant I was (and still am) forbidden by federal law to divulge their identity to anyone without their express permission. In the end, the interviews I conducted yielded detailed information about 113 incidents in which the officers I interviewed had shot citizens (several of the officers had been in more than one shooting) and thousands of pages of interview transcripts.[3] This book draws on this material to present a picture of the role that deadly force plays in police work from the point of view of officers who have used it.

I wrote it to shed light on one of the most intriguing, yet least understood, aspects of the American experience. Americans have been both drawn to and repulsed by deadly force since municipal police officers started carrying firearms in the 1850s. Psychologists would tell us that this is so because at some deep subconscious level humans are both drawn to and repulsed by violence of any sort.[4] But our schizophrenic posture toward police shootings springs also from a deep cultural well. Our nation has a long-standing tradition of clamoring for government protection from the actions of criminals, while at the same time rebelling against the constraints that those protective activities place on our lives.[5] So we are drawn to police shootings not just because they are violent acts but also because they are the most dramatic instance of government doing battle with the bad guys that threaten us. And we are repulsed by them not only because of the damage they inflict but also because they are the ultimate form of government intrusion.

In recent years, this sense of disquiet about deadly government power has repeatedly been expressed in the form of social unrest. A good many of the major civil disturbances (and many of the smaller ones) that have erupted in our nation in the last four decades have been spawned by anger over law enforcement activity, often the use of deadly force. Indeed one the first large-scale riots of the tumultuous 1960s occurred in July 1964, after an off-duty New York City police lieutenant fatally shot a black teenager who attacked him with a knife. Two days later, a riot that claimed one life and caused nearly two dozen injuries broke out when a crowd marched on the local police station house to protest the shooting. The rioting spread, and over the next few days the police battled brick-tossing crowds, and firefighters doused flames set by Molotov cocktails in the minority enclaves of Harlem and the Bedford-Stuyvesant area of Brooklyn.

Similar violence broke out following police shootings of minorities in Tampa, Florida, and other cities during the remainder of the decade.[6] This pattern was repeated in the 1970s, 1980s, and 1990s, as riots broke out in the wake of police shootings in several cities, including Miami and St. Petersburg, Florida, Washington, D.C., the Gotham suburb Teaneck, New Jersey, and New York City itself. The spectacle of community upheaval following police gunfire has carried into the new century. As I write these words in the fall of 2003, Cincinnati, Ohio, is still recovering from a series of disturbances that erupted in the summer of 2001 after a white police officer shot and killed an unarmed black man during a foot chase.

This book is not about police brutality or the response of minority communities to police violence. It does not explore why some officers go bad, nor the complex historical, social, and economic forces that give rise to violent conflict along racial lines when minority citizens perceive that officers have used too much force.[7] At the same time, however, I am painfully aware that it is commonly asserted by critics of the police that American law enforcement is full of bigoted officers who enjoy expressing their prejudice through the barrels of their guns. In making this argument, the critics point to the fact that although black citizens make up only about 12 percent of the U.S. population, blacks account for about half of all people felled by police bullets—and a much higher percentage in many large jurisdictions that have large black populations.[8] Although these numbers would at first glance seem to offer clear support for the assertion that officers use deadly force in a race-based fashion, careful consideration of the matter indicates that the issue is not so simple, and that the racial disparity in the likelihood of being shot by the police may be explained by patterns of criminal offending.

Criminological research consistently finds that black Americans—due to historical, economic, and social forces—are more likely than whites to commit serious crimes, and the research on the use of deadly force by police officers indicates that the racial disparity in shooting rates is quite similar to the racial disparity in serious criminal offending (especially in larger jurisdictions).[9] So a deeper look at the question indicates that it may well be that blacks are more likely to be shot because they are more likely to commit serious crimes, not because the police are quicker on the trigger when facing blacks.

That racial disparities in shooting statistics would seem to be explained by differential involvement in criminal activity does not mean, however, that all officers at all times use their firearms appropriately. Even though all of the available evidence indicates that it very rarely happens, there have in fact been cases in which officers apparently shot citizens with no lawful justification. The most recent notable examples of this come from Los Angeles and Miami, where small groups of officers stand accused of fabricating evidence to cover up illicit shootings. But these incidents do not suggest that racial bias motivated the accused, for many of the officers involved are themselves minorities.[10] So it would appear that the issue of illicit shootings is related more to problem officers, who arise from time to time in police work, than to a systematic bias or some other sort of generalized desire among police officers to abuse citizens.

Unfortunately, police departments are not required to report to any national body when their officers shoot someone, so there are no comprehensive national figures on how frequently officers fire their weapons.[11] But scholars who study deadly force have offered guesstimates based on the data that are available. In the late 1980s, for example, the low estimate for fatal shootings per year was six hundred, the high a thousand, and the estimates for nonfatal shootings ranged from twelve hundred to fifteen hundred per year.[12] If these estimates were correct, then American police were shooting between eighteen hundred and twenty-five hundred people each year during the 1980s.

These figures have not been updated, so current estimates of national police-shooting figures are not available. We do know, however, that the annual number of police shootings in many big cities declined substantially during the 1990s (in New York City, for example, from thirty-nine fatal shootings in 1990 to eleven in 1999).[13] This suggests that the number of people shot by police each year has likely decreased since the 1980s, perhaps to as low as twelve hundred. Whether this figure is correct—or too low by half or more—when one considers that there are more than 750,000 police officers in the United States and that these officers have tens of millions of interactions with citizens each year, it is clear that police shootings are extremely rare events and that few officers—less than one-half of 1 percent each year—ever shoot anyone.

The notion that officers rarely shoot runs counter to popular conceptions about the use of deadly force in police work, which are driven by fictionalized portrayals of police work in movies, TV shows, and other media; press accounts of police shootings; and the pronouncements of antipolice activists and other bloviators who are more concerned with promoting themselves or their cause than they are with an honest accounting of matters.

Incidents in which police officers shoot citizens are dramatic events that fit perfectly with the news media's "if it bleeds, it leads" dictum, so police shootings can generate substantial local press coverage. Any hint of controversy can turn a shooting into a cause célèbre that gets massive local, regional, and even national press play. Sensational reports of "garden variety" shootings and constant "updates" on the latest developments in controversial ones give the impression that police officers frequently use their firearms in the course of their duties. Popular entertainment reinforces the perception that officers often shoot people, serving up shoot-outs as regular fare in TV shows such as *Miami Vice* and movies about the police such as the "Dirty" Harry Callahan series. And people who make careers of complaining about alleged police misconduct have a vested interest in perpetuating the belief that officers shoot people on a regular basis.

In addition to presenting a false front about how often officers shoot, critics of the police typically gloss over or simply ignore an important fact about police work: it is an inherently dangerous job. According to FBI statistics, 644 police officers were murdered during the decade that ended in 2000. Most of these officers were slain with firearms: 452 of them with handguns, 114 with rifles, and 35 with shotguns. The other three-dozen-plus officers who were murdered during the decade were either stabbed or slashed to death with knives, swords, or other cutting instruments; purposely run down by motor vehicles; beaten to death with blunt instruments; punched or kicked to death; or fell victim to some other sort of gruesome fate. Tens of thousands of other officers survived assaults—many of them just barely—during the 1991 to 2000 span, including several thousand who were shot.[14]

It is in the context of this climate of ever present danger that officers operate with the power over life and death through their firearms. They have the responsibility to use their power judiciously: to protect themselves, fellow officers, and innocent citizens from harm, on the one hand, and to refrain from shooting if at all possible, on the other. It is hard for those who have not been police officers to understand what it is like to have the awesome responsibility to carry and possibly use firearms in the course of serving society. As we will see as this book unfolds, police officers often have to make their decisions about whether to shoot or hold their fire in split seconds, with limited information, in situations where the wrong choice can lead to needless injury or death and even the right choice can have substantial repercussions.

A major reason why it is hard for people who have not served in law enforcement to understand the immense responsibility that comes from carrying a gun is that there is a dearth of information about how officers actually think and feel about deadly force. This book seeks to at least partially remedy this by presenting a cop's eye view of the role deadly force plays in the lives of American police officers—from before they come on the job to the aftermath of shootings.

The first chapter deals with officers' expectations about the use of deadly force before they came on the job. The second chapter addresses officers' experiences during academy and field training and how these experiences shaped their attitudes about using deadly force. The third chapter focuses on cases in which officers hold their fire when shooting would have been legally permissible. The fourth chapter is devoted to shootings. And the final chapter depicts what occurs in the wake of shootings and how involvement in shootings affects officers who pull the trigger.

Each chapter consists of collections of stories that are presented in the words of the officers who told them to me. The stories, which vary in length from a single paragraph to several pages, were selected because they provide a set of accounts that represent the major themes that emerged during my research. The stories are presented in the officers' own words, but they do contain some modifications that enhance clarity and narrative structure.

In order to reduce the likelihood that some readers might be able to divine the identity of an officer from a given story, I typically changed the dates, the names of the involved officers, the locations, and other identifying information. The only exceptions are when changing potentially identifying information would substantially alter a major aspect of what occurred and the officers in question explicitly told me that they did not mind if some potentially identifying details remained.

The stories recounted in the pages that follow are as accurate and complete as I could make them. Nonetheless they do not convey everything the officers told me, for written words simply cannot express everything that people say when they talk. As is the case with all human speech, a decent bit of what officers conveyed about their experiences came through other modes of communication. Officers commonly punctuated their presentations with extreme animation: emotions surfaced and sometimes spilled over, as they used posture, gestures, tone of voice, facial expressions, and other means to help convey the anger, hatred, sadness, shock, fear, frustration, and other sentiments they felt before, during, and after their shootings. Tears welled up in—and occasionally spilled out of—some of the officers' eyes as they recounted particularly horrific aspects of a shooting or some aspect of its aftermath. Other officers visibly seethed with vitriol as they described the disdain they felt for specific individuals, including the suspects they shot, the suspects' lawyers, and members of the press. And some officers became still, subdued, and quiet as they told certain parts of their stories.

When turning the interviews into written narratives there is, unfortunately, no way to represent all of the various verbal intonations, tears, postures, gesticulations, averted gazes, and so on that framed officers' words without detracting substantially from the flow of their stories. I did all that I could to capture as much as possible of what officers were thinking and feeling by asking detailed questions and follow-ups that sought to get the officers to express with words as clearly and completely as possible what they were communicating through other means. These efforts yielded rich, detailed narratives that convey a tremendous amount of what the officers expressed.

At this point, it is worthwhile to note that a good deal of sociological, psychological, and legal research has established that people who are involved in or witness the same event often have different impressions of what transpired. This phenomenon (often referred to as *the Rashomon effect,* after Akira Kurosawa's classic film *Rashomon,* which presents four individuals' accounts of a rape-murder) indicates that what the officers told me about the shootings in which they were involved does not represent the complete story of the incidents they related, but rather the story from their point of view. Others who experienced the events would have told different stories. A different book might have included these stories, but the purpose of this book is to present officers' accounts of their shootings: what they saw, what they heard, what they thought, what they did, how they felt. And so it does.

In telling the stories of their shootings and other events, the officers I interviewed sometimes used technical terms and vernacular phrases and otherwise spoke in ways that could render understanding difficult for those lacking a background in law enforcement. Because the book uses officers' own words to tell their stories, the pages that follow contain a good deal of "police talk." To minimize any problem such language might present, I have included in the back of the book a Glossary, containing terms and phrases that readers can turn to for clarification when they encounter police idiom.

The definition of one idiomatic phrase should not wait for the back of the book, however, because it appears in the title. Police officers (and members of the military) use the term *kill zone* to refer to locations where a person is vulnerable to being killed by hostile action. The term is most often used to describe space into which someone possessing a firearm can shoot—the street in front of a house containing a sniper, for example. But it is also used more generally to describe the space that individuals occupy when they are vulnerable to being killed by any sort of weapon, be it a gun, a knife, or a motor vehicle. In police work, then, officers are in the kill zone when they are in positions where they could be shot, stabbed, run over, or otherwise mortally injured by citizens. Because the stories that make up this book are officers' accounts of how they prepared for, experienced, and dealt with the aftermath of spending time in the kill zone, they take the reader *Into the Kill Zone.*

CHAPTER ONE

Choosing the Badge and Gun

M en and women become police officers for many reasons. For some, police work is the realization of a childhood dream born of playing cops and robbers or family tradition. Others become officers because they wish to help people in need, protect innocents from evil, or render justice. I, for example, had a grand plan to save South Central Los Angeles from the persistent gang violence and other crime that had turned the area into a virtual war zone during the 1970s. Less romantic motives for becoming a police officer also abound, as considerations such as the desire for a steady job with benefits, a wish to avoid the drudgery of more traditional occupations, and simple happenstance lead many people into law enforcement. Whatever draws them into police work, most officers come to find that the job they have is quite different from the one they had envisioned. The fact is that most Americans' image of policing comes primarily from popular myths derived from media depictions of police work, which, as noted in the Introduction, provide at best shallow and at worst wildly inaccurate portrayals of the job.

Before coming on the job, most police officers are not aware that shootings are a rare occurrence. Prior to being hired, most officers are just ordinary folk, whose impressions of police work are shaped by the same media forces that frame those of any other member of the general public. So unless a future officer happens to have learned that shootings are rare events from a source such as a friend or family member already in law enforcement, he or she will likely share the general public's misperception that police officers shoot people on a regular basis.

Although their impressions of the odds that they will end up shooting someone may differ, all would-be officers know that firearms are a tool of the police trade and that there is some possibility that they might one day find themselves in a situation that calls for them to pull the trigger. The fact that being a police officer means that one might be called upon to shoot—and perhaps kill—another human being raises an important question for all who seek the job: Will they be able to do it?

Rooted in the biblical admonition "Thou shalt not kill," our American systems of law and civic morality stress the sanctity of human life and condemn the act of taking it. Even though our laws and morals have always provided for killing under certain circumstances—during war and in self-defense, for example—such provisions are narrow exceptions to the sweeping norm that we should not take the life of our fellow human beings. This powerful norm is not so easily overcome. Indeed some have argued that the norm reflects an innate human aversion to killing and, consequently, that police officers—like soldiers and anyone else whose job description includes the prospect of the destruction of fellow humans—must actually be taught to overcome their natural predisposition against shedding blood in order for them to take a life.[1]

Whatever its source, the sense that one should not kill is strong among Americans, and it can get in the way of doing one's job if one is a police officer. Men and women contemplating careers in law enforcement deal with the fact that the ability to kill is a job requirement in a variety of ways. Some think long and hard about whether they can take a life. I certainly did, spending countless hours reflecting on the issue and discussing the morality of killing with friends, family, professors, pastors, and police officers who shared my religious faith. Other would-be officers resolve the question in short order, and some don't really ponder it at all.

None of the officers I interviewed engaged in the degree of preemployment soul searching that I had, but some—such as the former theology student who took a police job after dropping out of seminary—came close. Several of the men and women that I spoke with had quickly put to rest the question about their ability to kill—some almost as soon it came up in their minds—and the majority never really contemplated the question as they were considering police careers. In fact, the only time many of these officers ever thought about the question was when it was put to them during their job interviews. Law enforcement agencies are keenly aware that some people are not capable of killing, so they try to avoid hiring such people. One way they do this is by asking applicants some variant of this simple question: "Do you believe that you could kill someone if you had to?"

Obviously, each of the eighty men and women who spoke with me had answered this question affirmatively. In this chapter we meet twenty-seven of them. Their stories were selected for two related reasons. The first is that the ways they dealt with the question of killing people before they came on the job cover the spectrum of how the officers that I interviewed approached the issue. The second is that the paths these officers took to police work are representative of those taken by the larger group. As a result, the stories in this chapter give the reader some idea of the types of journeys that people who aspire to law enforcement careers undertake on their way to an occupation where the job requirements include the ability to kill people.

The stories are presented in three groups, based on how and why the officers got into police work. This approach provides thematic threads that tie the stories together and allows the reader to see how people with similar motivations and backgrounds can have different ideas, attitudes, and expectations about deadly force. The stories begin with those of a set of officers who had a strong personal connection with law enforcement before they came on the job.

Friends and Family

The most common personal link to policing among officers was a parent or sibling who worked in law enforcement. The other sort of personal connection was through a close friend on the job. Officers who had a personal link to police work before they got into it typically possessed more knowledge about what the job entails than did their less-connected peers. As the stories in this section illustrate, however, officers who share similar backgrounds still can travel different paths to the job and possess substantially different perspectives on deadly force.

—◊◊◊—

I was pretty young when I started to think seriously about becoming a cop, seventeen or eighteen. The idea came from my brother, who was already in law enforcement. He encouraged me to pursue it, and I did. I didn't think much about being involved in shootings before I applied for the job. In fact, what first brought the possibility that I might shoot someone to my attention was a question that came up in an oral interview to come on the job. One of the people doing the interviewing asked me, "Do you think you could take somebody's life if you had to?" It kind of set me back a little bit because the questions prior to that had to do with mundane things like why I wanted to become a police officer and my religious beliefs and whatnot. So when the question about killing someone came up, it kind of threw me back a little bit. I had to really think about it. I told the oral board that if I was placed in a position where I had to shoot to save my life or somebody else's that I didn't think I'd have a problem with taking a life, and it was left at that. So that was my first introduction to the idea that I might have to shoot someone.

—◊◊◊—

I really started to consider becoming a cop when I was in high school. My dad was in law enforcement, but when I was young, he never would talk about things that were going on or things that had happened. When I was older and went to the station with him, the guys were always having fun and the stuff that was going on looked exciting. So police work looked exciting, and that was probably the main reason I got interested in it. When I told my mom I wanted to become a cop, she was concerned and proud at the same time. My dad tried to talk me out of it, but it was kind of a halfhearted attempt. His attitude was like, "It's a great job. I don't really want you to do it. But you'll love it." I went to a junior college for a couple of years, played some football there, then transferred to Randall State University and after a year there came on the sheriff's department when I was twenty-one.

The notion that I might have to shoot somebody was always in the back of my mind, from the time I first decided to become a cop. I knew that that was part of the job. I had gone on some ride-alongs with friends that were on the department, and I knew from that that I wanted to work the faster places. Those places had a lot of shootings, so I knew that that was part of the game, that getting in a shooting was a real possibility.

—◊—

Probably about a year before I came onto the force was the first time I thought about becoming a police officer. I was working for this import company that was facing a possible bankruptcy. My brother—who'd gotten on the force two years before—said my military background would probably help me get onto the police force if I were interested. I gave it some consideration and got accepted when I eventually applied.

I'd gone to college right out of high school and accumulated about ninety credit hours before I joined the army for a two-year hitch. I was a combat medic. Went overseas for a few months as part of a multinational peacekeeping force south of Beirut, Lebanon, called Operation Bright Star. It was fairly intense duty, but I was never involved in any combat. It was usually several miles away.

When I got out of the army, I came home, worked odd jobs, helped my dad in the family grocery business for a while, then found something that looked more promising at the import company that ended up facing bankruptcy. I decided to go on a ride-along with my brother when he mentioned that I should consider taking a police job. Nothing happened until the end of the shift, when he stopped by on a good shooting that involved a bad drug deal. The guy had half his face blown off. I had thought the ugliness of police work would not appeal to me, but it looked like I could handle the blood and gore, so I said, "This is for me." I liked the atmosphere, being around a police station, in a police car, the adrenaline involved. Plus I saw that the police department was structured very similar to that of a military environment, and that's something that I really enjoyed previously. In fact, I'd have stayed in the military for longer than two years, but I wanted to be near my family. I'm of Chinese descent and family is important to us. Besides that, I'm used to Mom's cooking, and you don't find much good Chinese food out in the sticks or in another country.

I gave some serious thought to the issue of using deadly force before I came on the department because I was involved in a shooting when I was eighteen years old. It was a hijacking at our family store. I saw the suspect come in, put a gun to my dad's head, lay him down, and shoot him execution-style. I witnessed the whole thing. I was standing by where my dad hid one of his pistols, and I pulled it out and shot the suspect after he fired a shot at me and missed. He got away, but I know I hit him because they recovered a bullet that had a lot of blood on it in the front door. I figured that round went through his arm because he dropped the money. I chased him out of the store, and when he was about half a block away, I shot him in the back. He actually did a flip before he fell; then the getaway car came and dragged him away.

I thought my dad was dead, but it turned out that the bullet the hijacker fired went through his ribs. The gun was a cheap .22, where the cylinder was misaligned with the barrel. A piece of junk. I swore up and down that the gun was raised over my dad's head, but he moved or something just when the guy pulled the trigger, and the bullet passed through two ribs, missed all the organs, and exited.

From that experience, I knew I could shoot someone, but I also thought about some other stuff regarding shootings. Besides my brother, I had some friends who came on the department before me, and they always told me about the liabilities involved. They said that every time you pull the trigger, you've got the chief's name on every bullet that comes out of your gun. I also thought about how I would act in a bad situation as a police officer because I'm not really the John Wayne type, the aggressive type. I'm a pretty laid-back person. More importantly, I didn't want to choke in a situation where I could get somebody else innocent killed, whether it'd be a civilian or my partner. I didn't have a problem with the notion of hurting someone. I was just concerned about whether I could react the way that I'm supposed to.

—⁓—

When I was a young kid growing up in the Midwest, my father had a very close friend named Ray Underwood, who was a police officer. He was a childhood hero of mine, so I started thinking about following him and becoming a cop when I was pretty young. He had been in the marines, and when we'd go over to visit, he'd show my brother and me his gun. He even gave us a bayonet he had from the Second World War. When I was nine or ten, he got in a horrendous shooting while handling a disturbance call at a local hospital one night. He took several rounds, but he put the suspects down. He stayed on the job for a long time after that, so I was always impressed with old Ray Underwood.

Even though I'd had a family friend who was shot when I was pretty young, I don't think that the seriousness of shootings registered when I was a kid. Where it really registered to me was when I was in the Marine Corps overseas in the Vietnam incident. I was in a force reconnaissance unit, a small group that would go out snooping and pooping around in the bush to bring back intelligence so the regular units could kick off a mission. Being in force recon was the best thing that ever happened to me in my life because I got intensive training and discipline. I went through all sorts of schools: guerrilla warfare, SCUBA, jump school, maneuvers over and over again about movement in the bush with a small group of people. I did all sorts of stuff like that for a year before heading overseas.

All that training helped keep me alive in Vietnam. That, plus when you're in force recon, you're not just one of the grunts. Those guys got hit terribly over there, but when you're in force recon, you're out there calling the shots. We had immediate air on station, immediate on-calls always set up to have artillery coming to our aid, and if we really got into the heat, we could get an emergency extraction. We'd just move to an LZ, a landing zone, and they would get you out of there. So it was a damn good thing as far as survival to be in a recon unit. We had a lot of contacts in the year I spent in Vietnam, but nobody from my unit ever got killed. We did OK, but we also ran missions where we set up as a reactionary force, and sometimes on those we had to go out and pick up the bodies of dead Americans. From that, I learned about what deadly force is all about and what guns can do.

I came back stateside in March of 1970. I put in my application with the police department in May, got released from the corps in late July, and started the academy two weeks later. So six months out of the bush and I was in the police academy.

———~~~———

Being that I grew up in a police family, I was pretty young when I first thought about becoming a cop, probably ten or eleven. My grandpa started the tradition back in the early '40s, right around '42. My dad got in it during the '60s. Then my sister and I came on the job in the late '80s. I'd gone away to college, came back from my first year at college, got a job with the Communications Division, and realized that police work was pretty much what I wanted to do. So I went back to school, got three more semesters under my belt, graduated, and came back. Two weeks after I came back from graduation, I started the academy.

When I was growing up, I never really thought about fights or shootings or anything like that. We didn't have *Cops,* and we didn't have *Real Stories of the Highway Patrol* on TV. That's something that has been so much more recent. I was a typical kid. I grew up playing cops and robbers and good guy–bad guy, and we had the cap guns and if some guy snuck around the corner of a building, we'd pop one at him. "Bang! You're dead" kind of thing. So we dealt with it, but we never had to deal with the seriousness of it. It's like these programs nowadays where they show chases and all this action-type stuff, but you don't see any of the aftermath of it. You don't see any report writing, the interviews that take place. You don't see really any of the investigation stuff. You see all the fun stuff, and that's what we dealt with as kids, we dealt with the fun stuff. We didn't have to deal with all the paperwork and stuff afterwards. So even though we did deal with it to an extent, we never really got in-depth with it.

Neither my dad nor my granddad were ever involved in a shooting, and they never talked about shooting people. When Dad would come home from work, I can remember he'd take his belt off and he'd set it on his dresser, and he left his gun in his holster. He very rarely would lock it up unless we left on vacation, and we all knew you don't touch the gun. If I wanted to touch it, I had to ask him first, and there'd better be a good reason why I wanted to touch it. So I asked him a few times, and he'd unload it and he'd sit down with me and say, "The bullets go in this way and this is how the barrel turns," stuff like that, because in those days they had the .38s. So my sister and I were curious about it and he never hid it from us, but we also knew that it was not a toy. I knew what it was capable of, but I guess I just never really thought about what it would do. So because Grandpa and Dad were never involved in anything, they never really talked about shootings, and looking at my father's gun was the extent of our dealings about that sort of thing.

I do remember when my dad was working the detective bureau, he went out one night to help a friend of his who owned a bar. They were having a problem with some people coming in and robbing the neighborhood bars, so my dad grabbed his 20-gauge shotgun, put it in the little bag, and went down and sat at the bar. I thought, "Boy, it would be terrible if this guy came in there." I was hoping that if he did that my dad could get him before he shot my dad, and I remember thinking, "I hope Dad comes home tonight." Luckily, that night everything went off without a hitch. There were no problems at the bar, and he never, as far as I know, ever went back. And that was the only time I ever worried about anything that he ever did. But like I said, neither he nor my grandpa were ever involved in any type of officer-involved shooting, so I never really thought anything about them.

Youthful Ambition

Kids with friends or family in police work are not the only ones who dream of a career in law enforcement. The stories in this section show how deep the desire to become a police officer can run and how individuals who set their minds on police work early in life can take quite different paths to realizing their youthful aspirations. Where deadly force is concerned, the stories once again demonstrate that future officers who share some sort of common bond can have very different approaches to the prospect of killing people.

—◊◊◊—

I decided to become a cop when I was seven. I was always getting into my parents' car and acting like I was chasing robbers. I even made a pretend *Kojak* light for that. I'd also make my little brother be a bad guy and chase him around the backyard. As I got older and started spending time around the police department in the city where I grew up, I started to realize that it wasn't all fun and games, that officers really do shoot people sometimes. That happened when I joined the police explorers when I was in high school. They had a program where we got to ride along with officers on Friday and Saturday nights, so through that I became good friends with the officers down there. One of them, Sam Wayne, got into two shootings within about a year, so I saw that shootings were obviously something that was part of the job.

I decided I didn't want to work in the place where I grew up, that I wanted to work in a big city. I looked into a few places and ended up coming here. At the time I hired on, the city had a reputation of having some pretty rough places, so I figured that there was a good possibility that I would have to shoot somebody someday. Having given it quite a bit of thought before I came on, I was satisfied that I'd be able to shoot. If you have to, you have to. It's part of the job.

—∿∿—

From the time I was very little, my ambition in life was to be either a veterinarian or a law enforcement officer. I've always loved animals, and police work always fascinated me. I had two Saint Bernards when I was growing up, so that's where the love for animals came from. The fascination with law enforcement just came from watching officers. I remember when I was a small kid, an officer came to school to talk with us about different things. I can't say I understood everything he was talking about, but it just grabbed me. He had my complete attention and my total respect. I liked that. I liked that people were willing to pay attention to him just because of his job. That was when I was a real little kid, and as I got older, that sense of awe just stuck with me.

Another thing that drew me to policing was that it seemed like a real active job. I've never been one to sit back and watch. I've always just liked to do things, and from what I saw of police work, it was clear that it wasn't the type of job where you sit behind a desk and punch in a card. It seemed like when I saw some cops, they were always doing something different, always dealing with different people, never the same thing. That fascinated me. When I was younger, I could watch cops doing their jobs all day, even if it was just writing out a little ticket. Plus I saw that they were almost always working together. I rarely saw just one officer doing something. It was usually a group of guys, doing their work together. I liked that because I played sports all my life, and the idea of working together for a common goal appealed to me. As I got older, my interest in being a vet declined, and my desire to become a police officer kept growing.

I wanted to be a cop so bad that I went down to apply with the PD as soon as I got out of high school. They told me to come back when I was twenty-one, so I did. I took the test, passed it, and went through the rest of the hiring procedures until I came to the physical. They knocked me out of the process because they found something wrong with my back, where one of my vertebrae was a bit off center. They discovered that the problem was something I was born with, not from an injury. But that didn't matter. They told me there were no ifs, ands, or buts; I couldn't come on. They did tell me that there was an appeal process, but I didn't bother with it because I didn't know any better. I just took the test a bunch of times over the next several years—at least five or six—and every time I'd pass, and every time I'd get rejected because of my back.

During that time, I worked a bunch of different jobs to support myself. I worked for Montgomery Wards, Coors Beer Company, and held some other jobs while I took some college courses. I drove a truck for a uniform company here in town for a couple of years, then started my own lawn and tree-trimming business on the side. That got to be pretty good, so I quit those other jobs and just did lawn care full-time. I was about ready to give up on becoming a police officer, but my dad suggested that I try it again. He told me that a buddy of his had told him that the PD had changed some of the hiring requirements. He fig-ured the physical might be one of them. I was doubtful about that, but I took the test again anyway. I went through the whole process again, and when I got called for the physical, I made it through. I didn't know how it happened, and I didn't ask, I didn't question it. Just kept my mouth shut, made it through the last step, and got into the academy in June of '88. Once I got hired, I let my lawn business go and just con-centrated on police work.

I never really gave much thought to shootings before I came on the job, but I was raised to take care of myself, so I knew I'd do whatever I had to if it came to that. That came from my dad. He was a boxer, and he got me involved in it when I was seven. I grew up in a real tough part of town, and my dad always told me from day one, he said, "Don't ever go looking for trouble, never. If you can, walk away from a fight, never look for trouble. But if someone is trying to hurt you or your family, you do whatever is necessary to take care of yourself and your family." So I've always thought that if someone was trying to hurt me bad enough, I wouldn't hesitate to kill them. I never really sat down before I got hired and thought about the issue of shooting someone. It was just engraved in the back of my mind that I would do whatever was necessary to take care of myself and my family, whether it be deadly force, or whatever.

I'd say I was about twelve years old when I first thought about becoming a cop. I think it was from watching TV and seeing LAPD out in my neighborhood doing their jobs. I grew up in a bad area, but the cops always treated me fairly. I had some positive contact with cops when I was growing up, and their job looked interesting, so from a young age I always felt like being a police officer was what I wanted to do. I think when I was twelve, the idea of getting into law enforcement was more of a fantasy, and then it grew into something more structured as I got older. By the middle to the end of high school, I decided that I really wanted to become a policeman.

I knew I couldn't be a cop until I was twenty-one, so about two or three days after high school graduation, I joined the Marine Corps. I stayed in the Marine Corps until right before I got on the department. In the marines, I worked the Presidential Honor Guard and security detail for President Carter. We were stationed in Washington, D.C., at Marine Barracks 8th and I, which is the oldest post in the Marine Corps. That's where they do all the ceremonial stuff. Then I worked the White House and also Camp David. So I worked different security assignments.

We carried loaded weapons and we got training on the rules of engagement, but I didn't think I'd ever have to fire on anyone. I knew that I was there more for show and that if I ended up in a shooting situation, the Secret Service would be putting holes in the guy before I got any rounds off. I mean, we weren't the primary defense for the president. Like I said, my position was more for show.

The only time we would be primary is in the case of a nuclear or terrorist attack. In that case, our actual primary duty was security for the president. For instance, if the president had to be evacuated, we'd land, secure the perimeter, the president would come in with the Secret Service, some of us would go to the bunkers with the president, and when he came out we would be his security force because the Secret Service wouldn't be big enough to handle that. We trained for stuff like that, but I didn't think it was ever really going to happen.

I think the first time I gave any serious thought to the possibility of getting in a shooting was right before I went into the academy. I had applied to the police department when I was still in the marines, done all the testing, cleared the background and all that, so I went almost straight from the marines to the PD. Just before I entered the academy, an officer from a neighboring department was shot and killed. He was a young guy just out of the military and still in training when it happened, so I identified with him. That got me thinking about shootings and the possibility of shooting someone. But up to that time, I never really thought about shootings. I knew that officers got into shootings, but I'd never really thought about me personally getting in a shooting. Up till then, my focus had been on working hard to get on the job.

—◊◊◊—

I've always been pretty sure I was going to do something either military or police related since I was a little kid. I'm not sure why. I guess the activity, the excitement. There has also always been the feeling within me that there are bad people, evil people, out there doing harm and killing people and that they need to be stopped. I have been around firearms all my life, started shooting competitive shotguns at a young age, so I've been an expert shooter since childhood. I've always felt that maybe that talent made me somewhat responsible to stop the bad people, that maybe I needed to be a sheriff or a policeman or something because that was one thing that I was good at. My parents taught me the difference in right and wrong, and since I can protect people with my area of expertise, I felt that maybe I should.

I read a lot as a kid. I read a lot of everything, from cowboy books, to quite a few police books, to a lot of spy novels. I knew from all this reading and from watching occasional news pieces that there were some seriously bad, evil people out there and that there was a potential that I would come into contact with them. I knew that I would be able to handle it. I never questioned my ability to take somebody's life if it was a situation of where it was them or me, or them or my family, or them or some innocent person they were trying to victimize. So I always felt that I would be able to shoot somebody if it was necessary.

—◊◊◊—

I wanted to be a police officer from when I was in junior high, or even before then. I remember watching *Adam 12* and just being fascinated with the idea of being a police officer. I think it was the responsibility of it, the pride involved, getting to work with people and to help people in need. I was also drawn to the excitement. I liked the idea of not knowing what's gonna happen when you go to work, of having to think on your feet and react. Also, I looked up to police officers, and I hoped that people would look up to me and that I'd be a positive example to people when I became a cop.

I don't recall ever thinking about shootings when I was young, but I did think about physical confrontations. The possibility of that. I worked on preparing myself physically and staying in shape. I remember that even at a very young age I'd go out and run for a certain length of time, then do pull-ups and push-ups. I've always been pretty small—thin boned and things like that—so I was working on my strength and building myself physically for the job from a young age.

Then I became a Christian when I was in high school, and I had a period of time in my mind where I felt that my calling in life was to be a church planter. I got a B.A. in philosophy and then started seminary. I planned to get a graduate degree in theology and go plant churches over in Australia among the Aborigines, or somewhere else in some Third World country, and I guess—had things kept going the way they were—that's what I would have done. But I had to support myself and seminary was very difficult. I couldn't handle classes and a full-time job because I worked more on school in that one semester in seminary than I did my entire four years of college before that. It was tough. I realized I couldn't do that and work at the same time, so I decided to fall back on the thing that I loved as a child—law enforcement. I said, "I'll give it a try." Never looked back since.

I thought quite a bit about the issue of killing people after I became a Christian. I remember that there were times during high school and college that I felt that I could never shoot anybody. Then, at some point, I realized, "Hey, if you gotta do it, you could do it." I wouldn't want to do it, but if I had to, I believed that I could. I think I just realized as I matured that life is not perfect, and we all have to react to things that life brings to us. Whether I was a cop, or I was just a citizen in my house and someone came in there to assault my family, I would do whatever was necessary to protect my family. I realized that protecting my family is the same thing that a cop does. He doesn't just protect himself, he's protecting the citizens. So I felt that I could do it.

I first got interested in law enforcement during my junior year in high school when I was called into the counseling office. At first, I thought I was in some kind of trouble, but when I got to the office, the counselor asked me what I was going to do when I got out of high school. I hadn't given it any thought. I knew my parents wanted me to go to college, but as far as career choice I had no idea. When I told the counselor that, he handed me this big pamphlet about a program called the

Regional Occupational Program that allowed high school students to get credit for taking occupational classes and working at these different places. He told me to look the pamphlet over to see if there was anything that interested me.

As I looked through it, the only jobs that interested me were things that would get me out of the building. I didn't want to be cooped up. I was a very active kid who lost interest quickly. In school, I found myself daydreaming, my mind wandering, stuff like that. So I didn't want a job where I'd have to be inside. Then I saw that there was this class on law enforcement/private security, and out of curiosity I decided to check it out. The class really piqued my interest because I learned that law enforcement was something that would get me outside a lot. So I thought, "Hey, that looks pretty good." It really interested me, and that's basically how I decided to get into law enforcement.

As I was contemplating a career in police work, I kind of asked myself about whether I thought I could shoot somebody. My dad had been a marine pilot in both World War II and Korea, so the issue of killing people wasn't foreign to me. He had also raised me to have a self-protection kind of mind-set. He taught me what to do if we had an intruder enter the home, stuff like that. I took it from there and decided that I could shoot somebody. So from an early age, I thought I could shoot if I had to.

Changing Jobs

Some officers become interested in policing later in life. In this section, we meet several officers who came into police work when they decided that a career change was in order, and we hear how they approached the prospect of having to shoot someone.

—⁓—

I got into law enforcement in my early twenties. I was working in the communications unit of a hospital's helicopter ambulance program, doing some PR and marketing coordination as well as managing calls. I was getting tired of that job, so I went down to the city hall to see what types of jobs they had to offer. I signed up for a bunch of things: communications dispatcher, lifeguard, some other stuff, and police officer. The police department called me up, I started going through the process, and it just snowballed from there.

I didn't really know what the job entailed, but as I went through the hiring process, it looked more and more interesting. The pay and fringe benefits looked good, but the things that appealed to me most were being able to work outdoors and being able to come into work wearing things like sweats and change into something. I know it sounds funny, but I'm a fairly laid-back, casual type of person and that really appealed to me.

Prior to getting hired, I never really thought about shootings. We had guns around the house when I was growing up. My father liked to hunt, but I didn't like it at all. He'd make me go sometimes, but I didn't care for it, so I was never big on guns. Now I did have a handgun when I got older, but it was just for target shooting. I'd shoot at an indoor range maybe once or twice a year. That was it. I didn't carry it around or even have it loaded at the house. I just had it for occasional target practice. The only time I can remember giving any thought to the notion of shooting someone was during the captain's interview, one of the final things in the hiring process. The guy asked me about how I would feel if I had to take a life; would I be able to do it? I obviously told him I could do it, because I knew that was what he wanted to hear. I mean, anyone would know that that's the right answer if you want to be a cop.

I got introduced to law enforcement–type work while I was in college. I was pursuing a broadcasting degree, wanted to get into some type of broadcasting or journalism. I took a part-time job as a security guard to get some extra money and I really enjoyed it. I got burned out on college, got tired of being poor, so I dropped out for a while to work full-time. I had grown up in a small rural area, so I decided to move to the big city, see what kind of job I could find. I had a friend that was going to college here, so I stayed with him for a few days. As I was looking around, I saw this big billboard that said, "Join the Police Department." I automatically correlated it with my security guard work and thought, "Hey, I know some guys who are cops. I could do that." So I decided to give it a try, thinking I'd do it for a couple of years maybe, then go back to college and finish my broadcasting degree. But I fell in love with the job, and I'm still here twenty years later.

Before I came on the job, I thought big-city cops got into shootings all the time. I fully expected to come here and get involved in a shooting before too long. I also thought that maybe I'd be shot. That crossed my mind a lot. I'd say the biggest thing that got me thinking that way was cop shows on TV. Those guys were in shootings every episode. Another thing was some stuff the guy I was staying with said. He tried to talk me out of joining. He told me that cops get killed here all the time. I remember thinking that maybe I ought to rethink this police job stuff, and then I thought it can't really be that dangerous. But I still thought that maybe I'd get shot. Then, after a little while on the streets, I came to understand that shootings don't happen very often. I never went back to college, and after twenty years I still haven't been shot.

—◊◊◊—

I was in the military, United States Army, assigned to a specialized recon platoon in an airborne unit. Then I got hurt and couldn't do that anymore. I knew that I wanted to do something with a paramilitary organization because I enjoyed that environment, so I thought about law enforcement. When I got out, the first thing I did was put in for police jobs. I applied to three departments—two sheriff's departments and the city PD. I got hired by all three on the same day but decided to go with the city. One of the county agencies told me, "You have to work the jail five years minimum." The other told me, "Probably five years in the jail." But the city said, "You'll be on the street right away." So I said, "That's where I'm going."

I had reconciled myself to the possibility that I might have to kill somebody even before I got into the military. When I decided to join up, I knew that there was always a possibility of war or skirmishes, police actions, and stuff like that. I knew that I could be involved in a shooting. I thought about it: "Would I be able to do it?" I made my mind up that if I was going to do that type of work that I was going to be able to do it. I'm a survivor, and the decision I made before the military just carried over to police work.

—◊◊◊—

I first started thinking about becoming a cop probably just a couple years before I came on the department. Part of it was that my husband applied for the department, and I kept being told that I had a better chance than he did. People told us that he was too white, too male, and since I'm American Indian, I'd have a better chance of getting on. The other part of it was that I'd always been interested in law enforcement, the legal aspect of it, the investigative part of it. My father's a lawyer, and I always liked the law. I was fascinated with it. I thought a long time ago about maybe being a lawyer but didn't really like lawyers too much so decided, no, that wasn't what I wanted to do. But I never thought I'd go into law enforcement. Never really even considered it. Then, when I kept being told that I'd have a better chance to get hired than my husband, it just sort of made me think, "Well, OK. I'm in for a career change anyway. So why not?"

I was in my late thirties, working at a medical office when I decided to apply to the police department. It took about a year from when I applied till they hired me. During that year, I was scared to death about whether I could get through the academy because of my age. I had always been athletic, but I'd had a kid, and I had never been the type to run or do all the physical things that you hear about in the academy. I never really thought about the possibility of shootings. My main concern was just getting through all the testing and all the interviews and getting ready for the physical part of the academy.

—∿—

I joined the Marine Corps on my seventeenth birthday, and I had planned on making it a career. When I had about ten years in, I was teaching a rappel class for a regional SWAT academy that was using the Marine Corps rappel tower. Everybody was telling their war stories; we had our war stories and they had their war stories, so it wasn't like it was that big of a deal. Then they started talking about working ten hours a day, four days a week, and anything over ten hours is time and a half. That got me thinking because I worked thirty days a month, twenty-four hours a day, and always got paid the same. When they talked about making $40,000 or more a year, I said, "I'm in the wrong profession." So about four months before my commitment was up, I applied to several law enforcement agencies and had a job waiting for me when I got out of the corps.

Before I became a cop, I never really thought about shootings because I was with the pretty active unit in the Marine Corps, and my primary MOS was all combat-related stuff. We practiced and trained a lot. Did close-quarter combat training, did hand to hand; we did all kinds of stuff that dealt with more violence than what I thought the police were dealing with. I just thought it would be a good career because you can promote, make a good income, you don't really have to worry about layoffs, issues like that. There were other issues too, like being in a profession where I could make a difference. But I thought it would definitely be an easy transition from the military to law enforcement.

—∿—

I had a regular job as a lab tech in a clinical laboratory in a hospital when I decided to apply for a job as a police officer. I was teaching music and working as a freelance musician for extra money. My wife was pregnant with my first daughter, and I knew I had to move into something where I was making more money and had a more secure future. I saw a recruitment poster. The PD happened to be hiring at the time. After I looked into the salary and benefits and what have you, it seemed like the thing to do. I didn't have a major commitment to law enforcement. Now I had thought about it on and off when I was a kid because my granddad was a firefighter. I thought about either becoming a firefighter or a policeman, like probably most all kids do. But I hadn't really thought about becoming a cop for a good many years before I saw that recruitment poster.

When I looked into getting on the PD, it crossed my mind a little bit that I could end up shooting someone, but it was never a real big deal to me. I grew up hunting. My dad's from eastern Kentucky, the good-ole-boy mold, and I grew up with a gun in my hands from the time I was very young, three or four years old. He'd take me out and teach me how to shoot a .22 and stuff, so I grew up with guns. I understood that deadly force was a very real part of the job and the potential was there. I knew what police officers did, and I knew that the possibility of having to shoot somebody was part of it, but I thought about it only in passing. I understood it was a serious part of the job, but it was just never a major issue for me.

—◊◊◊—

The men and women who choose police work bring with them an array of ideas, hopes, dreams, and desires; a variety of backgrounds and motives; and a diversity of perspectives on that most important aspect of policing: the power over life and death. Whatever they have been, done, thought, or felt in the past, once they become cops, they will be counted among that small number of Americans who have legal sanction to take life in a split second. The next chapter deals with how the transformation from ordinary citizen to police officer is accomplished.

CHAPTER TWO

Basic Training

W hen one of the twenty thousand or so law enforcement agencies that dot our nation wants to hire new police officers, they don't simply grab whoever applies for the job, give them a gun and a badge, and put them out on patrol. Rather, they choose new officers from a list of citizens who have passed through a selection process that may include a physical exam, written tests, a background check, and a visit to a psychologist—in addition to the interviews mentioned in the last chapter—which are designed to weed out people who are not physically, emotionally, or psychologically fit for the challenges of police work. Departments then train the men and women they select before sending them to work the streets on their own.

In all but some of the smaller departments, a new officer's training starts at a police academy, which can run from around two months to more than half a year, depending on the agency. There, recruits are taught the basics of policing, including how to shoot guns and when it is appropriate to do so. It is during this training that new police officers begin to shed whatever naive ideas they may have had about shooting people before they came on the job.

Police recruits spend many hours at the firing range learning how to shoot the pistols, shotguns, and rifles they will carry upon graduation and many more hours in classrooms learning the rules about when they may fire these weapons on the street. The broadest ring of instruction that recruits receive regarding when it is appropriate to shoot is the relevant federal law. Federal law has always allowed police officers to use deadly force to defend against attacks that could kill or seriously injure them or others, a standard commonly referred to as the *defense of life doctrine.* Until about twenty years ago, federal law also permitted the police to shoot citizens who ran from them if they believed the fleeing citizen had committed a felony. Then, in 1985, the United States Supreme Court changed things. In *Tennessee* v. *Garner*—a case involving an unarmed burglary suspect who was shot dead while running from the police in Memphis, Tennessee—the justices ruled that it is unconstitutional for police officers to shoot fleeing felony suspects unless the crime of which they are suspected involved violence.[1]

Tennessee v. *Garner* had a major impact on the second set of standards to which police recruits are trained: state law governing deadly force by police officers. States can place more restrictions on officers' use of deadly force than does the federal law, but they cannot be more permissive. Prior to 1985, about half the states had already restricted fatal police power to defense of life and apprehension of violent fleeing felons. After *Tennessee* v. *Garner* was handed down, those states that had allowed officers to shoot nonviolent felons tightened their laws.[2] For the last two decades, then, police recruits have been taught that they can lawfully shoot people only in defense of life and to stop the flight of violent felony suspects.

Federal and state deadly force standards are quite broad, setting only the outer bounds of when police officers may legally shoot citizens. Many police agencies offer additional guidance regarding firearms use in written directives called *shooting policies,* which detail the circumstances under which officers may fire their guns. Most shooting policies have some variant of the defense of life–violent felon standard, but some agencies limit the use of deadly force against people to defense of life, forbidding their officers from shooting violent felons who try to flee. And shooting policies often address many other aspects of police firearms use, such as shooting at or from moving vehicles, firing warning shots, and even when officers may draw and exhibit their weapons. Because shooting policies contain the specific guidelines for when officers working for a given police department are permitted to discharge their firearms, this is the final aspect of shooting rules that recruits learn about in the academy.[3]

Another thing that recruits learn in the academy is that the purpose of deadly force in police work is not to *kill,* but rather to *stop* whomever officers are shooting at from accomplishing an illegal act. Whether it is an individual who is threatening the life of the officer, or a third party, or a violent felon who is trying to escape, police officers are trained that they are permitted to shoot only so long as the citizen they take under fire continues to present an imminent threat or attempts to flee. Once the threat has passed or the felon halts, officers must stop shooting. Thus are police recruits disabused of the popular notion that police officers "shoot to kill."

This misapprehension likely comes from the fact that in being trained to shoot to stop officers are taught that the primary aim point for their weapons is what police trainers call *center mass*—the center of a suspect's torso—which reduces the likelihood that their bullets will miss their mark. A shot that is three inches wide of its aim point when the target is a suspect's sternum will still strike the person. The same off-target shot when the aim point is a suspect's arm will miss the suspect entirely. Because the center mass area contains the vital organs, when bullets hit there, they can do substantial damage, damage that frequently leads to death. But death is a by-product, not the intended purpose, of police gunfire.

The training that recruits receive on how and when to shoot goes hand in hand with instruction about things besides shooting that officers can do to protect themselves and their fellows. Police recruits are taught how to use nonfatal force (punches, kicks, and baton blows, for example); how to deal with the mental and emotional components of violent encounters; how to approach people, places, and vehicles in ways that reduce their exposure to danger; how to talk with the people they contact; how to work effectively with other officers; and many other tactics designed to lower the odds that citizens who wish to harm them can do so.

Classroom instruction and range instruction are often supplemented by other forms of training that put recruits' abilities to the test. Most academies conduct role-play training in which recruits handle simulated calls, with academy instructors (and sometimes fellow recruits) playing the role of citizens. Armed with blank guns or guns that fire some sort of projectile that leaves a mark when it hits, recruits must decide whether to shoot or hold their fire in a variety of circumstances. Many academies augment role-play training with video simulators that present recruits with prerecorded scenarios to test their shoot–don't shoot skill.

Such training gives recruits a glimpse of the sorts of situations they may confront on the street and serves as a transition between the academy and the second phase of the police apprenticeship: field training. During field training, academy graduates are paired with experienced officers, whose job it is to show rookies the ropes, evaluate them, and impart the final lessons they will receive before working the streets "untethered." In the weeks or months that young officers work with their training officers, they begin to apply the various lessons they learned in the academy to the real world and learn many other lessons from the school of hard knocks.

In this chapter, we hear from several officers whose stories about their academy and field training represent the range of what the officers I interviewed experienced during their rookie years. Although the stories focus on deadly force and related matters, they also reveal a good deal about the more general issue of how training prepares men and women for careers in law enforcement. They show, among other things, how young officers learn to deal with people and situations on the streets, the sorts of relationships rookies have with their trainers and their peers, and how their experiences begin to change their expectations about the job—in sum, the process through which novices pass on their way to becoming cops.

The stories are presented in three sets. The first two focus on officers' academy and field training experiences, respectively; the third one deals with how exposure to violence against fellow officers shapes the experience of some rookies.

The Academy

The teaching that recruits receive in firearms use and related topics has one primary objective: to equip young police officers with the ability to protect themselves and other officers from danger—within the confines of law and policy—as they carry out the rest of the policing tasks for which the academy is preparing them. Thus does academy training bring recruits face-to-face with two realities about their chosen occupation: first, that they may one day have to kill; second, that their own life might one day come to a violent end at the hand of another.

The stories in this section illustrate the sorts of training that recruits receive on shootings and related topics and the sorts of ways that young officers respond to this training. Their academy experiences made some officers nervous about the prospect of using force, gave others confidence, and set down lifelong survival habits for others. Some officers felt that the training they received was sound, others believed that it was wholly inadequate, and still others saw both good and bad in the instruction offered to them. The stories that follow show that whatever an officer's take on the time spent in the academy might be, the experience plays a pivotal role in the process of moving rookies from their previous lives and into the violent world of police work.

—◊◊◊—

They covered a lot of stuff in firearms training at the academy. They went over when you can shoot: the fleeing-felon rule, to save a life, your life, a citizen's life. They discussed all that. We did the dry firing, shooting at the academy range, and role-playing. The role-playing was important. They'd give us guns loaded with blanks and put us in different situations, like a family disturbance or a traffic stop, with police officers playing the roles of the citizens. We would have to react to what the guy was doing, and he would force us into a decision to either shoot or don't shoot. It was up to us to make the right call, and the instructors would evaluate us afterwards.

A lot of time also went into the mental part of preparing you for what you might feel afterwards. They told us that some people react different than other people. Between that and the officer survival books I read while I was going through college, I felt like I got good mental preparation for what I might have to do someday.

—✺—

The thing that really stands out in my mind about the deadly force issue in the academy was the officer survival part. One sergeant from the physical-training unit put on this class about building the foundation for officer survival. He showed us pictures of officers who were killed in shootings that are still set in my mind thirty years later. He told us the stories of how they got killed and pointed out some of the mistakes they might have made that gave the people who murdered them the chance to kill them. I vividly remember him talking about the stainless steel table that the officers were laying on at the morgue. He told us that we don't want to put ourselves in that position and asked us if we thought the officers could have done something differently to avoid getting killed. He said that we can't know for sure because we can't talk to the officer about what exactly happened but that they probably could have.

Another big thing I remember was weaponless defense. They'd have us wrestle with other recruits to the point where one of us had to render the other one unconscious. I wasn't about to let anybody put my lights out, so it was some really intense training. What stuck in my mind the most about that is the physical-fitness part. You have to be in shape to prevail. I'm fifty-four years old now. I've had three major surgeries in the last year from some complications that came up from getting shot twenty-seven years ago, but I know that I'm physically fit and strong. I probably can't do a lot of the things I did before, but the physical-fitness thing has stuck in my mind throughout my career. We know it goes hand in hand with survival, so what I learned about it early on in my career never left me.

—✺—

They spent a lot of time on deadly force in the academy. We got a lot on what the legal guidelines were, but I didn't find what the instructors that were lawyers or prosecutors had to say was that helpful or informative. One of the things that I found most helpful or informative was listening to experienced officers relate war stories or situations that they had been involved in. Hearing about what they went through, the feelings and thoughts they had, was important. That was probably what I found most interesting about the topic of deadly force. The prosecutors and lawyers would be discussing the topic from a different point of view than what I was going to be doing. I just felt like I was getting a more solid piece of information when an officer was talking because I was getting it from somebody that had been in it.

—◊◊◊—

Looking back on the academy, I'd say we got some good training on deadly force and some that was not so good. The instructors went through state law and what our manual states about when shootings are OK, what's legal and all that. They also talked about how the penal code in this state allows citizens to shoot a thief at night—but that police officers can't. They stressed that as police officers we would be held to a higher standard than Joe Citizen, particularly in civil court, where we could be held liable even if we got in a shooting that was justified by state law.

We also had a couple of officers who had been involved in shootings come in to talk to us, but they weren't real good at teaching. I think that if you're going to have officers who have been in shootings talk to a bunch of young cadets—the majority of them being twenty- to twenty-five-year-olds who have no clue of what's going to happen when they get out—you need officers who can open up and tell their stories effectively. The guys who talked to us weren't good at that, so we didn't learn that much from them. Probably the best training in the academy was from my tactics instructor. He stressed that when you hit the streets, you always have to be thinking, playing out scenarios in your mind, planning for situations that might occur. Asking questions like, How are we going to stop that car? What's going to happen if I stop that car? What if he pulls a gun on me? What if he pulls a knife? What am I going to do? The way he put it, you're not going to know how you're going to respond in a shooting situation until it happens, so you need to be ready. Be aware, be alert. Keep your mind there, and you'll be ready for it.

One of the things he talked about was that some officers start to get lax after a while. They get up on a nice side of town where nothing serious ever happens, where they aren't dealing with drug addicts, banditos, and other guys who are willing to mix it up, so they stop thinking about being alert. They get up there with Joe Q. Citizen, who pays his taxes and most of the time drives the speed limit. Maybe they catch him speeding once in a while, but that's about it. After a while, their minds go to shit. They aren't ready for it anymore. He warned us not to let that happen to us, because if you do, you stand to lose your life.

—∿∿—

They lectured to us extensively about when to use and when not to use lethal force. Probably not as much as they do now, because when I went through, it was only a four-month academy. Now it's six months. But they did touch on a lot of stuff about deadly force, and I think a lot of times they touched on it for liability's sake. They talked about the legal process of it, the department process, how the Homicide section investigates all the department's officer-involved shootings, but they didn't go into it from the officer's standpoint and how it's going to affect them. They never really sat there and said, "You'll probably feel something like this," or "You'll feel withdrawn," or "You'll feel mad, or upset, or glad." They never really covered anything like that, so I didn't really know exactly what to expect.

One thing they did talk about was how it feels to get shot. One of the guys that was on our hostage response team at the time came in and talked to us about that. He said that getting shot feels like a hot poker that just goes right through your body. It was sort of hard for me to relate to that because I had never had to deal with anything like that. I'd been cut before to the point where I needed stitches, I'd had broken bones, I'd had sprains, but you can't sit there and tell somebody, "Hey, this is how it's gonna feel to get shot. You're gonna have this tremendous pain" and whatnot. I don't think you can really relate to somebody how it feels if they haven't been through it. So I don't think there's anything that he could say that could've prepared us for how we could feel if we got shot. The only thing that he said that did make sense was that just because you're shot doesn't mean you're gonna die, so you should stay in the fight as long as you possibly can. Don't just sit there and freak out: "Oh, my God, I got shot." So he told us to just keep fighting until you just possibly can't fight anymore.

—∿∿—

Our firearms training instructor had been involved in multiple shootings, so I thought he was very qualified to teach that class. He said that the thing that stuck out from his first experience was seeing a dead officer laying in a ditch. That got my undivided attention, so I listened to everything he said. One thing I remember he always said was, "Never give up. No matter how dim it seems—even if you get shot—don't give up." That really stood out in my mind, and I think it kept me alive when I got in my shooting.

———~~~———

We had a lot of classes on arrest control/defensive tactics—twenty of those, so we had eighty hours of that. Then we had firearms training simulators that put us in "shoot" or "don't shoot" situations and a lot of scenario training. We also had a two-week officer survival block that covered shootings, deadly force, and lessons from officers that had been involved in shootings. So force issues were covered pretty well.

From all that, I knew that a shooting could happen to any officer, but I never really believed that it was gonna happen to me. It was something I thought other officers were going to get involved in. I wasn't naive to the fact that it could happen, but I didn't think it would. Everybody in my class talked about the prospect of getting in shootings. Even though I didn't think I'd get in any, I always knew that if it came down to it that I'd be able to react and do what I needed to do. So I never had those doubts that a lot of officers have.

———~~~———

My dad hunted all his life, so I grew up around guns and always felt comfortable that I'd be able to handle myself in a shooting situation. But one thing that happened in the academy showed me that maybe my level of confidence was too strong. It was a training scenario with the FATS machine where I got shot. I had a suspect at gunpoint who was holding a pistol in one of his hands that were raised above his head in a surrender position. Being the good shooter that I was, I was sure that I'd be able to shoot this guy before he could shoot me. He brought the gun down and shot me before I could get a shot off. That frightened me a lot and really illuminated my thinking on how to deal with noncompliant people in a deadly force situation. I thought, "Hmm, this is a good way to get killed. This is something that I never would have expected, and it's very dangerous, and it's something I need to be aware of to keep myself from getting killed."

Since then, I have done a lot of scenario training where I have been the suspect, and I can routinely shoot people who have their guns pointed at me before they shoot me. The first time happened shortly after I got shot in the FATS scenario. We were doing "hot stop" train-ing, and everybody in the class had to have the opportunity to be in each of the positions: the primary officer, the cover officer, and the assistant officer. By doing these rotations, we had to have people acting as the suspect each time. During one of my stints as the suspect, the trainers told me that they wanted me to be aggressive. I decided I was going to go down shooting. When my classmates that were playing the role of officers ordered me out of the car, I had the gun in my waistband. They ordered me to walk backwards toward them, and as I was doing that, I kept bringing my arm down to my face. I was coughing, pretending like I had a cough, and I kept bringing my hand down even though they told me not to. At one point when I did that, I just brought my hand all the way down to my waistband, drew the blank gun, spun around, and started shooting them. I got several shots off before they shot back. I thought, "Wow, this really does work. Even I can do it."

From those scenarios, I recognized that if someone on the street is holding a weapon and they are noncompliant, I am not going to get to the point where they are going to shoot me before I take some sort of protective action. So the scenarios were a big part of my firearms training, and they affected my decision-making process and how I felt about deadly force and shooting people.

—∿∿—

When I applied for the job, the testing process focused on English, math, and stuff like that. In the oral interview, they wanted to know what I believed the job entailed, but they didn't ask me any questions about shooting. That changed a lot once I got to the academy, however. There was a bunch of instruction on officer-involved shootings, what actions to take, what happens if officers get shot, if they die, how you relate to your family and stuff like that if you shoot someone. I remember seeing a lot of videotapes about shootings; the majority of them dealt with officers who lived through them, with a focus on how to mentally prepare yourself, to never give up if you find yourself in a gun battle, the will to survive, stuff like that.

Those tapes really made an impression on me because I remember thinking that if I ever did get into a shooting that I would want to know that I can react so that my partner wouldn't die due to my inability to act. I didn't dwell on it. I never thought that shootings were a big part of the job because I had always thought that dealing with people and whatnot were the major parts of police work. But in the back of my mind, I always thought that it could happen and that I had to prepare myself mentally for the possibility. I remember thinking that it's better to be prepared for it than to be caught off guard. I believed it when the instructors told us that we needed to be ready, even though the odds of getting into a shooting are slim. It probably won't happen, but if it does, you're behind the eight ball if you're not ready.

The two things that really, really stuck out in my mind about all this was the will-to-survive stuff that we saw on the videotapes and the emphasis the instructors put on being prepared, that fighting to the end is what is going to keep you alive and that messing up and getting killed or getting your partner killed may put you and/or your partner's family through a lot of emotional trauma. That you can screw up and cause your partner to get shot, and then you have to live with knowing that you could have avoided it if you'd been better prepared. I made up my mind in the academy that I didn't want to have to be one of those officers who ended up with a dead partner because I should have done something different. I decided that if a shooting came my way that I was going to perform right. After I got out of the academy, I came back up to the range about every week or so to practice my shooting. I just wasn't confident in my own proficiency in firearms. I had passed the minimum standards at the academy, but as far as I was concerned, that wasn't good enough. I figured that if I ever did get in a shooting, the minimum just wasn't gonna cut it, so I'd shoot every week. Just shoot, shoot, shoot. That way, I'd have one less thing to worry about if I got into a shooting. I also did a lot of what I call the "what if" games in my mind. What if this happened? What would I do? What if that happened? I figured that if I played things out in my mind that I'd be ready if it did happen in real life.

—◦◦◦—

When I went through the academy, the deadly force training focused on the legal aspects of shootings: civil liability, criminal liability, when you can and when you can't use deadly force. I paid close attention to that block of instruction, thinking to myself that I really needed to remember the stuff because I could get in trouble later if I made a wrong decision about pulling the trigger, so I really focused on those legal issues in the academy.

I took another class that dealt with shootings after I was out on the street, but the focus was completely different. The instructors talked about mental preparation and rehearsal for situations that could occur. That stuff interested me because rehearsing for things that might happen allows you quicker reaction time when and if they do come your way. The goal was to get us to where we didn't have to try to figure out a solution at the time of the stress, which is the worst time to be trying to think about stuff like that. You figure out how you are going to react to the situation prior to its happening; then, when it happens, all you have to do is basically draw it from your random-access memory. Then you can quickly respond to the situation, because you have already thought of what you are going to do; all you have to do is react instead of thinking of a reaction first. One of the things they taught us to do for this was to look at incidents that had happened within our department or incidents that realistically could happen to us and run through our minds what we would do in those particular situations. They taught us to condition ourselves to go to cover, to return fire if necessary, to change positions, to reload. They even covered follow-up as far as what to say on the radio—so you don't sound like an idiot if you do get in a shooting—and some other things you need to do: preserve the scene, render first aid, treat yourself if you're injured. So all those kinds of things were discussed in the mental-preparation class.

The one thing I didn't get any training on is how shootings can affect officers. Not in the academy, and even all the way up to my first shooting, I never received any training on that. No one ever mentioned anything to me about the aftermath of shootings. Then, when the first one happened, I wasn't prepared for it at all.

—◊◊◊—

I went into the marines in 1965 and served with the Thirty-Third Reconnaissance Battalion in Vietnam from '66 through '68. Our mission wasn't to seek contact, but I was involved in quite a few firefights. When I got into the academy, the differences between the military and police work surprised me. One of the biggest differences was the lethal-force issue. The difference between the military and the civilian sector is that when I was in the military, there were really no rules of engagement. When I was in Vietnam, we had a basic rule of engagement: you see the enemy, you shoot. In civilian law enforcement, it was a whole different concept. There were a whole lot of parameters assigned to it with the department rules and the state law you have to follow. So you have to make decisions regarding shootings, which was something that I never experienced in the military. In the military, they didn't encourage us to have a lot of independent thought. It was basically reaction to outside stimulus, so it was pretty easy to make decisions about shooting. There wasn't a whole lot of thought. In law enforcement, there's a lot more gray to deal with. I think the term that I remember the most from the academy was *discretionary decision making.* That was a term that was totally different from anything that I had heard before. And I think that's what probably translated into the biggest difference between the military and civilian law enforcement: in police work, you have to make decisions that fit the circumstances with the rules.

As a matter of fact, it seemed to me at first that the rules about shooting were a little limiting and restrictive. I thought, "Man, I've got to make that decision to shoot." There was a big difference between not having to really give it a whole lot of thought—that everything's a threat in the military—to having to evaluate each situation. Especially because you have a very limited period of time to make decisions. At first, I thought that was really confining. I thought, "How am I going to be able to react in such a short period of time?" Once I got through the academy, I realized that experience gives you the ability to evaluate things a lot quicker and react a lot quicker than I first thought was possible. In fact, I think that experience is probably the most important aspect of law enforcement. That and maturity. Together they give you the ability to make good decisions.

—◊◊◊—

The key thing they taught us about deadly force in the academy was to try to avoid being in a shooting. They said you can do that by just practicing officer safety to eliminate a lot of unnecessary risks: watching suspects' hands, keeping your distance, not charging up on a suspect if you think he has a weapon, giving vocal commands from behind cover. A lot of it involves common sense. They said that our job was to come home after that eight-hour shift. Not to be John Wayne or Audie Murphy and take a bullet or give a bullet, but just to come home.

—◊◊◊—

We were taught a force continuum in the academy that went from the spoken word, to empty-hand techniques, to minimal weapons like mace, to the dog, to impact weapons like the nightstick, and then on up to deadly force. What I really got out of it was that they emphasized that deadly force was the last thing to be used, that we shouldn't use it unless we absolutely have to. They made it clear to us that deadly force was our very last option, and they went through and taught us a lot of empty-hand techniques like hand-to-hand type combat, how to take people down, and the proper cuffing procedures. So they spent a lot of time showing us that there are other ways to handle things than to just go out and shoot somebody.

Field Training

Just as different police academies have different educational regimens, different law enforcement agencies structure their field training programs in different ways. Some agencies, for example, have formal field training programs, staffed by senior patrol officers who have gone through specialized training in how to train rookies and who have the formal title *field training officer*, whereas other agencies simply assign rookies to veteran officers, who are tasked with informally showing rookies the ropes. In some agencies, rookies ride with training officers for just a few weeks, and in others they patrol with trainers for several months. In some agencies, rookies ride patrol with several different training officers, whereas in others young officers work with the same one during their entire field training tenure.

Another major difference in how law enforcement agencies approach field training concerns the timing of it. Although the vast majority of agencies send academy graduates directly to the street, some—primarily large sheriff's departments that run the county lockup in addition to providing general police services—assign their newly minted rookies to work the jail for an extended period of time (up to five years) before sending them on to patrol. Such officers in essence remain rookies during the time they work at the jail before heading to the street. Only after successfully completing their field training do young officers who have spent years working the jail become full-fledged cops.

Most of the officers I interviewed went straight to the street from the academy, and I focused my questions about all of the officers' rookie experiences on the time they spent with training officers. Consequently, most of the following stories deal with the field training experiences of officers whose time on the street immediately followed graduation from the police academy. We hear from cops whose training officers stressed the importance of being prepared for gunfights and from those whose field trainers essentially ignored the issue. We hear them talk about the lessons they learned from their training officers, the sorts of interactions they had with citizens and how they reacted to these encounters, their thoughts and feelings about what they were going through, and much more about rookies' initial encounter with the potentially deadly world that lies beyond the protective cocoon of the academy.

—∿∿—

Everything about shootings was kind of sugarcoated in the academy. They'd do some stuff to try to scare you, but none of it seemed real. They'd tell you that you may have to shoot and that you have to be ready and so on and so forth, but it wasn't until well after the academy, when I was getting near the end of the two and a half years at the jail that just about all new deputies have to work before working the street, that I really started to think about deadly force issues. At that point, I knew that in not too long I was going to go out on patrol. That's when I started thinking about it.

We get to give them a list of stations we'd like to go to, and the stations I chose as my preferences were all very fast urban stations where officer-involved shootings were happening on a regular basis. When some of the supervisors who'd been around for a while found out where I wanted to go, they said, "Those places are crazy. Are you ready for that?" That type of thing.

So I thought about it and I talked about it with the other deputies who were about to get wheeled out. I told myself and the other deputies, "Yeah, I'll be able to do that. Sure, I could shoot somebody. Sure, no big deal." That was the talk. In hindsight, that's not the case. I wasn't even ready for the everyday stuff. I don't think anybody's ready when they first show up in a busy division. I don't care how prepared you think you are. The minute you show up there for the first time and everything's real, it's a whole different ball game. You're a baby. You start out from scratch. You don't know anything. So you may think you're ready, but you're not.

—∿—

In my agency, when you come out of the academy, you're given a field training officer, who you ride with for ten weeks. Mine was a guy by the name of Chris Cooper in the fifth district. We rode Hooker, which was kind of a rough neighborhood. I sometimes worked with other guys, and different FTOs had different policies. Some of 'em would say, "OK, you learned in the academy, but here's what you really need to know." The idea of field training was to get young officers involved in as many situations as they can while they have somebody there to help them make the right decisions. What they do is when you first start out, the first couple of weeks, the FTO makes all the decisions, and then gradually, as the weeks go by, you take a more active role. As you show that you can make the right decisions, they let you make 'em, and they sit back and become the observer. I felt it was a good training process. It's a good process as long as you have good, experienced FTOs.

On deadly force, they told me that at any given time, in any situation, you might be called to use your weapon. The one thing they always emphasized is that when you pull the gun and you're getting ready to point the gun, it's not to be used as a bluff. If you're gonna pull the trigger, it's because you need to take a life, not to wound the guy, not to shoot the gun out of his hand, but to take a life, so don't pull it out unless you plan on using it.

—∿∿—

I recall on my first day out of the academy, we went to do a warrant, and I remember just shaking and I couldn't stop. It was cold out, but it wasn't that cold. I was going, "Damn, I'm really scared." I'd never been that scared before. I'd jumped out of airplanes in the army, and there was fright there, but not like on that warrant. I was sitting there shaking, going, "Man, I can't stop myself from shaking." My training officer and I were standing outside next to this door, and the guys we were assisting told us the guy in there may be dealing narcotics. Well, I knew narcotics and guns go hand in hand, so I was thinking rounds were gonna be coming through the door any second. We were just standing out in front of a wall that based on my military experience I knew was not gonna stop a whole lot of types of rounds. I think that my fear was fear of the unknown: Is this guy just gonna be complacent and come out, or is he gonna just start shooting through the wall? That was probably the main reason for the intenseness at that point.

It was interesting to see myself doing that, and over time I learned to control it by focusing on what I need to do. I think fear is a good thing because fear will keep you alive. If you go into situations with your head up your ass and you have no fear, you can get hurt. I see guys out there that have no fear factor, and they just go in blindly and they sometimes get hurt. Fear to me is something I can control. I can contain it and then I use it to my advantage. If I'm fearing something, that means I'm missing some important information. So when I feel it, I try to pick up what I'm missing. Once I get all the info, it brings me back into a calmer state, a more controlled state, and I can do my job safely.

—∿∿—

Some of my training officers were better than others concerning deadly force. Some of them were out there just going through the motions, and you could tell which ones were and which ones weren't. The lousy ones never brought it up. The really good ones talked about it. Let's say we were in an alley, and we were gonna contact these two guys. The good ones would say, "If they turn around and start shooting, you need to think about where you're going to go, where your rounds are gonna go," things of that nature. That really clicked in: "Holy shit. It could happen." So that's what I do with the rookies I train now. I tell them, "Don't think that because you're at a slow division that you can't get in a shooting. It doesn't matter where you are. Seven days a week, twenty-four hours a day, you can get in a shooting. You should always think of that." So I've always remembered from when I was a rookie that no matter what you're doing, where you're at, what call you're on, it could turn into some kind of shooting situation.

—◊◊◊—

Some of my training officers talked with me about shootings and some didn't. When they did, most of it involved some sort of a lesson. The one I remember best was that my first FTO took me to Orange Avenue Park, where two officers had been shot—both fatally—a few years before. I had seen a video re-creation of what happened at the academy, but when I went to the park and actually saw where the officers had been shot, I started feeling sort of like, "Wow, this is where it happened." It felt a little eerie seeing the bench the suspects had been sitting on, the exact places the officers were standing when they were shot, the pond where the suspect hid for several hours before he was caught. It was kind of neat and kind of eerie to see where all this happened and brought it home to me that getting shot is a very real possibility.

—◊◊◊—

I had one FTO who was a SWAT officer, and he would drive to a place, stop, and ask questions like, "OK, if this was happening at this time what would you do?" One time we went to a 7-Eleven, and he asked me if someone had hostages inside and they came out by themselves with a gun, then turned to walk back in, if I would shoot that person in order to make sure they did not go back inside. I was fresh from the academy and was thinking about the legal aspects, but I was also trying to think of what I would do in that split second.

We had dealt with issues like that in the academy, but when you're sitting at a spot instead of just being told about it on the chalkboard or seeing it on video, I think it hits home more. Even though you think about these things in the academy, you're also thinking about a million other things, because you're pretty much overloaded—at least I was, mentally and physically overloaded—so not everything sinks in. But when you're out here in the field, and it's three o'clock in the morning, and you're sitting in front of a 7-Eleven, it makes you really think.

My first answer was, "Yes, I'd shoot him because I don't want a hostage situation." But then I thought, "Well, where are the hostages? Exactly where are the people in the store? Are they behind him? Are they within the range of being shot?" So it really makes you visually see a scenario. Even though you can visually see scenarios on tape in the academy, they're pretty much plotted out for you. But when you're in the field, you see that there are a lot of things to consider.

Baptism by Fire

Some officers don't make it very far into their apprenticeship before being hit in the face with the stark reality of the dangers involved in their new line of work. Some rookies see colleagues shoot people, others have colleagues who are shot or otherwise severely injured, and some experience both phenomena. Being witness to extreme violence by or against fellow officers can have a profound effect on how rookies view the job they are learning to do. As the following stories indicate, this was certainly the case for some of the officers I interviewed. From a recruit who is sent out to help search for a man who murdered a police officer and ends up witnessing other officers kill the suspect, to a young officer who had completed the academy but not yet started his field training who finds himself on the business end of a gang-banger's rifle, the stories show how exposure to police-involved violence fits into the overall picture of rookies learning the ropes.

—◦◦◦—

I applied to the PD when I was still on active duty, but I didn't get out on time because Desert Storm had everybody locked in. I had to turn down an academy start date, so the general I was bodyguarding for said, "As soon as the war is over, I'll get you out. I'll get you an early out, and we'll get you in the next academy." In fact, I was actually still active duty for thirty days when I started the academy. I came in with a lot of high expectations even though one of the guys who interviewed me said, "I'm gonna tell you this off the record 'cuz I don't want to see you dismayed by this job, but don't expect out of your peers what you expect out of yourself." At the time, I didn't really fully understand what he meant, but then once I got in the academy, I saw that there were people in my class who didn't really have a grasp on reality, who had no idea what they were getting themselves into. Then we also had people who got into it for paychecks. I got into it because it was something I always wanted to do, not just a paycheck. It was something I always wanted to do, and something I took pride in doing once I got in. So when I saw what some of the other people were all about, I understood what the interviewer meant.

Some of the differences between me and those other cadets became evident during what they called Hell Week, where the instructors went through all the officers from the PD who had been killed in the line of duty. They showed the autopsy photos and really delved into how they were killed. When I saw the photos, I thought, "I don't want to be in one of those pictures," so I focused on what the instructors said about mistakes the officers made. I tried to learn from it. There were several other people who thought the way I did, so there was a group of us that were really serious, really intense. Every day we went to the range, we focused on what we did. Our attitude was, "We're not gonna let what happened to those other guys happen to us." The other people didn't take the firearms training days seriously. Their attitude was, "Hey, it's just another day at work. Its just a job that's gonna pay the bills." Most of those people ended up quitting over the years. Once they saw the ugliness of the job, they quit and moved on to other things.

Besides the regular Hell Week, we had some other stuff happen during the academy. Not too long before we got out, a patrol officer was shot and killed in Northwest Division, and we got called out of the academy to do a quote "evidence search" while the scene was still hot. We had been out at the range, just about to start shooting class, when the instructors told us to put our guns away and meet at this CP. When we got there, they tried to feed us the line that they thought the suspect had already fled the area and that we were just going to be searching for the weapon. But I could tell—I knew from my military experience—that they were doing a grid search, not an evidence sweep.

Plus the SWAT guys were out there with Benellis and MP-5s, and they were searching some houses. We were probably about a hundred feet away when they found the suspect, shot and killed him. We could hear the rounds being fired. It was pretty wild.

When it was all over, there was a lot of anger in the class. Anger toward the suspect for killing the officer and anger toward the department for throwing us out there unarmed. It shocked a lot of the people who weren't really squared away. Probably about five of them. They started going, "You really can get killed doing this job." And we were like, "No kidding." Those of us in that group that was highly intense, we said, "You know what? You should have known this going in. It could happen. You may even have to kill somebody yourself."

—✿—

The academy taught us the normal procedures—patrol, how to handle certain situations, a lot of role-playing. We did a little red-handle training, where we'd have a nonworking gun and run scenarios, shooting scenarios. The emphasis was on instruction in the law, the state and federal laws about deadly force. Then we also did firearms training on the range. The state has a six-hundred-hour requirement, so I was at the academy eight hours a day, five days a week, for four months. Then I was out on the street.

None of my family members had ever been in any shootings, and I don't believe that I ever talked to any of the family friends who were officers about being in shootings, so I didn't really think much about shootings before I became a cop. That changed pretty early on in my career. Not too long after I started on the street, my sergeant was killed. I was working the desk on the midnight shift when an alarm came out at a women's clothing store in the Westpark Shopping Center. My sergeant responded; then the other units couldn't raise him on the radio. They kept calling for him, but there was no response. Then, when they arrived at the store, they found him lying in front of his car. He'd been murdered and his gun was missing. It turns out that he had interrupted a burglary and had the drop on two suspects. Unknown to him, there was a third one that was hiding behind a parked car. He came up from behind and jumped my sergeant. The guys ended up taking his gun. Then they pistol-whipped him and took his life; shot him with his own gun. The case went unresolved for about three years; then we finally caught two of the guys. They both stood trial, and one was acquitted and one was found guilty.

About a month and a half after my sergeant got murdered, we had an officer shot after he pulled over a vehicle. He had stopped a car with two occupants that was reported stolen. The passenger wouldn't show his hands at first, then he whipped out a gun, and shot. One round hit the officer in the lower abdomen and he went down. The suspects were gone by the time the first backup officers got there, but later on they found the guy hiding down in the business section of the city.

So even though I started out in a small town, it was by no means a slow town.

—∿—

I didn't take the possibility of getting into a shooting too seriously when I first came on the job. I'd been an MP in the army, worked on the DMZ in Korea, spent a few years as a guard in military prisons, and worked in the federal correctional system before becoming a cop. In all those experiences, though, the threats were pretty distant. Sure, it was tense sometimes in Korea, but when we weren't up in the trenches, it was really one big party. Back in the states, there wasn't much so far as crime on the bases I worked because the military community is pretty squared away. It was the same way in the military prisons. It's not like a state prison, where the inmates can grow their hair long and have mustaches and beards. These guys had to keep a military appearance, the whole business; even some of the lifers were real squared away. There was some inmate-on-inmate violence, but nothing really against the guards. When I was with the federal corrections system, I worked mostly a roaming patrol they had on the outside of the facility, so I didn't see much violence there. I mean, I knew that shootings could happen, but I never actually thought about it. Same thing in the academy and during my FTO phase. I got all the deadly force training and my training officers talked to me about shooting situations, but I never really gave it much thought.

That all changed not too long after I got done with the FTO phase of my training. I was still on probation when I got a call of a family disturbance where the son, who had just gotten out of prison, was supposedly threatening his mother and brothers. He was upset with them because they had some hand in getting him sent away about two years prior. He was over at their place threatening to kill them for what they did. There were no other patrol units available to cover me on the call, so my sergeant came over the air and said he'd back me up. When we were a few blocks away, the dispatcher gave us some more information. She told us that the mother had called back and reported that her son was standing outside with a gun. This didn't bother me much because citizens in that area regularly report that people have guns even when they don't in order to get us to respond quicker. Well, my sergeant got to the location just before I did. As I was pulling up and he was getting out of his car, a guy who matched the suspect's description to a tee ran out through a gate between some apartments just in front of my sergeant's car. My sergeant started to chase the suspect, and I got out of my car to help out. As I was running toward them, I couldn't see what was happening real well because the head- and spotlights of my sergeant's car were shining in my eyes. Just as I was breaking through the glare of the lights, the suspect pulled out a big chrome .357 revolver—I guess he had it in his pants. I was about one car length away when my sergeant dropped to his knees, brought his gun up, and fired a round that killed the guy.

That was a real wake-up call for me. It was when reality set in for me with this job. I mean, up until then I was really just a happy-go-lucky kid. The criminals I'd dealt with in the army and federal corrections were in a secured environment, and their weapons are limited to daggers and stuff. Then, when I first came on the job, I was just a young cop driving around in a police car, chasing bad guys and having a blast. But reality hit when my sergeant killed that guy. I realized that I was going to run into people like the guys I'd worked with in the pen, but they were going to have better weapons, and they weren't always going to do what I told them to. They weren't confined, so they could choose to fight to try to get away. The shooting made me realize that being a cop was different, that it's life and death.

—◇—

I worked for the sheriff's office for about two years before coming to work for the city. The agencies are different in a lot of ways, and that started in the academy. The sheriff's academy taught me more about how to be a better officer in the sense of contacting people, that you always need to be in command of any situation you come in contact with. The city academy expounded more on the officer survival mindset, basically the notion that you gotta be able to take care of yourself and your partner and the people that you're gonna be working for.

There were also some big differences in field training. I worked with the same partner for four months at the sheriff's department, and he basically was in charge of me. He would tell me what to do, and I was expected to do it. Where officer safety goes, he really stressed that if you get into a shooting, it will probably be when you're not expecting it, so he made sure I was aware of that and stressed that I had to be ready all the time. He told me to make sure that all the people we talk to have been patted down before we have any conversation with them, just for our safety. He basically told me, "Damn everybody else, damn who you're talking to, just make sure that they're not packing when you talk to 'em. Anybody who comes up asking information of you, you gotta go ahead and pat them down for your own safety because they know who you are and you don't know who they are." He made it very, very clear that he expected me to search everybody.

When I got to the city, I worked with several different training officers. There was more give-and-take with them compared to my first partner at the sheriff's department, because once they found out that I had prior police experience, they felt comfortable with me. They were more into just teaching policies and procedures, how things should be done. They would offer a couple of suggestions here and there on tactics and explain why they did things in particular ways. So it was more of a give-and-take situation, where I could make suggestions about things and we would agree on a solution.

One thing that was the same about being a young cop in both agencies is that I worked in places where there was a lot of violence going on. I saw officers die in the street in both places. When I was in the sheriff's department, a classmate of mine was shot and killed. I responded to the help call. It made me sit back and reevaluate the situation I was in: seeing a classmate lying on the sidewalk, shot in the head, blood running down the driveway into the gutter while the paramedics were trying to work on him. He died three days later. I stuck with law enforcement, but his death hit me with the reality that it could happen to me. Then, when I got to the city, one of the guys on my shift was deliberately run over by a suspect during a pursuit. I watched him die right there in the street. It's tough, seeing officers at roll call, and then a few hours later they're gone.

—◊◊◊—

I worked the jail for the first three years after I got out of the academy. I'd been there about two months when one of my partners from the jail, a guy named Harold, and I got in an off-duty shooting when this gang-banger recognized him from custody. I didn't fire any rounds, but my buddy got shot.

I lived in a rough area, and the guy recognized Harold when he came to pick me up at my house one night. He told me that these gang-bangers had yelled at him from a car a few blocks away, followed him a little bit, then turned off before he got to my house. We were in no rush to get going, so I took a shower, we relaxed, and then left my place about forty-five minutes after Harold got there.

When we got to the street where the carful of gang-bangers had turned off, Harold said, "Hey, why don't we roll down the street, get the plate number, and we'll give it to Ralph," a buddy of ours who worked patrol that was going to meet us later on that night. When he turned down the street, it was totally black because all the streetlights had been shot out. There was a big old gang party going on, and the car that had the guys who had yelled at my partner was parked in front of us in the street. As soon as we saw that, we decided to get out of there. As we took off, the guys from the car recognized us and started pointing at us and yelling. They jumped in their car and pulled out after us, along with another carful of gang-bangers. When we got to the corner, the second car pulled up pretty close to us, and I could see that one of the guys in that second car had a rifle.

We turned off real quick, went a few blocks, and pulled over at this 7-Eleven to call 9-1-1. We were going to tell them that there was a 417 with a rifle, the number of suspects in the cars, that sort of stuff. As we were talking on the phone, the second car came around the corner, and the suspect with the rifle popped up out of the window and started firing on us.

The backdrop behind the car was a hamburger stand across the parking lot where there were about forty people standing in line, so we couldn't fire back. Instead we dropped the phone and dove behind my buddy's car for cover. After the guy stopped shooting, the car drove off around the corner. We ran to the corner with our guns in our hands to see if they were stopping or if they were going to keep going. They continued, so we both ran back to the car, jumped in, and I said, "Let's get out of here!"

As we jumped in the car, the guys came back. There was a lot of commotion in the parking lot; people were running all over the place. My partner was looking over his shoulder, backing out the car, so he didn't see the guys coming at us from the left front part of his car. When I saw the gangsters' car, one of the suspects was hanging out the window with his rifle. I remember distinctly that another passenger in the rear was holding on to him as he leaned out the window so he wouldn't fall out of the car as he leveled his rifle at us.

I came up with my gun, getting ready to shoot the guy hanging out the window, and I saw Harold out of the corner of my eye. I was thinking that Harold was going to get shot, no doubt in my mind. I don't know what it was, but I knew he was going to get hit, so at that point I chose to grab him and pull him down rather than shoot. Well, as I grabbed Harold and pulled him down, the guy hanging out the window fired several rounds. At that point, he was right on top of us, about ten to twelve feet away. Three of the rounds struck Harold, one in the shoulder and two in his left forearm. We later found out—when the detectives did the trajectory thing where they put rods through the windshield and all that stuff—that the one that caught him in the shoulder would have been a fatal round, right in the middle of the chest.

After they went by, I jumped out of the car. By the time I got out, they had turned the corner and were gone, so I couldn't return fire. Harold was bleeding. He was wearing a white shirt and he was bleeding a lot. He said, "Man, I got shot. I got shot in my heart." I said, "No, stupid"—I mean, we grew up together—"No, stupid, it's your shoulder." He goes, "Yeah, yeah, it's my shoulder. I'm all right." So I drove Harold to the hospital, and they took care of him. I gave the officers who responded to the hospital the info on the car, and they ended up getting everybody except for the shooter that night. They got the shooter about a week or two later.

I had a hard time dealing with what happened for the longest time because I didn't know if I had done the right thing. I wondered if I should have dumped the guy with the rifle or if I did the right thing by pulling Harold down. I also thought that I could have reacted a little quicker the first time they came around and engaged them before they turned the corner, but I eventually came to grips with what I did. Harold was OK, he didn't sustain any long-term injuries, so I figured it worked out for the best. But I still think that if I would have reacted faster after the gangsters made their first pass that I could have got them. I was inexperienced and I hesitated a little bit. When the guy first started shooting, it caught me off guard. It was like, "Wow, this is for real."

—◦◦◦—

Whether it is the extreme intensity of the stories in the last section or the less dramatic introduction to policing that most rookies receive, what young officers go through in the academy and in their first months on the streets has a lasting impact on what type of cops they will become. All new officers have to make many choices about how they will carry out their duties once they graduate from rookie status. And no choice is more important than developing a personal sense of when they will be willing to shoot someone; for as the last story indicates, the proper course of action during tense, rapidly evolving circumstances is not always clear. Consideration of this issue is the subject of Chapter Three.

CHAPTER THREE

Holding Fire

T he federal laws, state statutes, and shooting policies that officers work under are quite broad, providing only general directions about firearms use. For the simple reason that no two encounters between cops and citizens are exactly alike, it is not possible for judges, legislators, and police administrators to develop laws and policies that provide specific details about whether officers should shoot in any particular case. Because legal and administrative deadly force standards are so broad and general, young officers must somehow make sense of them as they pass through their apprenticeship and head toward their unsupervised time on the street. As young officers do this, they develop their own personal set of standards about when they will use their firearms—in essence, their own shooting policies.

In developing their personal shooting policies, many officers choose standards for pulling the trigger that are more restrictive than those set forth in law and administrative directives. This is so because the written rules do not mandate that officers shoot whenever they are chasing a violent felon or each time someone's life is in jeopardy. Rather, legal and departmental standards say only that officers may use deadly force when such circumstances arise. Consequently, officers are free to decide that they will hold their fire in cases in which pulling the trigger would be justified by law and policy. And many officers do just that. Some, for example, will decide that they will not shoot fleeing suspects—the position I took during my academy training. Others will conclude that they will not shoot a gunman unless he points his weapon directly at them or someone else. And so on.[1]

Largely because the bounds that many officers set in their personal shooting policies are more narrow than those established by legal and administrative directives, the history of American policing is chock-full of cases in which officers did not shoot when they had legal cause to do so. Indeed police insiders have long known that officers hold their fire in the lion's share of instances in which their life or the life of another is in danger. Police hesitancy to fire even when life is in jeopardy was first formally reported outside of law enforcement circles in the early 1980s, when a study of police shootings in four major cities disclosed that officers in these departments shot in just a fraction of the cases that law and policy would allow.[2] This finding has received very little play around the nation in the last two decades, however, so the fact that officers exhibit substantial restraint in the face of deadly threat is not widely known.

I had been in several potential shooting situations during my brief tenure in Los Angeles—all face-to-face confrontations with gun-toting citizens—and I wanted to get some sense of the experiences that other officers who had shot people had in this regard. The first step I took to garner information about police forbearance in shooting situations was to ask the officers I interviewed if they had ever held their fire when they had legal cause to shoot. A dozen of the officers told me that the only situations they'd been in where they believed the use of deadly force would have been justified were the cases in which they fired. Among the other sixty-eight, most reported that they had been involved in fewer than a handful of cases in which they didn't shoot when they could have, about twenty reported that they held their fire in five to ten cases, and thirteen reported that they'd been in more than ten such situations (including a few who'd been in thirty or more). In total, then, the officers I interviewed held their fire in several hundred interactions in which they had legal cause to pull the trigger.

I asked those officers who had been in at least one situation in which they held their fire to tell me about them (or in the case of those who had been in more than three, to tell me about some of them). I asked them to describe the circumstances of the cases, why they held their fire, and how they felt about their decision afterward. In this way, I was able to gather information about more than 150 cases in which officers held their fire when they could have shot, which allowed me to develop a picture of the sorts of things officers consider during close calls, how they discern the difference between shooting and nonshooting situations, and what they think and feel after situations in which they hold their fire.

The following stories afford the reader a robust look at that picture, the most compelling facet of which is arguably the stark image of police officers showing remarkable restraint in the face of substantial danger. The unveiling begins with stories from the place where most policing is done, where most of the danger lurks, and where most of the near shootings occur: patrol work.

On Patrol

Patrol is the backbone of American policing, the place where nearly all young officers cut their police teeth, the place where the largest number of officers work, and the place where the vast majority of the contacts between the police and the public occur. It is therefore not surprising that patrol officers are involved in more near shootings than are officers assigned to other policing tasks: there are simply more of them, and they are involved in more interactions with people. The following stories offer a glimpse of the sorts of close calls experienced by the officers I interviewed during their time in patrol. From unarmed people who simulate that they are carrying weapons, to knife-wielding madmen apparently bent on their own destruction, to gunmen whose foolish behavior nearly gets them killed, these stories show how patrol officers manage to avoid shooting people during a variety of very tense situations.

———

We got a call one night out in the Tritopolis area about a suicidal guy with a knife backed up against a fence threatening to kill himself. He was holding the knife against his stomach when we got there. I stayed about twelve to fourteen feet away, just trying to keep some distance between us, and explained to him that cutting himself in the stomach was not gonna kill him, that it was just gonna hurt. He came at me with the knife in front of him about three or four times before we got enough officers there to contain him. He told us, "Shoot me. Kill me. I want to die. Shoot me. Kill me." I had my gun on him at all times, and each time he came at me, I probably could've shot him, but each time I chose to retreat instead. Each time I backed up, he turned around and acted like he was gonna stab himself in the stomach. The last time he actually did stab himself, decided it hurt too bad, and dropped the knife. He was yelling and screaming about the pain. I walked up to him and said, "Told you it was gonna hurt." It was sheer stupidity on his part.

I didn't shoot him because I felt pretty comfortable with my gun already out. I know twenty feet is the distance you want to keep from someone with a knife, but I felt I had a comfortable space between us at twelve to fourteen feet. As long as I kept that space, I felt the situation really wasn't that bad. We'd move back and forth. If he'd have run at me, I probably would've shot him, but he would only walk.

———

I've had a few situations where I almost shot someone over the years. One that sticks out in my mind happened when a call dropped about a guy inside this store who was harassing customers and the cashier. They said that he had something in his waistband that might be a weapon. When I pulled up, they had the guy locked out of the store. So he was standing there in front with his T-shirt hanging out, untucked in the front. Sure enough, I could see a bulge up under his T-shirt, so I stopped about twenty-five feet away from the guy, got out, drew my gun, and stood by the side of my car so the engine was between us. I kept my gun at my side and told the guy to put his hands up on the wall. Well, he looked at me and took a couple of steps toward me. I raised my pistol and told him to stop, to get his hands up on the wall. He got this angry look on his face and said, "What are you gonna do? You gonna shoot me with your pistol?" I said, "Yeah, if I have to." Then he said, "Well, what if I pull out my pistol?" At that point, I remember seeing all the other customers who were inside the store, all these Oriental people lying on the floor, waiting for the shots to go off. Then the guy reached down toward the bulge in his waistband. At that point, things went into slow motion, and I said to myself, "If he reaches under the shirt, I'm gonna shoot him."

Well, he brought his hand down, stuck it under the shirt, and then, real quick, pulled it up with the first finger extended toward me. When I saw that, I was doing everything I could do to keep from squeezing the trigger, because I had already started to shoot. Fortunately, the gun didn't go off. I don't know how it didn't go off, but it didn't. I mean, I had already made the decision to shoot, because from my training I knew that the best I could hope for with reaction time once his hand went under the shirt was to tie him, to get a shot off at the same time as he did. So I was trying to at least tie this guy. Then, when I realized he hadn't come up with a gun, it took everything I had to not squeeze all the way down.

After that, the guy got really verbally belligerent but didn't come any closer. I just stayed in my barricaded position behind the car with my gun on the guy until another unit arrived because I still didn't know what was under his shirt. When the other unit got there, we got him to put his hands on the car, and the other officer went up to take the guy into custody. Turns out the bulge was a damn *Green Sheet* newspaper, but it looked like a weapon when it was tucked in there.

That really pissed me off because I was gonna shoot this guy. It angered me that he did something stupid like that, trying to make me shoot him. It would have hit the news media as "Unarmed Suspect Gunned Down" and all that. So I was pissed, but we started talking to the guy, and he told us that he'd just come in from a B-52 flight and all this other shit. So we realized he was just psycho. Stuff like that happens, and you just have to deal with it.

———～～～———

I've worked some real highly active assignments over the years, so I've been in maybe thirty or more situations where I came close to shooting people but didn't. One of the ones that sticks out in my mind happened at dusk one day, when my partner and I spotted three gang members walking down the sidewalk, facing away from us. As we rolled up in the black and white, the subjects' heads start turning all over the place; it was evident they were looking for a place to run. The two guys on the ends split; one guy ran across the front of the car, and the other one jumped some fences to our right. The guy in the middle didn't know which way to go, and he just froze there in front of us. We were right on top of him when we stopped—maybe ten feet away. As I was getting out of the passenger door of the car, he started digging in his waistband with his right hand. Then I could see that he was reaching into his crotch area, then that he was trying to reach toward his left thigh area, as if he was trying to grab something that was falling down his pants leg.

He was starting to turn around toward me as he was fishing around in his pants. He was looking right at me and I was telling him not to move: "Stop! Don't move! Don't move! Don't move!" My partner was yelling at him too: "Stop! Stop! Stop!" As I was giving him commands, I drew my revolver. When I got about five feet from the guy, he came up with a chrome .25 auto. Then, as soon as his hand reached his center stomach area, he dropped the gun right on the sidewalk. We took him into custody, and that was that.

I think the only reason I didn't shoot him was his age. He was fourteen, looked like he was nine. If he was an adult, I think I probably would have shot him. I sure perceived the threat of that gun. I could see it clearly, that it was chrome and that it had pearl grips on it. But I knew that I had the drop on him, and I wanted to give him just a little more benefit of a doubt because he was so young looking. I think the fact that I was an experienced officer had a lot to do with my decision. I could see a lot of fear in his face, which I also perceived in other situations, and that led me to believe that if I would just give him just a little bit more time that he might give me an option to not shoot him. The bottom line was that I was looking at him, looking at what was coming out of his pants leg, identifying it as a gun, seeing where that muzzle was gonna go when it came up. If his hand would've come out a little higher from his waistband, if the gun had just cleared his stomach area a little bit more, to where I would have seen that muzzle walk my way, it would've been over with. But the barrel never came up, and something in my mind just told me I didn't have to shoot yet.

Some people do some incredibly stupid stuff that almost gets themselves shot. The first time I ran into one of these deals, I'd been on the street about two, two-and-a-half years. I got a call one afternoon that some guy was walking around the neighborhood pointing weapons at the kids who were playing outside. When I get in the area, I spotted this transient pushing a shopping cart up ahead of me a ways. He turned back to look at me, and when he did, I saw a chrome revolver in his waistband. So I got on the radio, let dispatch know where I was at, that I got a guy with a gun. I stopped about thirty yards behind him, opened the door, got a barricade behind it, and started shouting at him to put his hands up. He did that. Then I told him to turn around and face me. When he turned around, I saw that he had two more guns in his waistband. He was saying something to me, like he was trying to explain something to me. But he kept lowering his hands as he was talking. I couldn't hear what he had to say because I was too busy yelling at him to keep his hands up. All I could tell is that he was trying to tell me something, like, "Don't worry." I was screaming at him to keep his hands up, but he reached down toward the guns. When he grabbed the first one, he just grabbed the grip with his fingertips. Because he didn't have his finger near the trigger, I figured I still had time to react, so I held my fire. Then he pulled the gun out and dropped it on the ground. He did this four more times. Each time one of 'em hit the ground, it went with a sort of hollow "clink, clink, clink," and I realized they were all plastic. So he ended up having five guns, plastic guns, on him. Apparently, he found them in a dumpster next to a toy store. I got real angry at him for being so stupid, for almost getting killed over some toy guns. I let him know just how pissed I was.

I had a real similar situation a year or so later. I pulled some kids over, and when I walked up on the car, I spotted a gun on the center console. I told the guys to get out of the car. The driver realized that I had spotted the gun, looked at me, and he said, "But officer, this isn't a real gun." Then he reached down for it, I guess to show me it wasn't real. But I wasn't going to let him grab it because it looked real to me. I was close to the car, so I just grabbed him by the neck and pulled him out before he could reach to the gun. It turned out to be a toy gun. I could've shot him, but I figured that I could yank him out of there before he got to it. A lot of guys would have shot in that situation. Again, I got real angry at this kid, and I told him so, because he didn't realize how close he came to getting shot for doing something stupid.

I had another idiot I ran into when I was working patrol. I was off duty, heading into work in my uniform, driving a Honda Accord. This guy was next to me pulling a trailer, and he was trying to get in my lane. I honked at him, but then I slowed down and he eventually made it over. We went about another two blocks up and stopped at a traffic light. The guy opened his door up, leaned out, and pointed a revolver at me. I couldn't go left because the door was right there, so I dove to my right below the dashboard. It took me a couple of seconds to get my gun out because I was sort of lying on my holster. By the time I came up with my gun, he was driving off. Apparently, he saw the uniform. I didn't have a radio or anything, so there was no way I could call anybody for help. So I followed this guy. We had a little bit of a chase; of course he was pulling this great big trailer, so he wasn't getting away. He finally got caught up in traffic. I bailed out with my gun, and I called him out of the car. He came out with his hands up, left the gun in the truck. Come to find it was a real gun, but it wasn't loaded. He claimed to me that he just points it at people when people piss him off; it scares them away. I told him he was lucky to be alive. Again, one of the stupidity things.

My first close call came when I was fresh out of FTO—I don't think I'd been on the street but maybe a week or two on my own. I was on second shift, which would start at five o'clock in the evening. I'd just left headquarters when dispatch toned out a man with a gun that had threatened some people and fired off some shots about four blocks from where I was. I made a right turn, went four blocks, and was at the intersection where the call came from. As I drove up, this group of people standing in front of this old beat-up hotel started pointing down the street. I parked, looked down the street, and saw this guy walking down the street carrying a long gun. He was about a block to my east on the north sidewalk, walking away from me. He had the gun over his shoulder like Elmer Fudd going hunting for the wabbit. That's what I thought when I saw him, that he looked like Elmer Fudd in a cartoon walking with this gun over his shoulder.

He was oblivious to me, so I moved my patrol car down the street to get closer to him. I stopped about thirty yards from the guy, using my patrol car to block traffic and to provide me with some cover next to another vehicle that was parked on the north curb. Then I got out and challenged him: "Police, drop the gun! Police, freeze! Police, don't move!" Something like that. He just kept walking, so I challenged him again. He stopped for a second or two, like, "What was that?" then started walking away from me again. I challenged him again, then he kind of stopped again, like he could hear something but he wasn't really sure what he was hearing.

Once I got his attention, I kept challenging him. After I'd told him to drop the gun a couple of times, he took it off his shoulder and started to turn toward me, right shoulder first. As he was turning, he was holding the gun at port arms with his right hand behind the trigger guard and his left hand on the fore-grip. I could see that his index finger was not on the trigger, or even in a ready position. It was just behind the trigger guard. I was thinking that if he even starts to move that barrel toward my direction that I was going to shoot regardless of where his finger was. He kept moving the gun in my direction. Then he stopped, looked at me for a split second, and pitched his gun straight into some bushes next to where he was standing. I tried to order him into a handcuffing position, but he had a hard time following my directions because he was really drunk. So I just covered him until some other officers got there, and we took him into custody.

I didn't shoot him before he turned because I didn't perceive a big threat. The biggest thing was his reaction to my challenges. He didn't seem like he was really comprehending what was going on. I perceived him to be highly intoxicated, and I thought that that was the reason for his inability to follow my directions. I just didn't perceive him as being aggressive at that point in time. Then, when he turned around, I thought that I could beat him if he tried to point the gun at me. I got some training after the incident on reaction time where I learned that that was a false assumption, so I know better now. But at the time, I had a false belief that I could react quicker than he could, so I held my fire.

Things Ain't Always What They Seem

Because patrol officers are on the front lines of police work, they often find themselves thrust into situations with only the barest idea of what it is they are getting involved in. When the situation includes people armed with guns or other deadly weapons, patrol officers have to make split-second life-and-death decisions about whether to shoot. But sometimes on patrol, things aren't what they appear to be, and people who appear to be threatening are not. Sometimes what appears to be a bad guy is a crime victim—or another police officer. Officers know this and have to factor in the possibility that the person in front of them doing something that is about to get them shot means them no harm. The next three stories show just how close officers sometimes come to making a tragic error and how little things can prevent horrible accidents.

—∿∿—

The first time I almost shot someone was when I was still on probation. It was early in the morning on a Sunday, and we got a call that there was an auto burglar outside of a McDonald's restaurant. We got a description of the guy over the radio. A male Hispanic; I don't remember the height, weight, or clothing info, but when we got about a half a block away from the McDonald's, we saw a fellow matching the suspect's description, so we pulled over about fifty feet away to talk to him. As he walked toward our car, I could see that he had a .45 auto in his right hand. He was holding it down at about a forty-five-degree angle. The hammer was back. It was cocked and ready to go. I shouted, "Gun!" to let my partner know what was up, bailed out of the car, and drew down on the guy. I told him two or three times in both English and Spanish to drop the gun. He wouldn't drop the gun, and I was getting ready to cap him because he kept walking toward us with the gun in his hand. I was ready to rock-and-roll, but I decided to give one more set of commands before I dropped him because something wasn't adding up. It just made no sense for a car burglar holding a gun at low-ready to walk right at two cops. Plus his demeanor wasn't at all aggressive or threatening. Anyway, when I shouted at him for the last time, he was about twelve to fifteen feet away. I couldn't let him get any closer. But just as I was about to shoot, he stopped and dropped the gun.

We cuffed him up and asked him what was going on. He told us that he spotted someone taking his radio out of his car, so he got his gun to chase the guy off. Turns out some other citizen spotted him with the gun and put in the call that we got. That's why he fit the description so well. He was so distraught and pissed off at this guy who had just burglarized his car that he wasn't thinking clearly when he walked up on us. He knew he was in the right, so he didn't see us as a threat, even though we were pointing guns and screaming at him. I clearly could have shot him long before he got to within fifteen feet of us and been within my legal and moral rights. But something just told me not to do it, so I didn't.

Boy, was I glad I held my fire. Had a sense of relief you wouldn't believe. We never caught the burglar, but I was just absolutely relieved the whole rest of the day that I hadn't shot that poor bastard who had had his car stereo stolen.

———〰———

I was working with my regular partner, another female, and we were just driving down the street when all of a sudden we heard a shot ring out. We looked over to our right, where we thought the sound came from, and saw a guy waving a gun. It looked like he was robbing this other guy. We notified dispatch, opened our doors, and drew down on the guy. By this time, the guy with the gun had wrestled this other guy to the ground and was pointing the gun right at him. We could have shot the guy right then. I mean, he had this gun out, threatening this other guy with it, and we'd already heard one round go off. But from my angle, I saw something shiny on the belt of the guy with the gun. I didn't quite see what it was, but I know that sometimes cops carry their badge on their belt off duty, so I thought that maybe he was a policeman or a security guard, something like that. So I didn't shoot. I held back to try to get a better view. My partner on the other side of the car couldn't see whatever it was on his belt because of the angle she had. I heard her gun go that first click that happens when you start to squeeze the trigger, so I knew she was about to cap this guy. As soon as I realized what was happening, I shouted, "Wait, don't. Don't. He's a cop, he's a cop."

Turns out I was right. The guy with the gun was an off-duty transit cop, and the other guy had tried to rob him with a fake gun. They fought over it, and the transit cop pulled his gun and fired off a round that missed the other guy. No one got hurt, and we took the bad guy into custody, but I remember thinking how close we came to shooting the good guy. We sure could have. He was pointing the gun at this other guy, but something just wasn't right—that object on his belt. Because of that, I wanted to give it an extra second before shooting.

You know, he could have shot the other guy, and I'd have been wrong, but sometimes you just have to go with your instincts. And that's what I did.

<hr>

I had my brother-in-law on a ride-along with me when a broadcast came out that a narco buy-bust had gone bad with one of the street teams. They put out the description of the car and then said the suspects had fired at detectives and that the detectives were chasing the car. I happened to be coming off the freeway at 405 and Spring when I saw the car heading northbound on Spring. I got in behind it—aired that I was behind it—and all of a sudden, a Ford Mustang occupied by two Hispanic males flanked me to the left and passed the car I was chasing. One of the Hispanic males leaned out of the car and started shooting back at the suspect vehicle, back toward us.

So I yelled at my brother-in-law, "Shit, get down on the floorboard!" I was just concerned for him. I wasn't even thinking that a round could've deflected off the car and nailed me right in the forehead. I wouldn't have even known it. I was just concerned with getting him down on the ground. So he ducked down, the Hispanic male continued to fire, and the suspects' car came to a stop. All I could see in the car was two suspects like jumping beans inside, like they were trying to hide underneath the seat. So I got out of the car and went into a typical hot stop and then looked over to the Mustang. The Hispanic males were exiting their car, both firing into the suspects' car. I turned to engage them. I started to pull on the trigger and almost pulled a round off when I looked at the first guy—who was yelling toward the suspects' car—and I saw braces on his teeth. I said to myself, "Fuck, that guy was a cop at Central when I was a trainee," so I went off him and back onto the suspect vehicle. I was looking, looking, looking, looking, but I didn't see a threat. I was thinking, "Why are they still shooting? I don't see a threat. Am I missing something? Fuck."

Next thing you know, a bunch of plainclothes guys came up and yanked these two guys out of the suspects' car. As they were pulling them out, a third kid that I hadn't seen popped up into the driver's seat and the car took off. So I holstered up and went from a near shooting to chasing a car down the road that's full of bullets. After we got that kid into custody, I told the officer with the braces, "Goddamn, I almost shot you. Scared the shit out of me. I almost dropped you."

IA called me the next day and said, "You know, you would have been totally justified if you shot that officer." I said, "Yeah, but it would've been hell to live with." Then they said, "Yeah, but we just want you to know your train of thought, your thinking, was exactly right, because there was a threat. You didn't know that they were cops, and they were moving toward you and toward the suspects, still shooting." To this day, I don't know why they didn't ID themselves or what they were shooting at. It was pretty crazy.

SWAT

SWAT teams became a part of police work in the late 1960s, when a series of deadly events, including the Watts riots in Los Angeles and a sniper attack at the University of Texas at Austin in which more than three dozen people were shot, showed that the police were ill prepared to deal with unusually dangerous incidents. Realizing this, many large law enforcement agencies began to develop specialized units to handle crisis situations. Because these units carried weapons that were not standard police issue—such as assault rifles, submachine guns, and sniper rifles—and utilized tactics that were not typically used in other realms of police work, they came to be known as special weapons and tactics teams, or SWAT teams for short.

Over the years, more and more police agencies of all sizes have developed SWAT teams and have used them in a wide variety of special-threat situations besides riots and sniper attacks. In fact, most SWAT operations today involve the service of search-and-arrest warrants that are deemed to pose some sort of heightened risk to the police (typically called *high-risk warrants*), armed subjects who have refused to surrender to the officers who were initially handling the incident (typically called *barricaded suspects*), and situations in which armed subjects are holding someone against that person's will (hostage incidents).[3]

Because SWAT teams' bread and butter is dealing with the most dangerous sorts of policing situations, SWAT officers typically confront more threats than the average police officer. This section contains three of the more instructive close calls that the SWAT officers I interviewed had, including one in which the officer that I spoke with was shot. The other two stories—though not quite as dramatic—also show how experienced, well-trained police officers often avoid shooting suspects, even in the toughest of circumstances.

—⁓—

We got called in to serve a search warrant at this one-story house over in Baldwin on a subject known as 98 Frank, who was a very violent drug offender. One of our snitches had taken an undercover officer over there, and while they were trying to negotiate a deal with him, he had actually placed his .45 into the snitch's mouth and threatened to blow his brains out if he set him up, so we knew the man was very violent. We also knew he was very active in his own cocaine use.

After we got the warrant, we went up to the door, screamed, "County police!" knocked the door down, and stepped into the front room. I was the number-three man in. Our first guy broke left, second guy broke right, and I came straight into the front room. Straight ahead of me was 98 Frank in his bedroom. It had no door, and he was standing there with drugs in his hands and two pistols stuck in his waistband. I started advancing on him. He dropped the dope, and his hands started to come down. I told him to freeze, and I stopped my advance probably twelve feet from him. I was too far away to take him down physically, but close enough that I could see the guns clearly.

His eyes were glazed over, and the way he was looking—he had a very blank stare on his face—it was like he was looking at us but he didn't see us. I was yelling at him to freeze. Off to the right, his mother was in the other room screaming, "Don't kill him! Don't kill him!" As she was screaming this and I was telling him to freeze, his right hand started to come over near his waistband. I started telling him, "Don't touch the gun! Don't touch the gun!" because I knew that if a gun came up, I would have to fire because I had other officers in the room.

Well, he grabbed one of the guns by its handle and pulled it out of his waistband. I could feel the pressure on my trigger as I started to squeeze, and he dropped the first gun. He then immediately, but slowly, went for the second gun. He grabbed it and made a slight motion like he was coming up with it. I was again getting ready to squeeze the trigger; then he dropped the second gun. At that time, we pounced on him and took him to the ground.

After we cleared the rest of the house, I asked him what he doing with the guns. He told us he was so stoned that he didn't really realize who we were. His brain was just apparently fried from all the cocaine he used, which was a shame because the guy was a vet who had won several medals in the marines. He had used so much cocaine that when he sneezed, he would bleed from the nose. His mind was just frazzled. Maybe he just knew enough that he could realize that we must have been some kind of law enforcement, but he never gave me a very logical answer at all.

I know I could have shot him, but when I was looking at him— looking at his eyes—I just didn't feel he was a threat. I knew that I had my gun out, a fully automatic weapon shooting .223 rounds. At twelve feet away, I knew that if I had to pull the trigger, it would be over instantly. I just don't feel that because someone is armed that he's necessarily a threat. Even when you know ahead of time that someone is violent, you gotta judge the incident on what you're seeing at that time. Several of the guys there thought for sure I was going to shoot. And by the book, if I'd shot I'd been covered 'cuz the guns were in his hands, but to me he just wasn't a threat at the time.

Besides his eyes, when he grabbed the guns, his fingers never went inside the trigger guard. If a finger had gone inside a trigger guard, I would've definitely shot. The other thing that would've made me shoot was if a barrel would've started in my direction. If that happened, he could easily get the finger in the trigger guard before I could have gotten a shot off. So if either a finger went in a trigger guard or a barrel came toward me, then I'd have pulled the trigger. No doubt.

—◊◊◊—

Since I came over to SWAT, we've had several cases where guys have shot at us, but we never returned any fire. Probably the craziest one happened in 1993 when I got shot in the leg. It was a boyfriend-girlfriend deal. He was upset about his girlfriend working at this video store at this strip center on the north side of town. He went over there and started slapping his girlfriend around. Somebody there at the store told him to leave her alone. The boyfriend shot this other guy, in the leg I think. So the guy crawled out and called the police. By the time patrol got there, the boyfriend had beat the poor girl pretty good. I don't know how much time went by after patrol arrived, but he finally let her go. So by the time we got there, he was inside the video store by himself.

The guy was nonresponsive to all the negotiators' attempts to contact him, so some of the other guys and I went into a restaurant that shared a common wall to the video store at the strip center to see what we could figure out. I ended up getting on top of the freezer, had a body bunker in front of me so I could get access to the ceiling because nobody knew where he was. He was hiding somewhere, apparently. So I took off some ceiling tiles over the video store and started looking around for him. Couldn't see him, couldn't see him. So I got up on my tippy-toes. I was looking, looking, looking, peering over the top of the shield. Finally, I looked just about straight down, and when I did, I spotted him just behind the front counter. Right then, he looked up. I don't know if I made some noise or what. But he saw me at the same time I saw him, so I got down behind the shield real fast. As I was ducking, I heard, "boom, boom." Both of his rounds hit the shield and flew off somewhere.

I told the CP what happened and got down from the ceiling. The negotiators got the speakers going, trying to talk to him, saying, "Yes, we know you're behind the counter, give up," and stuff like that. He didn't respond. After a bunch of attempts that got nothing, they finally asked me if I could get to that ceiling again and pump some gas in there. I said sure, went back up with a big tube of pepper mace spray and the shield, and started to fill the store with gas. Well, he shot at me again. Bounced a few more rounds off the shield.

That just got me going even more. I'm an adrenaline junkie; it didn't bother me any. We'd found the first two rounds he fired. He had a .25 auto. Those rounds can kill you if they hit, but they weren't going to go through the shield, so I felt pretty safe. Some of the other guys got worried, but I'm like the guy in the cereal commercial, "Let's get Mikey to do it, he'll do anything." Yeah, that's me, I like that stuff, I live off that adrenaline. I mean, I know it's dangerous stuff that we do, but I don't get scared when we're doing it. I guess maybe I get scared afterwards, but not during.

He shot a couple more times, then the guys in the front saw him scamper into what turned out to be the bathroom. We figured out that the storeroom for this little restaurant we were in shared a common wall with the bathroom in the video store. So we got in there, being real quiet, and set the four-foot big body bunker against the wall. We decided to try to put a hole in the wall and pump some gas into the bathroom. Because I'm the guy that'll do anything, I moved up behind the shield with a keyhole saw and started cutting a hole in the Sheetrock about five feet off the ground. The only thing that was exposed was my right hand, so I figured the worst-case scenario was that he might get off a lucky shot that hits my hand.

Well, I got all the way through the layer of drywall on the storeroom side of the wall, but on the bathroom side I started hitting something. "Clunk, clunk, clunk." I was thinking, "What the hell!" Then it hit me, it was the damn mirror over the sink!

Randy was with me and he said, "We'll go up higher."

I told him, "I'm not getting up over that shield." You know I'm an adrenaline junkie, but I'm not dumb.

So he said, "Well, just set it up on a chair." That made good sense. My lower legs would be exposed, but the rest of my body and head, except one hand, would be protected. So we slid a chair up and set the shield up on it. The idiot must have heard me, because when I reached up to start cutting the hole, he fired a shot through the wall about two feet off the ground. The damn round went through the wall and hit me in the left shin bone, right below the knee. It bounced off, hit the wall in front of me, dropped, and went spinning along the floor a little bit.

It didn't hurt too badly. I was still standing, so I moved away from the wall to get some better cover. My team leader got on the air and put out that an officer had been shot. I stopped him and told him that we shouldn't get this blown out of proportion. I knew the bullet hadn't penetrated much because it bounced right off. I reached down and cut my pant leg open. There wasn't much blood, just a frickin' groove in my leg. I showed it to him and said it was no big deal.

He asked me if I was sure and I told him, "Yeah." We were about to get back to work when one of the sergeants showed up. He asked what happened. I told him I got nicked by a bullet and showed him the little cut. He wanted to pull me out of there, but I didn't want to leave. I told him that I'd scratched my leg on a nail worse than what the bullet did. Apparently, I convinced him, because he let me stay there.

We ended up putting another shield on the floor in front of the one on the chair so that we had cover all the way down. I cut a hole all the way through, and we got the gas in there. The gas pushed him back out to the front part of the store. Then I left the restaurant and took a position outside near the front door of the video shop. After about another hour or so of him not responding, we set a light at the door. I was holding it on a fire pole, so I was out of the way around the corner. He fired a few rounds at it but missed. Then he stopped shooting and started throwing videotapes at the light, trying to knock it down. It got to be a game, where I was holding the light out there, kind of dancing that light around, while he threw videotapes at it. I figured the poor owner of the store was gonna have a heart attack when it was all over 'cuz the guy must've thrown three hundred videotapes out the door trying to hit that light.

Well, the idiot finally came out holding his gun to his head and sat down on the curb in front of the store. He was facing right at me. I was behind cover, but I could see him clearly. I could tell he was tired. It had been going on for hours. He was sort of nodding off every now and then, his eyes shutting a little bit, his head drooping, then snapping back up. Well, after a while, his head dropped again and the gun went off. I remember that his eyes opened up for a split second, and he had this surprised look on his face. Then I saw the blood gushing down the right side of his head, and the guy fell over. The react team, which was staged in the doorway of the restaurant, ran up and covered down on him, but he was DOA.

I figured from that surprised look that guy didn't mean to kill himself, that he shot himself by accident. When I saw him do it, I thought to myself, "Serves him right for shooting me."

Veterans of Restraint

As noted in this chapter's introduction, some officers are involved in dozens of close encounters. The man whose words appear in this section's primary story is one such person. He has spent most of his twenty-five-year police career as a SWAT officer in one of the nation's biggest cities. He has also worked patrol in some of his city's busiest beats, spent a short stint assigned to the city's jail, and nearly four years in Narcotics hunting dope dealers. Over the years, he has shot three people, witnessed partners or teammates shoot at least ten other people, and held his fire in at least two dozen cases in which he could clearly have shot. The cases he talks about in this section are those that were most salient in his mind and therefore those that give the best view into how at least one busy cop handles and thinks about the many close calls that have come his way.

The second officer who speaks in this section has also spent many years on his department's SWAT team (also one of the nation's largest and most active). His words are included because they present the single best accounting from the interviews I conducted of why it is that police officers shoot so few of the people that they have legal cause to kill.

I've been involved in at least two dozen cases, maybe three, where I could have shot people but held my fire. The first time I came really, really close to shooting somebody was at a disturbance call at a beer joint when I was still on probation. I was working a night shift with my training officer when we got the call. Shots had been fired. We responded, but the suspect was gone. The witnesses gave us a description of the vehicle he'd left in, said he had a gun, was involved in a fight with his girlfriend, and the bouncer threw him out of the bar. He went out and got in his car, started it up, and as he was driving out of the parking lot, he cranked off a couple of rounds into the bar. He didn't hit anybody, but there was a couple of bullet holes in the walls. So we put out a description and started looking around the area for this vehicle.

A few minutes later, we got a return call that he was back at the bar. When we got back there, he was gone again. He had just done another drive-by shooting on the bar. So we put out another broadcast that he was in the area and started to drive around again when we got another call that he was back at the bar. We go back this third time and saw his car sitting there. He had gone into the bar, grabbed his girlfriend at gunpoint, and taken her back out to his car. He threw her into the front seat of his car and jumped in behind the wheel. It was a bench seat. When we pulled in behind him, he had his right arm around her, over her shoulder in an affectionate-looking way. But he had a pistol, turned out to be a .357 Magnum, in his right hand, hanging down in front of her chest. She was sobbing.

It was summertime, very hot, and all four windows on his car were down. We drew our guns, and my partner told me to approach from the passenger side while he moved up on the driver's side to a point where he would be in a good position to make verbal contact with the guy. I moved up and stopped just outside his rear passenger-side door, where I could see his right hand with the gun in it. I was about five feet away from him with my front sight focused on the back of his head. I could hear what he was telling her. Very affectionate stuff like, "It's OK, honey, I still love you. Everything's gonna be all right." It was obvious from the way he was slurring his words that he was highly intoxicated. She was sobbing, not responding to him.

My partner was positioned just outside the driver's-side back door. He had a perfect bead on the back of his head as well. My partner made voice contact with him and told him to drop the gun. For some reason, instead of looking in the direction of my partner's voice, the suspect turned and looked at me. We made eye contact right over the front sight of my gun. Then he focused on the end of my gun, said, "Oh, my God, don't kill me," and dropped his gun. I heard it drop. It hit the seat and bounced onto the floorboard. I started giving him commands, and he very slowly raised his hands. Then my partner opened the driver's door, yanked the guy out by his hair, and wrestled him to the ground while I reached in and got the gun.

I came very, very close to killing that guy. I was in fear for the girl's life because he had that gun in his hand. I had a tactical advantage because I was behind him. He was going to have to rotate quite a bit to get a shot at me. So I was basically concerned for her safety, that he might suddenly try to shoot her. But when I realized how intoxicated he was, I felt I had a big advantage over him because he wasn't going to be able to move real quick. I thought I could get him before he could do it to her because I was real close and I felt very confident of the head shot that I had. I remember thinking that I really might have to kill this guy, but I wasn't going to unless he made some overt move to hurt her. If he would have made any sudden or aggressive move, I'd have pulled the trigger. He never did, so I didn't have to shoot.

I had another real close call while I was still on probation. I was working with a different partner, when we were dispatched to a disturbance call at an apartment complex. We went to arrest this one guy, and he took off running. We chased him through the apartment complex. As he went around the first corner, we lost sight of him for just a second. Turns out he threw this gun he was carrying over a redwood fence and onto this lady's back patio when we lost sight of him. We didn't even know he had a gun, but this lady saw him throw it. When it was all over, she brought it to us, so we were able to make a case on it with her testimony. Anyway, we finally caught the guy, had to fight him, kinda bloodied him up a little bit, got him handcuffed, and took him back to our patrol car, which was near the apartment where this all started. When we got there, about five of his buddies were there. They asked us where we were taking the guy. We told his buddies we were taking him to jail. They said, "No, you're not." We said, "Yes, we are." We went back and forth like that a few times, when, all of a sudden, they just jumped us.

I had already gotten the prisoner into the back of the patrol car, and as I was in the process of trying to secure him there, one of the other guys came at me with a club. I was partway in the backseat, so I pushed the prisoner down onto the floorboard and started kicking at the guy, trying to kick him off of me. He was swinging this club at me, trying to get my feet, so I pulled my feet into the car. I drew my pistol, thinking that would make him back off, but it didn't. I was sitting in the backseat with one hand pushing down on the prisoner while I had my pistol pointed at the guy with the club. He was right on top of me, no more than two or three feet away. I was screaming, "Back off! I'm gonna kill you! I'm gonna kill you!" It didn't make any difference to him. I was thinking, "Oh, man, you've made your bluff, now you gonna back it up or what?"

Out of the corner of my eye, I saw my partner on the hood of the patrol car, fighting with two other guys. I had already put out an "assist the officer" call, but I was real worried about my partner. He was getting the crap beaten out of him. I was afraid those two guys were going to get his gun, shoot him, and then come after me. I was pretty safe in the car right then. The guy with the club couldn't really get to me, but I had to do something to help my partner because I didn't know how much longer he could hold out. I couldn't get out without getting hit by the guy with the club, so I decided to shoot the guy, then go help my partner.

Just as I was about to pull the trigger, this bystander, a big guy, grabbed the guy with the club in a headlock and yanked him back. The bystander beat the crap out of the guy with the club while my partner and I finally got the upper hand on the other two guys. Then some other units showed up and it was all over. But I was in the process of pulling the trigger when this other guy grabbed the guy with the club. All I saw at first was this arm come over the guy's head. My initial thought was that some other officers had arrived. As I came out from the backseat, I saw this guy in regular clothes, and I was wondering if he was an officer working plainclothes, or narcotics, or what? Turns out he was just Joe Blow Citizen who was watching everything and decided he had seen enough, that he was going to get involved. He didn't know it, but by getting involved he saved that other guy's life.

Another close one happened during my first stint at SWAT. We got called up on a highly intoxicated female who had run her family out of their house with a gun. She was extremely erratic. She was on Prozac, Thorazine, all that. She had quit taking her meds and was high on some other drugs and alcohol. When patrol got there, she confronted them. They backed off and called us. It was nighttime when we got there. We were establishing a perimeter, and I was on the front side of the objective, behind a vehicle parked in the street. She didn't know I was there. Billy Dale was trying to move into position behind a car that was parked in her driveway. Billy was almost at the car when she came out of her house holding her gun and saw him. He made it behind the car, but she spotted him before he got there. She started walking his way and said, "I see you, you son of a bitch." The car was between her and Billy, but the closer she got, the more dangerous it was for him. She was pointing the gun in his direction, telling him she was going to kill him. She didn't see me, and I had her in the sights of my M-16. I was thinking that if she pops a cap, it could skip underneath the car and hit Billy, that I was gonna have to shoot her if she got much closer.

Billy was crouched down behind the car, just trying to maintain cover. Now one of the patrol sergeants and one of the other assault team guys had moved around behind the house and were coming around to the side with the driveway. I didn't know exactly where they were, but they were somewhere behind the woman. I was worried that they were in my line of fire. I was concerned that if I shot the woman, the bullets might go through her and hit them. Well, she kept moving toward the car, then stopped just a few feet away, and said, "I know you're behind there, you son of a bitch. Come out, come out." I was thinking, "How much closer am I going to let her get?" She had the gun pointed at the car this whole time, because she knew Billy was behind it. I had a perfect shot on her. She was no more than twenty yards away, and I was lined up right on her, but she had no idea I was there.

Then she started to move around to the side of the car, and Billy started playing ring-around-the-rosy with her, trying to keep the car between himself and the woman. Some other officers were telling Billy to get out of there, but he was scared to run for it. I was sure that if he took off that she'd pop the cap at him. I was thinking, "What if she gets off a lucky shot that kills him? Can I live with that? If he does decide to run, am I going to let her shoot? Do I need to nail her now before she even gets a shot off?" All this was going through my mind, "Do I need to kill her now? Do I want to kill her, this drunk lady waving a gun around?" My safety was off, I had my finger on the trigger, it was no longer indexed. I was there, ready to squeeze. She was at the left front-door panel of the vehicle; Billy was at the right rear. If she moved any closer or fired a round, I was gonna take her right there. I wasn't going to let her get any closer. I wasn't going to let her get a second shot off. She started to move, and I was just about to drop her, when she turned around, then walked back inside the house. We eventually talked her out, so it turned out OK.

Looking back on it though, I don't know if I made the right decision. It turned out for the best, but it would have been really hard to take if she had gotten a shot off and killed Billy. It would have been hard to live with the knowledge that I had the shot but didn't take it. To this day, I still wonder whether maybe I should have taken that shot.

After three and a half years in SWAT, I went to work a raid team in Narcotics. The narco guys had been in a bunch of shootings where search warrants had gone bad for some reason, and the cops had to shoot it out with the dealers. The administration decided that this had to stop, so they figured the best way to accomplish this was to put together a team that does nothing but run warrants. The thinking was that if that's all the team does, then they will do things better, fewer things will go wrong, and fewer people will get shot. So all I did for about three-and-a-half years was serve dope warrants and train. We had a team of eight guys. We were all clean-cut. Short hair. They didn't allow any beards. You could have a mustache, but the bosses didn't want a bunch of longhaired dudes with beards busting into peoples' houses, where the folks inside might not believe it's the cops. So they wanted us all clean-cut looking. We always wore blue jeans, sneakers, and raid jackets that said "POLICE" over full tactical vests. That way, we looked like a bunch of cops when we hit a place.

When we weren't out serving warrants, we were shooting or doing some other sort of training. We did an occasional buy-bust—maybe one a week—but other than that, all we did was train and run warrants. Other Narcotics guys would make the case, bring the info back to us, we'd go take a look at the location—usually take some pictures—head back to the office, draw up a plan, get in the van, and go out and execute the warrant. We averaged one warrant every working day, about 250 a year, for nearly four years. During this time, our team proved the bosses' thinking to be correct. After a while, the shootings went to almost nil. But we did get into a few shootings, and we had a lot of close calls.

I remember one incident where we did a raid on this pimp's place. He was running whores and selling dope. As we pulled up in the van, I saw the guy standing outside. He saw us and took off into the house. I chased after him. He ran down a hallway and made it into a bathroom and slammed the door before I could catch him.

I came up and kicked the door while my guys were coming in behind me. When I kicked the door open, I heard a gunshot. At first, I thought, "Oh, my God, I'm shot." I backed up, and the door swung back until it was almost closed. I looked around, trying to figure out who shot me. Then I realized I hadn't been hit. A few seconds later, the door swung back open, and I saw the crook lying back in a half-full bathtub with both his hands in the air. So I figured he hadn't shot. I started looking around again. Everybody else was stopped, just covering their own areas of responsibility and looking around. Someone said, "Who shot?" I said, "I don't know, who shot?" This one guy on the team was always a little gun happy, and I always thought if anybody was going to have an accidental discharge, it would be him. So I looked at him and asked, "Did you shoot?" He said that he hadn't, but he was looking at his gun like he wasn't sure that he hadn't shot. It turns out he didn't. It was the guy in the bathtub who shot.

After we all calmed down, my sergeant and I stepped into the bathroom and got the pimp out of the bathtub, stuck him against the wall, cuffed him up, and patted him down. Then I get to noticing the smell of gunpowder and a cloud of smoke up near the ceiling. When I looked up, I saw a bullet hole in the ceiling, but there were no guns that I could see in the bathroom. Where's the gun? After a few seconds, another one of the guys came into the bathroom, reached down into the bathtub water, which was so filthy you couldn't even see through it, and came up with a gun. What this guy had done was run in the bathroom, slam the door, pull his gun, and point it at the door. He was about to shoot it when I kicked in the door. The door hitting him sent a round into the ceiling, knocked the gun out of his hand and into the bathtub, and knocked him into the tub on top of the gun.

When I realized what had happened, it scared the hell out of me. He totally had me. He could have taken me out right there. I was lucky to be alive. I was also real pissed off at the guy. I wanted to beat the hell out of him right there, but he was handcuffed and you can't beat handcuffed prisoners. But I wanted to kill him. I looked him right in the eye, thinking, "I could kill you." But I didn't do anything, and that was the right thing to do.

A few months later, I came real close to killing this one gal. We were serving a warrant on this place that was supposed to have a whole lot of Mandrix. The main crook wasn't even home, just his old lady and her girlfriend. My assignment was to go down to the bedrooms and secure them. I had my pistol out, and I was leading the charge down the hallway to the back bedroom. It was kind of a dark hallway, and I was hollering, "Police," as I moved. I was dressed in my raid jacket and all that. I knew the rest of the team was coming behind me; I could hear them all coming. I hadn't seen anybody so far when, all of a sudden, I spotted this woman sitting up on a bed in the bedroom at the end of the hallway. It was a big house, so she was about ten or fifteen yards away, looking directly at me.

I started screaming at her, "Police! Police!" as I continued down the hallway. She leaned over real quick, so her upper body went out of my line of vision. I was figuring she was trying to dump the dope, get rid of it somehow. Then she came back up with a handgun pointed right at me. I just happened to be at this little alcove off the hallway that led to another door, so I jumped in there and barricaded up with my gun pointed right at her. She was holding her gun with both hands, still pointing it at me. She was kind of shaking and nervous looking. I could tell by the way she was holding the damn gun that she didn't know what the hell she was doing. She was trying to hold it like it was a revolver, but it was an automatic. She was sort of fumbling it between her hands, like she wasn't sure what hand to put it in. She was very awkward in the way she was holding the weapon. She looked really nervous and scared. That look, and the fact that I could tell that she didn't know what the shit she was doing with the gun, gave me a little bit of confidence. I felt fairly secure. I was somewhat barricaded up, had my tac vest on with very little of my body exposed, really just my head and arms.

I started screaming at her, "Drop the gun! Drop the gun!" I started to get more peripheral vision on the room, and I could tell there was another female in there. She was just sitting there like she couldn't believe what was happening. The girl with the gun was just looking at me, and I was going, "Drop the gun! Drop the gun!" over and over.

Finally, she said, "Who are you?"

I said, "I'm a police officer. Drop the goddamn gun!"

Then she said something like, "How do I know you're a cop?"

Some ideas started running through my mind, like maybe I should take my badge off and throw it into the room or maybe show my ID card. Then I thought, "This is bullshit. I need to kill her." I mean, I should have already killed her, I should have shot her. She was pointing her gun at me. What if she shot down the hallway and hit one of my buddies behind me? I decided that it had gone far enough, that I was going to ask her one more time to drop the gun, and then I was going to pull the trigger.

I shouted at her, "You're fixin' to die! Drop the goddamn gun!"

The girl next to her was pleading with her, saying her name, "Suzy," or whatever it was, "Suzy, drop the gun." I was thinking, "This is it, do her." And I started to pull the trigger. The girl with the gun took her eyes off of me real quick and looked over at her friend. Then she looked back at me and threw the gun down. We rushed into the bedroom and took her and the other girl down and cuffed them up.

I got a chief's commendation for not shooting that gal. But I don't think I made the correct tactical decision. I felt confident with my vest on and confident in the position I was in, but looking back on it, I could have easily died that day. Any of the guys behind me could have easily died. If it would have been a guy holding that gun, there is no doubt in my mind that I would have fired. I looked at it differently because she was a woman, took too much for granted in my position and my perception that a woman is less dangerous than a man. I put the lives of the officers behind me at risk. I knew guys would be barricaded up, but they'd be sticking their heads out and looking. If she fired a round, it could have gone past me and hit one of them. I risked their lives without their consent, and I don't really feel like I had the right to do that. I think I should have fired. If I had handled it the way I'd been trained, I would have shot her. That's what I should have done. I felt a little guilty about jeopardizing my teammates' lives. If I want to take chances in my life, that's fine, but I shouldn't be taking chances with theirs. That's the conclusion I came to. The chief's commendation is all well and good, but it doesn't stop me from wondering what would have happened if she had gotten a round off. Where would that round have gone?

There have been a bunch of other close calls since I came back to SWAT about ten years ago—none where I wonder if I made the right decision, but several cases where suspects shot at us but we didn't return fire. Probably somewhere between ten and fifteen of them where people shoot at us, but we just take cover. Sometimes people try to shoot us through walls; sometimes they pop a cap at us when we're moving around on the perimeter. The bullets come pretty close, but we don't shoot back because we've got cover.

I was behind a big pine tree one time, and the suspect was shooting his deer rifle my way, putting rounds into the tree. But it was a huge pine tree, so he wasn't going to hit me. I never was in any real danger, but it was a little unnerving having those bullets hitting the other side of the tree. Cases like that where we could kill the guy, but there was really no need. There have also been a few times when we were poking lights fixed to poles around corners or into rooms when the suspect shot the light. It tends to scare the crap out of you, but it's not real dangerous because you're behind cover at the other end of the pole. Most of the time, we are able to resolve these situations without using deadly force. We almost always find ways to end them without shooting anybody.

—⁓—

I could have shot a lot more than one person in my twenty-five-plus years, but I didn't because I didn't need to. To me, there's legal justification for shooting, moral justification for shooting, and then, "Was a shooting necessary?" That's the most important question and the one that guides my decision making. I think that maybe that's what makes a good policeman: the ability to make a decision based on that question. After a situation is over, he says, "I could have shot him, but

I didn't, because it didn't need to be done." I've been in a bunch of those, where I could have legally fired, but for some reason it just wasn't appropriate. It's that third criterion, it wasn't necessary. So I've been in a lot of situations where, yeah, I could have shot, but it just wasn't necessary.

—∿—

The words of this last veteran officer sum up what good cops all over the nation know: that the legal sanction they have to shoot is not a license to kill, but rather a power that should be invoked only when they believe they have no other choice. As the next chapter shows, however, deciding when it is absolutely necessary to pull the trigger is not a simple matter.

CHAPTER FOUR

Pulling the Trigger

The line separating close calls from shootings is razor thin. As we saw in the last chapter, police officers hold their fire in the face of all sorts of threatening actions, including gunfire directed at them. So when officers do shoot, it is because something—the way armed individuals stand, the way they hold their weapons, the way they move, the words they speak, the look on their faces, some cue—tells them that this moment is different, that it is for keeps, that they can't hesitate, that they have to fire. The last chapter illustrated the sorts of things that officers consider as they contemplate pulling the trigger but stop short of the act. This one completes the shooting picture by showing how and why officers cross the line, and what happens when they send police bullets plowing through citizens' flesh and bone.

In some instances, the decision to shoot is the end point of a deliberative process. In others, it is a split-second reaction that involves no conscious thought at all. Sometimes a shooting is the culmination of a protracted encounter during which officers had plenty of time to consider the possibility that they might need to shoot. Other times, officers are thrown into dangerous situations without warning and fire right away. And shootings happen in any sort of situation: burglary investigations; disputes between family members, friends, or neighbors; traffic stops; noise complaints; and even when officers are minding their own business off duty. Because shootings can (and do) unfold in a variety of ways, during situations of every conceivable stripe, there is no such thing as a typical shooting scenario.

The same is true about the people officers shoot: there is no such thing as a typical police opponent. Although some of the people the police shoot are hardened criminals, many are folks who were not in serious trouble with the law before the incident that brought them to the attention of the police. Some souls are enraged about some real or imagined affront they have suffered, some are high on alcohol or other drugs (or both), some suffer from some type of long-standing emotional or mental problem, and some are suicidal. Indeed the most thorough research to date indicates that some 10 percent of the people struck by police gunfire in recent years were suicides who goaded officers into shooting them. This unorthodox form of self-destruction, commonly called *suicide-by-cop* in law enforcement circles, is sometimes chosen by troubled individuals (such as the disturbed man who stabbed himself in the stomach from the previous chapter) who wish to end their lives but can't do it by their own hand.[1]

Whatever the circumstances that bring officer and assailant together, and whatever the assailant's motive for the behavior that prompts police gunfire, all shootings boil down to the same point: police officers decide that the person they face will do them or another innocent person grave harm if they don't shoot.

The stories in this chapter show what happens when officers reach that critical point. Readers will meet young officers thrown into violent shoot-outs while they were still wet behind the ears, veteran officers who kill knife-wielding madmen, and officers and shootings of every sort and stripe in between. More than a dozen of the officers I interviewed were injured during their shootings. We will hear from a few of them. Although—as detailed in the Introduction—most officers never shoot anyone, a small number are involved in two or more shootings. Several of the officers I interviewed fall into the multiple-shooter category, and we will hear from two of them here. Finally, I was occasionally able to interview two or more officers who fired their weapons in the same incident. To provide the reader an idea of how different officers experience the same shooting, I have included a handful of stories that deal with a single incident.

As was the case in the first three chapters, the stories are presented in a series of groups, starting with two of the more dramatic shootings, both of which happened when the involved officers were mere novices.

Baptism by Fire

One of the reasons police agencies put newly minted academy graduates through a probationary period that includes substantial time riding with senior officers is to allow young officers the opportunity to break into the rigors of police work slowly. Fate is no respecter of time on the job, however, and some officers find themselves in deadly straits before they have learned the ropes. We saw in previous chapters that this can include witnessing fellow officers struck down in the line of duty, watching other officers shoot citizens, and nearly shooting people themselves. This section completes the picture of rookies' exposure to deadly violence with a pair of stories from young officers who shot people long before they had a chance to get their police legs under them; in the case of the first officer we hear from, just ten days after he hit the streets.

—◊—

My first training officer was a fairly young guy, who spent a lot of time talking with me about deadly force. At the time I showed up at the station, he had been in two shootings in less than two years. So he was one of those guys that was just always in the middle of whatever action was going on in the division. Because of that, he put a major emphasis on deadly force in training.

When he told me about those shootings, I figured that couldn't happen to me. I was just getting out on the street. I was like, "Well, yeah, I know it happens, but it's probably not going to happen to me." I mean, I knew that something like that could happen, but in my mind I thought it wouldn't, at least not early on in my career. Then, on my tenth day in the field, it happened.

It was a Monday and we were working day shift. We were very busy because of this gas station across the street from a housing project that was a real crime magnet. The gang-bangers who lived in the projects would run across the street, rob the patrons at the gas station, and then run back into the projects. As a trainee, I had to write all the crime reports for our car, and I was getting report after report after report of robberies at that gas station. My training officer wanted to make sure he got off duty on time that day—I can't remember why— so he said, "Let's park our car near the gas station and sit and write your reports there. Maybe we can keep them from robbing it, so we can go home on time." So that's what we did. We parked in a visible area to the rear of this little tiny hot dog stand that was right next to the gas station.

So we were parked there in a marked black-and-white radio car writing our reports when both me and my partner saw this guy walk up to a customer who was putting gas in his car about thirty to forty feet away from us. The guy didn't look at us. He just reached into the back of his waistband, pulled out an automatic, jacked a round into the gun, and stuck it into the customer's stomach. The guy then took the customer's wallet and started going through his pockets.

My training officer grabbed the radio and put out the emergency traffic that we had an armed robbery in progress and where we were. I don't even remember drawing my gun, but by the time my training officer got off the air, I had my gun out and I was ready to go. He told me, "OK, wait till he gets away from the victim," because the crook still had the gun in the guy's stomach.

After a little while, the suspect finally looked over and saw us sitting there. My training officer said, "We're going to let him walk away, and then we're going to pull forward." And that's exactly what happened. The guy pretended like maybe we didn't see this whole thing in front of us, put the gun down by his side, and started to walk away. As we started to pull forward in the car, the guy started to run. When he got to the curb, he slowed down, then ran out into the street. It's a major street—four lanes across—and when he got to the middle of it, he turned around and started firing at us.

I was still sitting in the radio car with the door open, one foot on the ground. I knew the guy was shooting at us because I saw him shooting, but I didn't really hear the rounds going off. The audible start-up and "BANG!" that usually happens when you pull the trigger wasn't there. It was just a soft "pop, pop, pop." He fired nine rounds at us—all misses. My partner fired four, and I fired two. At the time, I didn't know my partner fired because I didn't hear his shots. In fact, when it was over, I asked him, "Did you shoot, or was it just me?"

When the shooting started, there was this Housing Authority police unit right there, almost between us. When they saw what was happening, they just left. I remember them watching us in this gunfight, looking at us, and putting it in reverse. I remember their tires screeching as they left. I couldn't believe it.

Another thing I remember is that when the guy turned and started firing, I got tunnel vision on him. I also remember that I had a sight picture on him as I was firing, because I remember seeing my front sights as I was shooting and wondering why he wasn't falling. I remember actually thinking, "Why isn't he falling?" Then I wondered, "Why is he still running?" because after he fired his rounds, he took off running again. It turns out that we hit him four times, but we didn't know it because he just ran into the projects.

As soon as the guy disappeared into the projects, everything got loud. My partner said to me, "We're not going to chase him. We got to get the victim and make sure he's OK." Not chasing the guy was a judgment call on his part, and it turned out to be a sound decision, because all the witnesses said that the guy went around the first corner and waited there to ambush us. He waited there for us for quite a while. It wasn't until the first assisting unit got there that he got up from his ambush position. The witnesses said that when that first unit arrived, the guy took off running a little ways, then fell in some bushes and died. And that was probably a good minute to two minutes after we shot him.

Now we didn't know any of that at the time. In fact, after he disappeared, I thought he was gone. I thought our rounds missed him, and I didn't think we were going to find him because, traditionally, once suspects disappear in the projects, they're gone. So I thought the incident was over. I noticed at that point that I was breathing real heavy, like I had just run a hundred yards, when I hadn't moved even ten feet. Because I thought it was over, I started to calm down for a couple of minutes. Then the world started to fall apart again.

When the other units got there, we started to set up a crime scene, and some other guys went into the projects to try to find this guy. Well, when they located him, a miniriot broke out. Four to five hundred people came out of the projects, and our units started taking bottles and rocks. They were upset that we'd shot one of their people. We had to get the help from all the sheriff's stations in the region, and then the city sent us one-hundred-plus officers right away. When the city units started showing up, a lot of the anger turned on them because some of the gangsters were telling people that some city officers had simply walked up to the guy where he lay and shot him for no reason. So the city units started taking bottles and rocks. It went from a real quick incident—a matter of seconds—with the shooting, then it mellowed for a couple of minutes, and then it turned into a major civil disturbance. I mean, we were standing there in the middle of hundreds of radio cars, hundreds of cops, two helicopters, and sirens everywhere. It was quite a production.

We were trying to maintain a crime scene where the shooting occurred. Other deputies were looking for where his rounds hit, for his expended shell casings, all that kind of stuff. City units were trying to maintain the scene where the guy fell. There were hundreds of angry people, and there were bottles and rocks flying in the projects. After about half an hour, they pulled my partner and me out of there and took us back to the station while the riot continued. About another half hour after that, the city units started taking people to jail, and things slowly started to calm down.

I had been a little bit worried about things when we were still back at the scene, but my training officer was real reassuring. He told me that I had done a good job and that I shouldn't second-guess myself, because it was so cut-and-dried: armed robbery right there. Crook started shooting at us. That's as clean a shooting as you can get. When he told me that, it was a big load off my mind, because I knew that if it wasn't that way that he'd have told me so.

I tell you, that was one crazy baptism by fire.

—∿∿—

I got out of the academy in the springtime, completed my FTO program in the summer, and was patrolling by myself in the early fall when the shooting went down. It was a Friday, my first day back at work after my normal two days off. There was another guy on my shift, named Mike Mural, that I had gone to the academy with, so we were still full of excitement for our jobs, glad to be back at work on our Monday. It was a beautiful fall day. It was cool and the sun was out. There wasn't a cloud in the sky. In fact, I remember telling Mike what a beautiful day it was.

We took some calls that morning. We ate breakfast. We took a few more calls, then met to talk and write our reports that we were catching up on. When we finished up, he went off to his beat, and I went the other way to mine. Shortly after that, a burglary-in-progress call came out. Dispatch told us that there were two men trying to get into the sliding glass door of an apartment and that the complainant was inside the house with a small child.

Mike said he was en route, and I heard another unit say they were en route too. I was pretty far away, but I responded anyway because it was a felony in progress—one of those calls where more than just two people should go. Before I arrived, Mike broadcast that he was going to go out on two guys walking out of the complex that matched the description of the burglars. Then, a few seconds after that, he advised that he was in foot pursuit, and I heard the sound of the foot pursuit on the radio. He was gasping for breath, giving out directions, giving out descriptions of the suspects, and then the radio was quiet. Then the dispatcher prompted him, asked him to advise. No response. Prompted him again. No response. Some other units arrived on the scene. Then I got there, and we started to set up a perimeter on this large wooded area that was just adjacent to the apartment complex, because that was the direction the foot pursuit had been traveling before Mike's radio went dead.

Soon thereafter, one of the officers on the scene broadcast that a citizen had advised him that he had seen a police officer being led into the woods at gunpoint. I was thinking, "Man, this is not good." But instead of staying where I should and manning the perimeter, I said to myself, "This is my buddy. I got to go in and find him." So I just trudged off into the woods looking for my buddy. I didn't put out a broadcast of what I was doing; I just took off looking for Mike.

I had my gun out. I was walking slowly. Being careful. Being real deliberate. Looking around, trying not to stumble upon them and make whatever the situation was worse. There was a lot of commotion on the radio as I was walking. Other units were checking out an equipment shed at a baseball diamond on the other side of the woods, thinking they might have made it that far. Someone called for the SWAT team, and a supervisor called for an ambulance to respond to the scene. The radio was abuzz with all sorts of chatter. There were sirens wailing all over the place. I couldn't believe what was happening. I couldn't believe someone had taken Mike hostage. I couldn't believe I was walking through the woods looking for my buddy who had disappeared.

Then I came to a small clearing and saw something worse than the worst nightmare I ever had. Just on the other side of the clearing, I saw Mike standing there with his hands up and some guy standing right in front of him holding a gun to his head. I could see that Mike's holster was empty, so I figured the guy had disarmed Mike and was holding his own gun to his head. Mike's back was facing toward me, so the guy could look past Mike and see me. Then the guy said, "You better get out of here or I'm going to blow his fucking head off!" I was in the open, so I took about three or four quick steps to the right through a bunch of thorns and tried to get behind a nearby tree. As I did that, the guy kind of shifted so he could use Mike as a shield. Now I really couldn't believe what was happening. I just couldn't believe that I was looking at this guy pointing a gun at Mike.

I tried to get on the radio to advise the other units, but I couldn't get through, so I just put my radio away and we had a standoff. I remember thinking at that point that I was in a no-win situation. The guy kept telling me to get away, to get back, but I wasn't going to leave. I came there, I found him, and I was not going to back off. I was not going to give ground. We stood there for about a minute or two. Then I told myself that something bad was going to happen sometime soon if I didn't do something. The guy was looking back and forth. He would look at me, then he would look at Mike. Me, then Mike, back and forth, with the gun pointed at Mike's head the whole time.

The guy wasn't moving his head, just his eyes. He was trying to keep Mike like a shield between us, staying where he could make eye contact with me and see where I was at. At one point, when the guy shifted his eyes toward me, Mike reached up and grabbed the gun. When he grabbed it, he grabbed it around the cylinder. It wasn't cocked, so that made it real hard for the guy to pull the trigger.

As soon as Mike grabbed the gun, I tore out of the bushes like a rhino. I put my gun in front of me, thinking that I had to shoot this guy as soon as I could. As I was running up, I could see that the guy wasn't trying to shoot Mike. He was struggling with Mike to get the gun pointed at me, and he was trying to pull the trigger. I didn't know it at the time, but the cylinder was half rotated. The guy had pulled the trigger far enough to start the cylinder rotating, but Mike had a grip on the cylinder that was keeping it from moving a round into the firing position. So the guy was trying with all his might to shoot me as I ran up, but Mike's grip kept him from doing that.

When I got there, I stuck my gun into what I thought was the center of his stomach and pulled the trigger. It was almost like an instantaneous reaction. I ran there so fast that we had a collision. Boom, I got there, my gun went off, and we all fell to the ground like a bunch of bowling pins.

When we fell to the ground, the guy dropped the gun and Mike said, "Get the gun, get the gun!" So I reached over and just kind of swept it to the side, put my gun away, and then we commenced to pummeling the shit out of the guy. He was resisting at first, then he quit fighting, and we got the handcuffs on him. Once we got the cuffs on, it dawned on me that the guy was still alive. I could see a big powder burn on his shirt, so I raised it up. He was an obese guy, and I could see two holes on his big belly, an entry wound and an exit wound. There was a little bit of blood coming out of the holes, but I really couldn't tell how bad he was hurt. It turns out that the gunshot wasn't that bad at all. The round had gone in at an angle on one side of his belly, traveled between the dermis of the skin and the peritoneum, and went out the other side. It never entered his abdominal cavity, so it was basically just a superficial wound. Now I didn't know any of this at the time. All I knew is that he was still alive and that sort of shocked me, given the fact that I'd just put a contact shot into his gut.

A few minutes later, some other officers arrived and one of them took the guy away. Then I remember saying something that was just totally stupid and irrelevant. I'd left the headlights on my car on from running code over to the scene, so I asked the other officers if they could send someone over to turn the headlights off. I don't know why that thought even entered my mind. Why would I remember leaving my headlights on? I hadn't even remembered leaving them on up to that point. I'd just been involved in a hostage situation and in a shooting, and I'm worried about the battery running dead on my car? Who knows?

But I was still pretty juiced up from what had happened. When I first spotted them in the clearing, I could feel these chemicals running through my body, like I'd just seen a lion or some other dangerous animal running loose. It felt like my body had just been charged with something, and it was very powerful. It wasn't fear. I never felt any fear in the situation. That was pretty amazing because, like I said, what happened was worse than my worst nightmare, but I wasn't afraid. It was like fear was not an option, like there was no room for the emotion of fear at the time.

I was so juiced up that I didn't even realize that I was cut up pretty bad from running through the patch of briars to get behind that tree when I first spotted Mike and the guy. I had on a short-sleeved shirt, and some of the thorns tore my arm up, just scratched and lacerated the hell out of my right arm. It looked like shit, but during the situation, I hadn't even realized I was injured, that I was bleeding. When I first spotted the cuts, I didn't know where they came from. I said to myself, "How in the hell did this happen?" Then I looked around where I was at and figured out what happened.

After that, a supervisor came up to me and asked me to give him my gun. I was expecting that because we'd been told in the academy that it was department policy to hold the guns from officers who get involved in shootings as evidence. They told us that the gun would be taken away at the scene and that the officer would be given another gun right away, and that's what happened that day. The supervisor took my gun and gave me another one to put in my holster.

Then my sergeant showed up, we walked back to his car, and we drove to Homicide to talk to the detectives.

More from Patrol

Both of the preceding shootings have unusual features besides the fact that the officers involved were so short in experience when they occurred. For example, although citizens attack police officers on a regular basis, one thing that crooks hardly ever do to officers is kidnap them. So when the officer in the second story found himself in the middle of the woods living something worse than his worst nightmare, he was involved in an event that occurs only once in a blue moon. It is therefore no wonder that he experienced such a strong sense of incredulity.

The first shooting included two unusual features. First, for obvious reasons, robbers rarely stick up victims who are standing only a few yards from a marked police car with two officers in it. The second unusual feature of this shooting concerns what happened after the smoke had cleared. Even though police gunfire has sparked many a riot in the last few decades, the vast majority of police shootings do not prompt any sort of civil unrest. So when a brand-new rookie witnesses a robbery that leads to a shooting that leads to a riot, he has indeed had quite a baptism by fire.

The lion's share of the five-dozen-plus other shootings that happened when the officers I interviewed were on patrol were, in comparison to these two rookies' shootings, ordinary events. But a few, in one way or another, were highly unusual. The stories in this section include shootings of both sorts, providing a more complete sense of the range of deadly circumstances that patrol officers can find themselves in, and highlighting some of the things that most police shootings have in common.

The first point of commonality across most shootings has to do with the distance between police officers and suspects. Although fictional portrayals of police shootings often place officers a substantial distance from the citizens with whom they do battle, the vast majority of real-life shootings involve a separation of a few yards or less, and in many cases less than an arm's length. So the two-lane distance separating the first rookie from the suspect he shot was near the outer range of what typifies police shootings, and the extremely close quarters in which the second rookie fired was not at all unusual. Similarly close distances are involved in most of the shootings in this section (and in most of the shootings that make up the rest of this chapter as well).

Another thing that is common to most shootings is that officers usually fire only a small number of rounds. Although patrol officers occasionally shoot gobs of bullets, they usually fire fewer than a handful, and a single shot is quite common. In a related vein, most shootings happen quite quickly. Quite obviously, the time spent shooting when firing a single shot is quite brief, but human beings can pull a trigger multiple times in a single second, so officers can—and usually do—fire all the rounds they shoot in just a second or two.[2] It is important to keep this in mind when considering the stories in this section (as well as the other stories in this chapter), because the pace of narratives is often much slower than the pace of the action as events unfolded in real time.

At this point, it is worthwhile to briefly revisit our second rookie's shooting, for there is one aspect of it that deserves some mention—the fact that the suspect took his kidnapped partner's gun from him. Although suspects almost never kidnap officers, they do try to disarm them on a fairly regular basis. A decent number of suspects succeed, but when they do, they typically shoot the officer in short order. Indeed just under 10 percent of officers murdered with firearms in the decade ending in the year 2000 were slain with their own guns, usually within moments of being disarmed.[3] Because officers know that they are liable to be killed if they are disarmed, they often shoot suspects who try to take their weapons. Because suspects attempt to disarm officers on a regular basis, a sizable minority of police shootings occur in situations in which suspects try to take officers' guns from them. In order to provide some sense of what a more typical disarming case looks like, this section includes a shooting in which the officer in question shot the suspect before he could complete his potentially lethal theft.

This chapter also talks about mistakes. The rules that govern officers' use of deadly force do not require that an actual deadly threat be present before officers fire, only that officers have a *reasonable belief* that this is the case. The standard of reasonable belief allows officers to make what the law calls *good faith mistakes* in their use of deadly force. One sort of good faith mistake that officers sometimes make is shooting people who wield objects that appear to be deadly weapons, such as toy guns. Another sort of good faith mistake officers sometimes make is shooting unarmed individuals whose actions immediately prior to being shot led the officers to form the reasonable belief that they were in fact armed with a deadly weapon with which they were about to harm the officer or others.

Incidents in which officers mistakenly use deadly force against nonthreatening people are quite different from those exceptionally rare cases in which a brutal officer purposely shoots someone without cause, and readers should be careful to note the difference. This may be difficult, however, as many people have a hard time understanding shootings in which the person shot posed no actual deadly threat to anyone— particularly those cases in which the person was unarmed—because they believe officers should be able to easily discern real threats from innocuous action. But in many cases, it is not in fact easy for officers to determine whether an individual confronting them is armed or whether what an armed individual is carrying is a deadly weapon or some less harmful object. The nature of the problems that officers must deal with often is unclear: lighting often is poor, circumstances often are evolving (or devolving) rapidly, and officers often have to make decisions about whether to shoot in split seconds, before they have a chance to obtain all relevant information. So officers sometimes shoot when the facts established in the aftermath of incidents indicate that they really didn't need to.[4]

The stories in this section shed light on this matter by relating two shootings in which officers came to believe they were in imminent peril when the people they shot, in fact, posed no deadly threat. Together, they illustrate how officers' interpretations of citizens' actions during tense, fast-moving, uncertain circumstances can lead them to believe that they must shoot to protect themselves or others from deadly threats that do not really exist.

But in the vast majority of cases in which officers fire, they do so to defeat real threats. In fact, only three of the officers I interviewed shot unarmed individuals, and fewer than a handful of others were involved in cases in which they mistook objects such as toy guns for deadly weapons. Consequently, most of the stories in this section (as well as the vast majority of those in the rest of the chapter) deal with shootings in which officers' opponents in fact had deadly weapons, including one in which the suspect was armed with arguably the most unusual deadly weapon officers ever faced in the history of American law enforcement: a stolen army tank.

—◊◊◊—

I was working a ten-hour shift that started at 9:00 on Halloween night when I got in my first shooting. I had taken my kids trick-or-treating, dropped them off back home, grabbed my gear, kissed the wife and kids good-bye, and went into work. I was working with my regular partner, and we figured it would be a busy shift, but it was cold out, and that really put a crimp on the trick-or-treaters. We had some calls at first, but after about 11:00 it was just dead. We couldn't find any-thing—nobody walking around, nothing at all. Then, about 3:00 or so in the morning, we spotted something. I was driving. We had the heat on, but the windows open. I was going eastbound down this four-lane road real slow, five or ten miles an hour, just kind of daydream-ing, looking around. We were coming up on some apartments when I noticed an open door on a car facing us on the other side of the street. I kind of gave my partner a shot in the shoulder 'cause he was fading in and out and said, "Hey Dave, there's an open car door. Let's check it out."

As I was making a U-turn to come up behind the car, our head-lights went across the open door. I saw two guys there, one in the seat of the car with a screwdriver, working on the steering column, and the other one squatting down next to him. The second guy was holding something I couldn't make out in one hand and a lighter in the other that he was using to light up the interior of the car. The guy squatting was kind of tall and thin. The guy behind the steering wheel was really big, a real muscular-looking guy—I could tell by the size of his jacket. There wasn't enough room to complete the U-turn, so we actually ended up facing the side of the other car at a slight angle, like a K minus the bottom leg, with our spotlights and headlights shining on the side of the car.

The guy who was squatting stood up real quick. We were both expecting these guys to beat feet out of there, so we were ready for a foot chase. Dave went to run around to the rear of the car to pin them in, and I was going to pin them the other way so that we could catch them before they ran. The thin guy, who had his back to me, dropped the stuff he was holding. I shouted for him to stop, and he kind of put his hands out to his side.

The other guy started to get out of the car, and I could see that he was wearing jeans, but no shirt under his big, black, 1950s Fonzie-style leather jacket. As he turned, I could see that he was a big, muscular, weight-lifter-type guy. As soon as I saw his build, I said to myself, "This guy is a parolee." The other guy I wasn't so sure about, but I was certain the big guy had done some time. I was thinking, "He doesn't want to go back to the pen," so I figured we had a fight on our hands.

I started to move around my open door to grab the thin guy 'cause I was pretty close to him. As I was doing this, the big guy took two quick steps toward the back of the car—where Dave was heading to cut him off—and he reached back to the rear of his right side, which was facing me. This movement caught my eye, and I saw the outline of his hand going onto the grip of a pistol—some type of semiautomatic—that was tucked in the waistband of his jeans. I start yelling, "GUN!!" to let Dave know what was going on. As I was yelling, I started to draw my gun, and the big guy started to pull his gun out. I could see that it had a long slide on it, and I thought, "Holy shit! This guy's got a .45!"

Everything started to slow down at that point. I was really worried that he was going to shoot Dave, and I wanted to shoot him before he did, but I couldn't seem to make my body move fast enough. He seemed to be moving slowly, too; his gun was coming out slow. I fired a round as soon as I got my gun out of my holster. I saw the muzzle flash and some smoke. The shot sounded real muffled, not like a regular gunshot. Then I heard my casing hit the windshield of my squad car, slide down, and hit the windshield wiper. I brought my gun up to eye level to take a second shot, but before I could pull the trigger, Dave ran into the guy at full speed. He grabbed the gun as it was coming up, pushed it down, and tackled the guy into the trunk of the car that they were trying to steal.

Dave and the big guy fell off the trunk and onto the ground. As they were fighting, I heard the gun hit the ground and slide on the cement. The other suspect then started to turn and face toward me. I had closed the ground between the two of us as I was shooting, so I grabbed him by the scruff of the neck and shirt and slammed him onto the hood of the car. I put my gun in the back of his neck and told him not to move or I was going to shoot him. At that point, time started to return to normal. The slow-motion stuff stopped. Then I got on the radio and called for help.

It turns out the round I fired went through the big guy's right forearm, into his stomach, traveled around his hip bone, went into his colon, and ended up somewhere near his scrotum. He was injured pretty bad, but at the time I wasn't sure I'd hit him because he was still fighting with Dave. They were on the ground. The suspect was on his stomach, and Dave had him from behind in a choke hold. He was holding on for dear life. Just riding him, basically. He had one arm around the suspect's neck, and he was trying to pin the guy's arm down with his other one. He had his legs wrapped around the suspect's waist and thighs, and they were sort of rolling around. I looked at Dave and asked him if he was OK. I thought maybe I shot him by mistake because he was so close when I fired.

He said, "I don't think I'm hit," and started to look at his legs as he was fighting the guy.

I kept asking, "Are you OK? Are you OK?" He said he was OK, so I asked him where the gun was. He told me he thought the guy had fallen on top of it, and I thought, "Oh, my God, he's still got the gun!"

I leaned down and put my gun into the suspect's side to put a couple of contact shots into his ribs. I'd seen a training tape during lineup one night about doing contact shots to the head and the ribs. It explained how you can be pretty sure that when you press the barrel against the bone that the bullets will go right in where you press, so in close quarters you don't have to worry about bullets flying around. So that's what I was thinking—put my gun in this guy's ribs and put a couple of shots into him sideways so no rounds would come through and hit my partner.

Just as I was about to pull the trigger, Dave spun the guy over and the suspect's arms came free. There was no gun in his hands, so I held my fire. I could see that the suspect was bleeding from his arm and stomach. There was blood all over the place. That's when I realized I'd hit him with my first shot. The guy was still fighting with Dave, but Dave was holding his own. I just held onto the thin guy until the rest of our squad arrived about a minute later. They took the thin guy from me, cuffed him, and helped Dave cuff the guy I shot. He kept fighting, even after they got the cuffs on him. He didn't even know he'd been shot until one of the other officers told him, "Quit fighting. You've been shot!" Then he looked down, realized that he had been shot, and gave up.

After the guy finally gave up, my attention turned to finding the gun. I looked everywhere around where he and Dave had fought, but I couldn't find it. I was really, really afraid because I knew I saw a gun, but I was worried that maybe I saw something that wasn't there. I was thinking, "The media is going to love that," and worrying about how I was going to explain my actions to the detectives. As I was thinking this stuff, one of the other officers found the gun on the other side of the car the suspects were trying to steal. It was on the street by the sidewalk. It had gone across the trunk and landed on the other side when Dave tackled him. When I saw that gun, I had a sense of relief like you wouldn't believe.

My emotions changed pretty quickly, though, because it turned out the gun was a Crossman air pistol. Damn replica of Colt .45. It even says "Replica .45" on it. You can go to K-Mart and buy them. I thought, "Why did this idiot pull a BB gun?" After it was all over, Dave and I discussed what he was planning on doing with the gun. We were thinking maybe he was going to try to bluff us and escape. Maybe he was going to try to throw it because he was on parole and didn't want to get caught with it. Who knows? Whatever he was thinking, he's obviously not the brightest guy in the world.

Thirty days later, Dave killed an ex-con who attacked him, and seven months after that we got in another shooting. We were working day watch when a call came out on a disturbance at a house that we knew. Dave and I had been there numerous times. We had arrested a guy there who was a crystal meth user. He was an asshole, always doing something to get us called out there. He lived in a camper on the bed of a pickup in the driveway of his uncle's house, a beautiful home. The house is in the area we usually work, but we weren't working that beat that day. The call went out to some other units, but we decided to respond because we knew the guy. So Dave drove like a maniac. I mean, he broke a thousand vehicle code sections. The guy can drive. He went ninety-some miles an hour. He was flying. The dispatch said the suspect was armed with a screwdriver that he was using to pry the bars off the window to get into the house. It gave his description, said he was wearing a red shirt and blue jeans. We knew who it was.

We worked out a plan so that when we got there, Dave would drop me of in front, then take the car around back in the alley. That way, if the guy took off when he saw me, we'd have him trapped. We'd take him to jail and put an end to these repeat calls for a while. Unbe-knownst to us, a few days prior he'd threatened some other cops with a knife. They had to mace him. He spent a couple of days in custody, talked to some mental health people and such, then they released him. Since getting out, he'd been talking about how he was going to kill the next cop he came in contact with. All this stuff had gone on the last couple of nights, but nobody put anything in the books about it or anything, so we didn't know about it.

When we got there, we saw that one of our K-9 guys, Dan Franklin, was already there. Dave let me off by Dan's patrol car, which still had the dog in it, and he took off to get to the alley. When I started walk-ing up the driveway, I saw Dan fighting with the guy in the backyard of the house. He had him by the neck from behind like he was trying to put a carotid on him or just hold him, and they were banging against the side of the house. There was no easy way for me to get to him because there were some fences between us. The people who let Dan in weren't there anymore, so I took off running along the side of another fence that went back to where they were fighting. There were actually two fences—a six-foot wooden fence and a three-foot chain-link fence—that were up against each other.

I pulled my pepper spray so that when I got to where they were fighting, I could hop the fences and help Dan get the guy into custody. I was running full speed through the yard—I couldn't see how the fight was going because of the six-foot wood fence—and as I got par-allel to the camper, I heard, "BOOM," a gunshot, loud as can be, right in the area where they were fighting. I figured Dan had shot the guy because he pulled the screwdriver and tried to stab him. I jumped up on the chain-link fence to look over the wood fence to see what was going on. I dropped my mace as I was coming up and drew my gun 'cause I figured Dan might need me to cover down on the guy while he cuffed him up.

When I looked over, I saw a whole different scenario from the one I was expecting. The suspect was sitting upright on his butt, legs spread. Dan was sitting between his legs in front of him. The suspect had Dan from behind. He had Dan in a headlock with his left arm, and he had Dan's Smith & Wesson 5903 in his right hand. He was try-ing to turn it toward Dan's head. Dan had grabbed the gun with his left hand and was trying to push it away from his head. With his right hand, Dan was reaching down, trying to pull his backup gun from his ankle holster. Because one round had already been fired, I was thinking that Dan had already been shot once. I was about twelve feet away, standing on the chain-link fence, looking right at them. They were facing right at me. I saw the whole picture in detail. I saw Dan reaching for his backup gun. I saw that it was a Walther PPK, just by the handle of it. I saw Dan's 5903. I saw the suspect's hands. I saw the three fingers and thumb of his right hand around the pistol grip, and I saw his finger on the trigger. I saw that it was Dan's left hand on his 5903, and I saw fear in his eyes. Dan's head was centered on the suspect's chest, so all I could see of the suspect was his head and his gun arm.

He looked up, saw me, and said, "Oh, shit." Not like, "Oh, shit, I'm scared." But like, "Oh, shit, now here's somebody else I gotta kill"—real aggressive and mean. Instead of continuing to push the gun at Dan's head, he started to try to bring it around on me. This all happened real fast—in milliseconds—and at the same time, I was bringing my gun up. Dan was still fighting with him, and the only thought that came through my mind was, "Oh, dear God, don't let me hit Dan." I fired five rounds. My vision changed as soon as I started to shoot. It went from seeing the whole picture to just the suspect's head. Everything else just disappeared. I didn't see Dan anymore, didn't see anything else. All I could see was the suspect's head.

I saw four of my five rounds hit. The first one hit him on his left eyebrow. It opened up a hole, and the guy's head snapped back, and he said, "Ooh," like, "Ooh, you got me." He still continued to turn the gun toward me, and I fired my second round. I saw a red dot right below the base of his left eye, and his head kind of turned sideways. I fired another round. It hit on the outside of his left eye, and his eye exploded, just ruptured and came out. My fourth round hit just in front of his left ear. The third round had moved his head even further sideways to me, and when the fourth round hit, I saw a red dot open on the side of his head, then close up. I didn't see where my last round went. Then I heard the guy fall backwards and hit the ground. He was still holding Dan's gun in his right hand when he hit. A second later, Dan jumped up, holding his backup, reached down and took his Smith & Wesson back from the suspect.

I got on the air, put out a broadcast that we'd had a shooting, and hopped the fence. The guy was obviously dead. I asked Dan if the suspect had fired his gun, and he said, "Yeah, he tried to shoot me." I said, "OK, let's inspect you." So as we were waiting for people to show up, we looked at his arms, looked at his legs, making sure he hadn't been shot. As we were inspecting Dan, Dave came running up. He'd had the windows rolled up and air conditioner on, so he hadn't heard any of the shots. All he'd heard was my "shots fired" broadcast. He looked over at me and asked, "Was this you?"

I said, "Yeah."

He said, "Go ahead out front. The sergeant will be here in a couple of minutes."

I hopped the fence, then Dan hopped the fence, and we just went out and sat on the curb while Dave stood over the body. Then my boss came, same sergeant who had been at the other two shootings. He separated us, and after a few minutes we went down to headquarters to talk to the detectives one more time.

It was back in '86, and I was working the area around Sherman Park, which the FBI said was the most violent three-square-mile area in the United States. There were more homicides and more police activity and more police shootings in that area than any other area in the United States for three years running in the late '80s, so it was pretty heavy at that time.

We'd just arrived in our patrol area after clearing midnight roll call when we saw somebody lying down on the sidewalk. Looked like he was a drunk down. When we got out of the car, I saw that this drunk guy had a hole in him about the size of my fist from the back to the front and that there was a shotgun shell laying next to him. We called an RA unit in, a supervisor showed up, and we started setting up for a homicide scene when another round went off, probably about a hundred yards away. It sounded like it was probably another shotgun round, because it was real loud and it wasn't a sharp crack like a rifle round.

I was working with a probationer, and I told the sergeant that we should head to the area the shot came from because we had no units over there, and I thought that maybe the shot was related to the scene we were sitting on. So my partner and I went down there, and lo and behold, there was another body on the ground. So we put out the information that we had some clown running around shooting people. After that, we could hear shots being fired down the block, going to the west and coming back up north again.

We got some more units there, and we got the whole area basically cordoned off. We got RA units in there, taking care of the people who were shot, and set up for Homicide for those that were killed. We talked to a couple of civilians, who were telling us that they saw a guy with a black coat walk up the right side, the east side, of the street a little ways from us, and it looked like he went into one of the apartment buildings up there. So we decided to take a team of four, maybe five, officers and clear the street as far as we could in order to make the perimeter smaller and more manageable.

We were walking, clearing the area house by house as we went along. Even though it was real early in the morning, a lot of people were out in the neighborhood. With people all over the place, it was going pretty slowly. Then, finally, we heard some screaming and saw somebody running up the street about four or five houses in front of us. Three of us ran up there—me, my probationer, and a guy named Greg Davis. It turned out to be a fistfight, where a friend of one of the people who was shot was beating up on this other guy who he thought was the guy who shot his friend. Turned out the beating victim wasn't involved in the shooting. He was just one of the people standing out there watching.

So we were breaking up the fight when Greg Davis saw somebody standing in an alcove of this nearby apartment building. The alcove was all brick and concrete, with a walkway going through it and a roof overhead—it looked like a bunker. When he saw the guy, Greg said, "It's him, he's got a shotgun!" Then the suspect came up on Greg with a sawed-off, pistol-grip shotgun. He had a bandoleer of 00-buck under his jacket, which I could see as he raised the shotgun. Greg was about twenty-five feet from the guy. I was probably fifteen or twenty feet from Greg and probably about thirty feet from the suspect. I didn't have a real good view of the suspect, but I could see the bandoleer, and I could see the shotgun come out between the sides of the little entry to the alcove.

Greg had a shotgun, and he fired two rounds real quick—"boom, boom"—at the suspect, but the way the suspect was in this little alcove, he was pretty much protected from the rounds. The rounds were gonna hit the concrete; they weren't gonna penetrate where he was. The other officers and I were out in the open, and I thought Greg had some protection from this brick wall next to these bushes he was standing by, so I told him to slow down his fire and let us get some cover, to keep the suspect pinned in the alcove. Greg did that, but his shotgun jammed after he fired his third round. It turned out that there was no wall next to the bushes he was standing by, so he was out in the open when his shotgun jammed.

He yelled out, "It's jammed!" and the suspect stepped out into the open a little bit. As he fired a round or two, I fired three rounds. I knew I hit him good—because I could hear the rounds hit, like a "smack" on the skin, and he went down instantly—but I also knew I had hit him low, maybe the pelvis area, because I was looking over the top of my sights when I fired. I ran toward Greg and told him to get rid of the shotgun and draw his handgun. Then we went over to where I thought this wall was. Like I said, it turned out to be bushes, so we really had no protection at all, but from the bushes we could look straight into the alcove opening and see the suspect clearly. Around that time, there was another round fired from my left side. Came from my probationer who basically fired into the alcove where the suspect was. He didn't hit anything—it just bounced off the concrete.

The suspect wasn't moving anymore, so now somebody had to go up and check him out. By that time, other officers had arrived, and we were putting together a plan for two of them to slowly move up on the suspect. But before we got the plan squared away, another officer started going up there by himself. As that officer got to the opening of the alcove, I could see that the suspect was obviously not out of commission, because I saw him start to move the shotgun. He was holding the pistol grip in his left hand, and he had his right hand on the pump handle, and he was starting to lean forward. He was doing that just as the officer started to lean around the wall to check him out. I yelled for the officer to move back, but he didn't hear me and continued forward. When the officer looked around the wall, the suspect brought the shotgun up. I thought he was going to shoot the officer in the face, so I fired one more round. It hit the suspect in the chest, knocked him back, the shotgun went off, and the officer fired one round from the shotgun—almost a contact shot—into the guy's side. He died at the scene.

The other officer was upset with me for firing that last shot—thought I fired too close to him. He didn't realize that the guy was trying to shoot him because even though he was on top of the guy, he never heard the suspect's shotgun go off. We couldn't find where this guy fired—into the wall, across the street, or anything like that. We couldn't figure out where the round went. I was saying that he fired, Greg said he fired, but the officer that was up there was upset, saying the suspect didn't fire. So everybody was a little tense about that.

After everything was secured, they transported us back to the station, where we gave our statements to the shooting team. We found out what happened to that last shotgun blast when we came back to the scene for the walk-through. Some detectives from the shooting team asked the officer, "Where were you standing?" then put him where he'd been. He told them that the guy couldn't have fired a round when he was there because he'd have heard it. Then they pointed up to the ceiling of the alcove and showed him a bunch of pellets in this crease where one part of the ceiling overlapped with another. Turns out the blast went over his head by about a foot. When he realized that, he said, "Oh, my God!" Kind of a rude awakening for him.

When it was all over, it turned out that the guy had killed two people—shot five total—before we found him. We knew he'd shot at least two when we caught up to him, and that gave a bit of a sense of fear because it was obvious to me that this guy wasn't finished killing people and that he was waiting for us. But there was also something humorous about what happened. It was when Greg Davis's shotgun jammed. After telling us that it had jammed, he said, "Goddamn shotgun. I knew I should've changed that damn ammo," as he threw it to the ground. We had old ammo, and what had happened was we had gone to the sergeant before the shift started and asked him for some new shotgun rounds.

We're supposed to trade our rounds in if they're old or scuffed up, and some of Greg's were. Greg had gone to the sergeant that night and asked him for some new shotgun rounds. He looked at Greg's rounds, and he said, "Oh, your rounds are good enough." What occurred during the shooting was that the brass on the fourth round that was in there was oblong, and it jammed the shotgun. So that was the remark that I remember Greg saying: "I should've got some new ammo." Right in the middle of a shoot-out, he threw the shotgun down and said, "Should've got some new ammo." So after it was all over and we were talking about what had happened, I thought that was sort of humorous.

—∿—

I was at home nursing my daughter right before the shooting. She was about four months old, so I would take my dinner breaks at home in order to nurse her. I finished up about nine o'clock, gave her to my husband, and went back on patrol. Right after I told dispatch I was back in service, I was driving through a parking lot, and this Hispanic lady came running up to my car. She was in a big panic, screaming something about her husband chasing this guy who didn't pay for his dinner at their restaurant. I got her calmed down a little bit, and she told me that she and her husband owned this Mexican restaurant next to where we were talking and that the guy her husband was chasing had a gun. She was terrified that her husband had gone after this guy who had a gun because he didn't have one himself. I got descriptions and the direction the guy and her husband were running in, broadcast what I had over the air, and went looking for her husband.

I hadn't gone very far—maybe two blocks—when some citizens flashed their headlights and flagged me down in front of this car dealership. When I pulled into the front end of the parking lot and stopped, I could see a commotion about a hundred feet away at the back. One of the citizens, a Mexican guy, pointed to the back of the lot and said, "They're in the back, they're over there, they're over there!" When I got out of my car, I saw two other Hispanics in restaurant outfits fighting on the ground with this guy who matched the description given by the woman who flagged me down. He was a white guy wearing a jacket.

It was obvious that these were the guys I was looking for, so I broadcast what I had, drew my gun, and started to move toward the back of the lot. Normally, I would have waited for some backup before doing anything in a case where I had a guy with a gun, but I was worried that the guy might hurt the other citizens if I waited. When I got to a position about thirty or forty feet from where the fight was, the two Mexican guys let go and started to move away from the white guy.

Then the white guy stood up real quick. Not all the way, but in a low crouch. I yelled at him to get back down on the ground, but he didn't move, so I kept yelling, "Get on the ground! Get on the ground!" Then, all of a sudden, he stood straight up and started sprinting toward me. As he was running at me, he started yelling, "Shoot me! Shoot me! Shoot me!" over and over.

When he started to run at me, I started backpedaling as fast as I could go. I kept yelling, "Get on the ground! Get on the ground!" as I was moving back with my gun pointed at him. He kept yelling, "Shoot me, shoot me, shoot me, shoot me," as he was closing in on me. I don't have a clear memory of what happened next, but the citizens who where right there all told the investigators that the guy reached across his body and into his coat with his right hand. All I remember is that I thought that he was going to kill me, so I shot him. I wanted to go home that night, that was all that mattered.

I thought that the guy was about eight to ten feet away when I pulled the trigger, but the citizens said we were almost touching, that we were close enough to shake hands. They even remember that I had the trigger indexed as I was backpedaling. Part of their statement was that they thought I was going to die if I didn't put my finger on the trigger and shoot, that the guy was going to kill me. At any rate, right after I fired, the guy fell to the ground, holding his stomach. Then another officer who had arrived just as the shooting went down ran up, patted the guy down, and handcuffed him.

I didn't want to be there. I didn't want to stand there and watch the guy bleed to death, so I backed away and walked down this little driveway toward where some other officers were coming in. My lieutenant came up and asked me to tell him what happened. I briefly told him, then I gave him my gun because I knew that was part of the procedure. He told me to go sit in the car with one of the officers on the scene, who had been in a shooting before. I talked with him a little bit about what I could remember. Then the lieutenant told me I could go, and the other officer drove me back to the station.

About an hour or two later, somebody told me the guy I shot didn't have a gun on him. That made me feel pretty bad. It turns out that the guy's a drunk and mentally ill. He'd been sitting around the restaurant that night, looking at a picture of his dead nephew lying in a coffin. He kept reaching into the pocket of his coat as if he had a gun in there and telling the workers that he was going to shoot them. I think the guy wanted to die. That's why he ran at me shouting for me to shoot him, but hearing that I had just shot an unarmed man made me feel shitty.

—◦◦◦—

I was supposed to get off at seven o' clock that night, so about 6:45 I was in the locker room taking my gun belt off. I still had my radio turned on, and a call came out that an army tank was running things over not too far away. I thought, "You know, that'd be a pretty cool call to go to," so I put my gun belt back on and jumped in my car. Another officer jumped in the passenger seat and off we went. I started driving through some streets where the tank had already been, and I couldn't believe what I saw. There were crushed cars, knocked-over fire hydrants, and telephone poles down. I was just like, "Holy cow!" I remember thinking it looked like something you'd see on CNN out of Bosnia or something, not here.

When I got to the intersection of DeSoto and Mesa Vista, I looked to my left and saw a tank rolling down the street. It had dragged a streetlight that came off when the driver turned the corner, leaving the pole blocking the intersection. To avoid it, I drove through the driveway of the Jack in the Box on the corner and got behind the tank. There was a crapload of other cops there too, so we just kind of traded places back and forth, all in a line abreast from the intersection, and then down onto the freeway. We were all just following along, kind of looking through our windows at each other, going like, "Hey, how you doing?" because there was nothing much we could do.

I remember thinking that the guy was either gonna stop and give up, or some knucklehead was gonna have to jump up there and shoot the driver. He had already run over a van that was occupied with civilians, and he'd been trying to ram police cars throughout the pursuit. Anytime somebody would get up close to him, he'd turn toward 'em and try to hit 'em. Of course, our cars were faster than he was, so we were able to get out of the way, but he was definitely trying to kill some cops. Somebody got on the radio and asked if SWAT could do anything. They said they couldn't, so there was no way we could stop him. If he wanted to keep going, he was gonna keep going. I knew that eventually he would have to stop somewhere, but I didn't know what was gonna happen then. So I figured that there were only two options: either he was gonna give up or somebody was gonna shoot him.

Tom Jackson, one of the guys in the pursuit, was a tank commander in Desert Storm, so I figured if anyone could figure out some way to stop the guy, it'd be him. He had actually been ordered to go up behind the tank by his sergeant, who knew he had tank experience, so he was in the unit closest to the tank, along with a sergeant and another officer.

After we'd been on the freeway for a little while, the guy started to drive toward the center divider, heading for the oncoming traffic. I thought, "Oh, shit, there he goes." We were heading southbound, and no one had stopped the northbound traffic. It was still pretty much rush hour, and I knew that there wasn't enough room for both his tank and all the traffic in the northbound lanes, so somebody was going to get run over once he made it over to the other side. I was thinking that he was about to kill a bunch of people.

When he hit the Jersey wall separating the north and southbound traffic, he sent up a huge cloud of dust that I couldn't see through. When the dust settled a few seconds later, I could see that he had high-centered the tank on the center divider wall so that the left tracks were on the northbound side and the right tracks were on the southbound lanes. He kept moving the tank back and forth, just crushing the concrete wall underneath him. I stopped my car just a little forward of the tank and jumped out.

There were cops all over the place, and by the time I got over to the tank, Tom Jackson and a robbery detective named Henry Beard were already up on it. The tank was still moving, going back and forth, crabbing along the wall, crushing the concrete. I stood there for a few seconds. Then it stopped for a moment. At that point, a guy named Bill Kingwood boosted me up onto the tank. Just as I got up on it, it started moving again. When that happened, I got a little bit worried because I didn't want to get caught in the track or get flipped off the tank and end up under the track.

I was able to hang on and get all the way up onto the turret, where I felt a little bit safer. The tank was still moving pretty violently, but I got a handhold on a bar up there, so I was pretty stable where I was—even though the three of us were constantly swaying as the tank was jerking left and right and moving forward along the wall. I was on Tom's right side, which put me on the southbound side of the freeway, just hanging on. He was trying to open the periscope hatch, which is about an eight-inch-long by four-inch-wide hatch in the middle of the big hatch that you actually climb through to get inside the tank. From the inside, you can open it and stick a little periscope up to see what's going on outside. I let go of my handhold and pulled my gun out when Tom got the periscope hatch open. Just then, the tank lurched, and I almost fell off. Tom reached out and grabbed me. Then I put my gun back in my holster and grabbed the handhold again. We looked down through the periscope hatch, but we couldn't see the driver, so Tom reached inside and popped the lever that opens the big hatch. When he got the big hatch open, I found another hold for my left hand, grabbed it, and pulled my gun out again.

When we looked inside, the only thing we could see of the driver was the top of the back of his head and the tops of his shoulders. He wasn't wearing a shirt, and I could see his shoulders moving back and forth as he was turning the levers to steer the tank. We started yelling at him, and he looked back up at us, so he knew we were up there, and he knew we had the hatch open. The guy looked real tweakerish, like a methamphetamine user. He had long, stringy, greasy hair down to his shoulders, a bad complexion, real dirty, not quite a transient, but on the way there. We were yelling at him to stop the tank, to let us see his hands, to come out of there, just the general police stuff. All three of us were yelling at the same time. In fact, the next day all three of us were hoarse, so I guess we were yelling that stuff pretty loud. After a little while, the driver took his eyes off us and looked forward again. He never looked back up at us again.

I know it was real noisy up there from the tank engine and from the concrete breaking underneath us, but I don't remember hearing any of that noise. I could hear the three of us yelling, plus I had a brief conversation with my sergeant, who was standing on the ground to the right side of the tank, that sounded just like two people chatting at a table. I looked over at him and said, "I'm gonna have to bust a cap in this guy." He looked back at me and said, "You gotta do what you gotta do." I know we were yelling because I know it was loud, but it sounded like we were just talking.

I remember a strong smell of hydraulic fluid, 'cause the guy had popped a hydraulic line when he hit the wall. I also remember looking up and seeing all the officers standing on the freeway and all the traffic going by, but it didn't seem like things were moving very fast. I know the traffic going northbound was still going at a pretty good clip, but when I looked up and saw the cars, it wasn't like they were whipping past like they'd normally be. Another thing that was weird was that I looked over where the other officers were on the ground a few times, and sometimes I would see them, but sometimes they weren't there. I don't really know how to describe it other than to say it was a like a strobe light effect. I remember looking around and thinking, "Wow, this is pretty cool." Then I started thinking, "What the hell are you thinking about that for? There's a guy inside the tank. Think about him." It was odd, but I remember thinking those things. I was like, "What the hell are you thinking about this for now?"

Then I heard Tom yelling some more, and I saw him pull out his OC to spray it into the tank. While he did that, I was thinking, "Oh, crap, that's just gonna screw up the whole inside of that tank, and we still gotta get in there." I know how that stuff affects me, and it's not a good thing. I thought that if we ended up having to go in there, I was gonna have to fight the guy while Tom stopped the tank, and I didn't want to fight this guy inside a tank full of OC. I was about to knock Tom's hand away so that he couldn't spray the inside of the tank when he pulled it back and put it away. He told me later on that he had thought the same stuff I was thinking about the OC, so that's why he pulled it away and put it back.

I was thinking that we were getting pretty close to where we were going to have to shoot this guy because Tom had to get inside the tank and stop it before it made it all the way over the center divider. Based on the way the tank was moving, I knew that he wasn't gonna stay on that wall forever, and we were gonna come off the wall and into the northbound traffic pretty soon. We had to do something before he started rolling again, but none of us wanted to go down into the tank because we didn't know if the driver had guns with him, and we also didn't know if there was anybody else in the tank with him. I was pretty sure that one of three of us up there on the tank was gonna shoot him if he didn't give up. I just didn't know it was gonna be me.

I stuck my gun into the tank and yelled at the guy, "Hey, last chance. Stop the tank or I'm gonna shoot!" Just then, the tank lurched real heavily to the left toward the oncoming traffic. I thought he had finally broken enough of the concrete to where we were on our way to the northbound lanes. It turns out that the left track had come off the tank at that time, but I didn't know that until it was all over. I thought that he was about to drive into the oncoming traffic, so I aimed my gun at the back of his head and pulled the trigger. I didn't want to miss him because I didn't want the bullet to bounce around on all that steel in there 'cause with my luck, I figured it'd bounce back up and pop me right between the eyes.

Just as I pulled the trigger, he moved his head forward and to the left a little bit, so I knew the bullet wasn't gonna hit his head. I heard the round go off, but it wasn't real loud. It sounded exactly like it does at the firing range when you have mufflers on your ears. Then I saw the bullet strike the guy's right shoulder. I actually saw the projectile hit his shoulder, I saw the hole open up, I saw the blood spurt out, I saw my slide come back, and I saw my casing come out of my pistol. I thought that was pretty weird, seeing all that. Then my next thought was, "Oh, shit, now I'm gonna get sued." I wasn't afraid of getting sued; it was just a thought that crossed my mind. I knew that officers who shoot people sometimes get sued. I don't know why it went through my mind, but it did. Then the tank stopped moving.

A few seconds later, Tom told me to go down into the tank, so I hopped on in. Once I was down inside, I could see that the guy had fallen forward but that he was still in a seated position with his hands on his thighs. I could see that he had no gun, so I put my gun away, put on my rubber gloves, and felt for a pulse. I couldn't feel anything. As I was doing that stuff, Tom came in, checked the rest of the tank to make sure there were no more suspects inside, then told me to shut the tank off. He told me how to do it. Then he grabbed the guy and pulled him to the side so I could lean over and pull the levers. It got real quiet when I shut the tank down.

I looked over and saw that the guy was still bleeding a little bit. I thought, "How do we get him out of here?" Then I reached over him, and I grabbed both of his hands in both of mine and started pulling him up. When I got to a point where I was standing up in the turret with him right in front of me, all this blood started spurting out all over the place. By that time, other officers had climbed up onto the tank, and one of them reached down and stuck his finger in the hole in his shoulder to stop the blood flow. I thought, "Well, what do we do now?" Then a bunch of hands reached down through the hatch, grabbed him, and just sucked him right out. Tom and I sat inside there for a few minutes. Then I thought, "This is boring," so I got out and jumped off the tank. One of the sergeants there grabbed me, threw me in his car, and drove me back to the station.

—◊◊◊—

I was working a crime suppression detail with Roger, my regular partner. Our job was to go into the housing projects and gang areas that were known for narcotics activity and see what was going on. At about 2145, we were cruising through a place called Kennedy Court, a high-crime area with a lot of crack cocaine dealers. Roger was driving. We spotted these two guys at the corner who were making some type of exchange. Automatically, we thought narcotics. They saw us, turned, and started walking away. Roger pulled up just behind them as I opened up the patrol car door. I asked them, "Hey, guys, what's going on?" One of them replied, "Nothing." So I asked, "Have you all got any ID on you?" The other guy then said, "We're just going to the store." And I said, "Well, that's fine. I understand that, but could I still see some ID?" About that time, the guy who said they were going to the store took off running. I figured he had dope on him, so I took off after him, leaving the other guy behind. I was chasing him down the sidewalk. Roger was in the car so he pulled ahead, then swung the car to block the guy in before he got to the corner. I had been about ten feet behind the guy as I was chasing him, but I caught up to him when Roger cut him off.

I was just about to grab him, couldn't have been more than three feet away, when the guy turned around and shot me. I never saw the gun. He was a black guy, the gun was black, and it was dark out. All I remember is that when he turned around, he was firing. I don't remember seeing the muzzle flash, but I did hear the round go off. It was kind of muted though, not as loud as it should be. The bullet hit me in the inside of my right forearm. It didn't really hurt, but it stung, like somebody had slapped me real hard.

As soon as I got hit, I yelled, "I'm hit!" Then I remember spinning around, falling down, taking my gun out of my holster, getting up, drawing down on the guy as he ran away, hearing Roger shooting at the guy, then seeing the guy on the ground. Roger went over to him, got the gun away, and cuffed him up. Then Roger came back to the car to check on me, and we started arguing about who was going to get on the radio to tell the other units what had happened and where we were at. I guess he thought that I was hurt pretty bad, but I didn't feel I was injured bad at all. I knew I was hit, but I figured I could still do my job. So we had a little argument:

"I'll call it in"

"No, I got it."

"No, I'll call it in."

"No, I got it."

Back and forth like that for a few seconds, then I finally got on the radio and advised dispatch about the shooting.

Other marked units started arriving just a short time later. They made sure the guy was secure and kept the crowd that had gathered away from the scene. I was feeling real hyper, just walking around. Then a detective arrived, and he made me sit down in the patrol car. He asked me how I was and I said, "I'm fine."

He said, "No, you're not! Look at your arm! You've been shot! Just calm down."

I said, "I'm fine."

And he said, "No, no, you're not. You've been shot!"

I replied, "I know. But I'm fine, I'm fine." I lost that argument, and they took me to the hospital. Turns out it was a through-and-through wound. No bones hit. No serious damage. I was out of there in a couple of hours.

Before going to the hospital, the detectives asked me if I had fired my gun. I told them I hadn't. They checked my gun, and it turned out one round was missing. To this day, I don't remember firing my gun, but I did. All I remember is getting shot, spinning around, drawing, coming up, Roger shooting, and then seeing the guy on the ground. The only thing I can think is that I just reacted to my training. I have a real good friend who was one of the instructors in the academy.

We've had some long talks about officer survival and what happens in life-threatening situations. He's helped me out a whole lot in how to think when you go into situations like that, because he's been there, and he's told me that sometimes you just respond automatically. It's like someone presses this button and you just shoot. So when the guy shot me, he pressed that button, and I just responded.

—∿—

The detail we were working was this combination antigang–crime suppression deal, where the city councilmen call the chief and say, "Hey, I've got a constituent here saying she's having problems with this gang-banger down the street. Send me some guys over here." So we go and flood the whole neighborhood with officers and just basically shut it down for a couple of days. Pick up everybody we can, put as many people in jail as we can.

Johnny and I just seemed to attract criminals. We just picked the right guys, and one night we spotted these two guys about a block from us looking like they were exchanging some money, so we decided to stop and check them out. We were in a known dope area, so we figured they might be doing a dope deal. They spotted us coming up in our car, and they started to walk away on this cross street. We lost sight of them for a few seconds, then spotted them again when we turned the corner.

I slid up behind them and Johnny got out. I stayed in the car, figuring that he was going to hand me the driver's licenses, and I'd run them on the computer. He said, "Guys, I need some ID," real nicely. No big deal. One guy said, "Well, I don't have any ID. I'm just going to the store, and I don't need my ID." Johnny said, "Well, look, man, I'm just checking you out. If you don't have any warrants, we'll let you go." Right after he said that, the guy took off running. Johnny took off after him, so I threw the car in gear and started paralleling them. They were running right along the sidewalk, and as we got up to this little parking lot in front of this market, just a little place where you turn in to park diagonal-like, I got just in front of him and cut the car to the right to block the suspect off. He ran into the car and turned around just as my partner was closing in on him.

I was starting to get out of the car when I heard a shot go off. I didn't know if my partner had shot the guy or if the guy had shot my partner, so for a split second I wasn't sure what was going on. Then I heard Johnny yell, "I'm hit!" and I saw the guy running back the way we came. When I heard, "I'm hit!" this rush of adrenaline came over me, and all my attention focused on the suspect as he was running away.

I could feel my hair on my arms sort of standing on end, and I just had this sense of where everyone else was. I didn't have to look; I just knew where Johnny was, where all the people who were out on the street were. I couldn't really hear much of anything at that point, but I had this heightened sense of awareness.

As I was noticing all this, I was thinking all sorts of thoughts. I didn't know how bad Johnny was hit, but I was thinking that he bought it. He always wore his vest, but I was thinking that he might have taken the round between the panels, or in his head or neck. I was thinking that "I'm hit!" might be the last words I was ever going to hear him say. We weren't just partners, we're best friends, and I was thinking that I'd let him down, that I should have been up there with him when we first stopped the two guys. I should have gotten out of the car, but I was being lazy, staying in the car to make it easier to run the guys on the computer. If I had gotten out, the guy wouldn't have run, we'd have found the gun and gotten it from him right then, and this wouldn't have happened. So I told myself, "I've got to get this guy, no matter what." I wasn't going to let the guy get away.

All this was going through my mind as I was getting the rest of the way out of the car and moving toward the trunk. It couldn't have taken more than a couple of seconds to get to the back of the car, but it seemed like I was moving in slow motion. I felt like I couldn't move fast enough. It just seemed like I was being a slug, not getting my ass out of the car fast enough. I wanted to get to the back of the car that instant, but it just wasn't happening quick enough.

When I finally got to the back of the car, I considered shooting at him, but I thought that maybe he had dropped the gun. I couldn't see it in his hand. He was a real dark black guy, and he was wearing dark clothes. There were no streetlights where all this went down, so all I could really see was his outline; he looked like a shadow.

Then he suddenly stopped and turned toward me. Like a dumb ass, I stepped out from behind the car so that we were facing each other in the middle of the street, just like an Old West showdown. Then I saw a muzzle flash, and I knew he still had the gun. I thought, "Man, that son of a bitch is shooting at me." Then I remembered some training I'd had that if you get caught out in the open in a gunfight that it's a good idea to try to make yourself a smaller target, so I knelt down and commenced to let loose. I fired three rounds, the guy went down, and I stopped shooting.

I took my eyes off the suspect for a second to look over and check on Johnny. He was holding his arm, so I figured he wasn't hurt too bad after all. I still had to secure the suspect, so I started moving up to where he went down. He had dropped the gun, but he was reaching for it as I was closing in on him. I probably could have shot him again right then. I was ready. I still had my gun out, and I had my sights right on the back of his head, but I figured I could reach him before he grabbed the gun. So I just ran up and kicked him as hard as I could. Then I got his arm back, got the gun secured, and handcuffed him.

I left him there in the street and went back to the squad car. We put out some broadcasts to let everyone know we'd been in a shooting, that one officer and one citizen were hit, that we needed two ambulances. Guys were all over the air saying they were going to respond. We didn't want anyone to get hurt in an accident trying to get to us, so Johnny got back on the air and told everyone to slow down, that we were OK. A crowd started to gather as we waited for the troops to arrive. Every time another unit arrived, they wanted to know what happened and if we were OK. I told them we were OK, that Johnny got shot, I shot the guy, that it looked like the guy was going to be OK. After a while, the detectives arrived, Johnny and the suspect went to the hospital, and I stayed behind to tell the dicks what happened. They told me that some Housing Authority security officers had caught the other guy, and I gave them the lowdown on the shooting. It took a couple of hours to get that taken care of. Then I went to the station to write up my formal statement.

On the way to the station, my big toe on my right foot started to hurt, so I took my boot off to figure out what was going on. I didn't look at the boot, but I noticed that my toe was sticking out of my sock. When I looked at my toe from the top and I could see a little scratch at the tip, I said to myself, "Goddamn, look at that," and figured that it might be the boots. They were kind of old, needed to be resoled. I thought that maybe one of the nails was sticking up in there, and when I kicked the suspect, it split the sock open and cut my toe. I put my boot back on and we went on to the station.

My toe still hurt, so I took my boot off again once I got inside the Homicide office. Some guys came in, looked at my foot, and asked me what had happened to my toe. I said, "Well, I kicked this guy who shot my partner."

"That all you did?"

"Yeah."

"He didn't shoot you?"

"Well, he shot at me. It looked like he was shooting for my head and missed."

They were like, "Are you sure?"

I was like, "Well, yeah. I mean, it just hurts a little bit. No big deal. Just bandage it up. It'll be all right."

They were looking at it from a different angle, where they could see that the whole bottom half of my toe was gone. They were saying, "No way," but no one ever told me to look at the bottom of my foot.

About a half an hour or forty-five minutes later, somewhere around two in the morning, I was talking with my mom on the phone, when this night sergeant came in and asked me what happened to my toe. I told my mom to hang on, then told him that I kicked a guy and cut my toe doing it. He asked me where my boot was, and I told him it was over there in his office. He left and I went back to talking to my mom. I told her that everything was fine, that Johnny got shot, that he's OK, that I had to shoot a guy, that it was no big deal, that I wasn't hurt—just scratched my toe a little bit—stuff like that. About five minutes after the sergeant left, here comes my boot, sailing across the office, followed by the sergeant, saying, "You stupid kid, you got shot. Get your ass to the hospital!" So I said, "Mom, change that. I got shot. I'll be at the hospital. No big deal though."

She freaked out, said, "I'll be right down."

I told her, "Don't worry about it. It's late. Come down tomorrow if you get a chance. It's just a minor wound." I was still thinking it was a little bitty cut. But when I got to the hospital, they showed me in this mirror that most of my toe was gone. I was surprised that it didn't hurt more. In fact, the worst part was when they hit me with Novocain before patching up the toe. That hurt much worse than getting shot. That was painful.

It turned out that the bullet the guy fired entered my boot near the outside, missed the first four toes, hit the big one, and fragmented into the sole of my boot. That's why the sergeant was so ticked off; they had stayed out there an extra hour looking for the bullet the guy fired, when all along the fragments of it were in my boot.

Officer Down

Although the injuries suffered by the two officers we just heard from were relatively minor, many other officers who are struck down in the kill zone do not fare so well. I pointed out in the Introduction that each year some five dozen or so officers don't survive the wounds they suffer at the hands of criminals and that scores of additional officers are maimed or otherwise grievously wounded. In this section, we hear from some officers who were very seriously injured, as they talk about their brushes with death: how the incidents went down, what they were thinking when Death came knocking on their doors, what they did to stave off his call, and—in two cases—how what they endured influenced their actions in subsequent situations.

The stories underscore several things already addressed about the dangers of police work. One is that people armed with sharp objects can be very dangerous: two of the officers we will hear from were felled by knives (one in a shooting that was eerily similar to mine). Another is that officers are at extreme risk when they are disarmed: we see in the starkest of terms what typically happens when officers have their guns taken from them. On a different tack, this section also shows how training, lessons officers learned long before coming into law enforcement, mental preparation, determination in the face of danger, and the will to survive can help officers overcome the most harrowing of circumstances.

The stories begin with the tale of the officer who suffered the most severe injuries among those I interviewed, a woman who very nearly didn't make it out of the kill zone.

—◊◊◊—

My shooting happened real early in the morning. I played softball the night before on a team with my partner and his wife, went out for pizza afterwards, then over to their house to watch a video of that Tom Hanks movie *Big*. On the way home from their house, I swung by the police station and dropped off my request for days off for the upcoming month because it was now Saturday morning and they needed to be turned in that day. After visiting a bit with the officers at the station, I took off for home at about 1:30 A.M. I wasn't really thinking much, just heading home on autopilot for the thirty-mile drive. I pulled up in front of my house somewhere around 2:00. My roommate had parked in the driveway, so I parked on the street. Like I usually do, I drove with my gun slid in between my seat and the center console. That way, when I get home, I can grab it with my right hand, step out of my truck, tuck it under my left armpit, grab my ball bag, and head into the house.

Well, as soon as I stepped out of the truck, I saw the barrel of a .357 Magnum pointed right at me. What had happened is that a carful of gangsters had followed me home to rip off my truck. Apparently, the fifteen-year-old girlfriend of the fourteen-year-old boy pointing the gun at me had seen my truck, liked it, and wanted him to steal it for her. So these two characters, along with three of their buddies, had followed me home. When I pulled up, the fourteen- and fifteen-year-old jumped out while the other three waited in their car.

At any rate, when I opened the door and stepped out, there was this fourteen-year-old standing there with this gun pointed at me. Now I never saw him. All I saw was the gun. I had no idea who was holding it. It could have been an eight-foot-tall transvestite or a ninety-year-old lady for all I knew. All I saw was the barrel, the cylinder, the trigger guard, and the trigger. The barrel looked really big. It looked like a cannon.

I hadn't yet tucked my gun under my arm, so it was still in my hand when I saw the barrel of the .357. I began to raise my gun, and I was getting ready to say, "Police officer—drop the gun!" because that's what I had been programmed to do from training. I about got "police" out of my mouth when I saw a muzzle flash and heard a loud "BOOM!" The bullet hit me square in the chest, tore right through it, and went out my back. I was dumbfounded. I truly thought that if I said, "Police—drop the gun" that he would drop it, so I simply couldn't believe that he had shot me. I was so programmed from watching TV and from all the training in the academy where we would tell people to drop their guns and they do it that I was certain that he was gonna drop it. Boy was I wrong.

Well, right after he shot me, the kid turned and ran toward the back of my truck. As he was turning, I cranked off a round at him. I remember thinking, "You little coward, you're gonna just shoot me and run away?" I was pissed. He fired a few more rounds at me as he was running away. Then he disappeared behind the back of my truck. I started to chase him 'cause I needed to stop him. I figured that if he'd shoot me, he'd shoot anybody, and I couldn't let him do that. It only took a few steps to get from my door to the back of my truck, and I stopped at the bumper to kind of hide out because I knew that if I went straight out behind my truck that he could light me up because I'd have no cover. I was peeking around the corner when I saw him coming back around with his gun. He started firing, so I fired. I put three rounds into him, and he went down.

At that point, I realized that I needed to get into my house and get some help because I was bleeding out pretty good. I also figured that this guy wasn't acting alone, that someone had dropped him off, so I was concerned that there might be other suspects in the area. Because I needed to get help and because I was worried about other threats, I just left the kid there and headed toward my house. I made it to my driveway, when I started to pass out from the loss of blood. I was thinking that I had to get to the house, but I was too weak to make it. I grabbed my chest with my right hand and could feel blood running down my side. I remember thinking how warm it was and that it wasn't sticky. For some reason, I was thinking that blood was supposed to be sticky, but it was real smooth. I was also a little bit pissed off because other people had told me that when you get shot you go numb, but I wasn't numb at all.

First off, when the bullet went through me, I felt a real bad burning sensation, and it really hurt when it tore through my back. Then, there in the driveway, I just hurt like crazy. But as I was thinking all this stuff, I was getting weaker. I remember thinking that I was about to pass out and that I didn't want to smash my face on the ground when I lost consciousness. So I just dropped to my knees, rolled onto my back, and laid down there in the driveway. The last thought that passed through my mind before I faded to black was that I was really going to be sore when I woke up.

I woke up in the hospital two days after I was shot. My partner and another friend were there in my room. The first thing I asked them was, "What happened?" My partner told me, "You did a good job. Get some rest." That's all he said. I was real groggy, so I went back to sleep. I woke up about an hour later, and my partner was still there. This time, when I asked him what happened, he told me that I'd been shot and that I'd been in the hospital for two days. I couldn't believe it. I remembered the shooting, but nothing about what happened after I passed out. I asked him how I got to the hospital, and he filled me in.

My roommate had heard the shots. She came out, saw me down in the driveway, ran into the house, called 9-1-1, called our neighbor who was a cop, and told him to hurry on over. Meanwhile the girlfriend of the kid I shot had dived into some bushes around my neighbor's house when the shooting started, and the three who were in the car took off and left the other two there. When my neighbor got there, he saw the kid lying behind my truck on his back with the gun up near his head. He checked on the kid, then came over to help me. By the time the ambulance got there, my heart had stopped. They put the MAST suit on me, defibrillated me there in the driveway, loaded me up, and rushed me to the hospital.

I also wanted to know what happened to the kid I shot. I knew he went down behind the truck, and I knew I hit him, but I just didn't know if he had survived. I needed to know if he was alive or dead. I'm not sure why, but I just needed to know. My partner told me he couldn't tell me because I hadn't talked to the detectives yet. He just said, "Relax, you did good." When he said that, I knew the kid had died. But there were still a few holes about the incident I wanted filled in. I wanted to know how he got there, if other people were involved, if anyone else got hurt, and whether I hit him with all four rounds. He told me that he couldn't answer any of those questions either because I needed to talk to the detectives first. So I said, "Well then, bring 'em on." I wanted all the blanks filled in.

The detectives didn't show up till the next morning, and in the meantime I started feeling better. The nurses asked me if I minded getting a couple of other visitors. I said, "Sure, I don't care. Is there someone out there wanting to see me?" They told me there was about three hundred people outside my room who wanted to see me. So I said, "Well, send 'em five or ten at a time." The nurses were all freaking out, but I said, "You gotta let them in."

After a few hours of that, they gave me a break, and I asked the aide who was in my room why there were so many people there to see me. I mean, I knew I was shot, but people get shot all the time, and they don't get hundreds of visitors. I just didn't understand why there were so many people out there. That's when I found out what had happened to me after I passed out.

The medical people told me that when I got to the hospital, they had cracked my chest open almost right away. Turns out the bullet had gone through the front rib cage; fragmented and nicked the stomach, liver, and intestines; cut some veins and arteries; shattered the spleen; and hit the diaphragm, while the main part of it passed through the base of my heart and cracked a rib as it went out my back. Blood was just pouring out of everywhere. They had to call in a specialist to handle the hole in my heart, and then the surgeons just sewed up all the other holes they could find. At some point, as they were trying to repair all this damage, I flat-lined again. They defibbed me again and kept on going. I was on some major life support. My heart was beating on its own, but I had a ventilator to help me breathe. I had blood being pumped into my system through my femoral arteries, a trach tube in my throat, and a line in my chest so they could directly pump adrenaline or something to my heart if it stopped again.

About an hour after they closed me up, I started to bleed pretty bad inside my chest. I had come out of the anesthesia, but I don't remember that. Fortunately, I don't remember anything from the time I passed out until the time I woke up two days later. At any rate, they told me that I was conscious and that the doctor came into the room to tell me about the bleeding. I had so many tubes in me I couldn't talk, so the doctor told me to squeeze his hand if I understood what he was saying. He told me that I was going through a lot of blood, which meant that they must have missed something and that they were going to have to crack me open again. He asked me if I understood, and I squeezed his hand. Then he told me that because I'd only been in recovery for an hour or so that they were gonna have to do it without any anesthesia. I squeezed his hand to let him know that I understood, and they wheeled me in to the operating room. As soon as they opened me up that second time, my heart went into full arrest. They did a heart massage for about forty-five minutes, till it started working on its own. As they were working on me, they found what the problem was, where the bleeding was coming from. An artery along one of my ribs in the back had been hit, but some muscle spasms around it had initially prevented it from bleeding much. When I started to relax a bit, it just opened up and the blood started to pour into my chest cavity.

After they repaired that and got my heart working again, I was still in real bad shape.

I was on life support big time, machines keeping everything going, and the docs figured that because of the trauma that my body would shut down in about two hours. So they told my family to come in and say their last good-byes. In fact, one doctor took my brother aside and told him that I was already dead, that the machines were keeping me alive, and that they were giving my family a couple of hours so that they could deal with it however they wanted but that I wasn't coming back.

About an hour or so later, my mom made it to the hospital, and she started yelling at me, "You're not a quitter. You've never been a quitter, so don't quit on me now!" Stuff like that. She and other family members then started telling me to do things like move my fingers if I could hear them. So I moved my hands, and they ran out and told the doctor, "Hey, she's going to be OK. We told her to move her fingers and she did." The doctor told them, "No, what's happening is her body is shutting down, and she's doing involuntary muscle twitches. You think she's responding to you because you hope she's somehow going to make it."

My mom said, "No, it's not spasms, you try it!" So the doc did the same thing. He asked me some questions, and I moved my fingers. He did a few other things, I responded, and he told my family, "You know what? You're right. I don't know why, but she's fighting back." I slowly started to recover, and they started to take the tubes out. I think they started with the femoral tubes because I was now holding blood. Then they took out some of the zillion tubes in my arms. During that second day, they took the trach tube out to see if I could breathe on my own, without the ventilator. I guess I gasped a little bit at first, then I breathed OK after that. A little bit later, I woke up.

After I got out of the hospital, I was off work recuperating for about eight months. Early on, they had to do lots of testing and stuff. I had a lot of pains in my chest and back, and they had to drain my lungs a few times from the back, and—let me tell you—that was a real joy. After about the third month, I started getting some sharp pains every now and then, like someone was sticking an ice pick in my back. When I asked my doc what it was, he told me that they had left a few bullet fragments inside me because it was more dangerous to cut them out than to just leave them there. Every now and then, they would shift, and I'd get little sharp stabs. The doc just said that was normal. They're still there. They just float around and poke my ribs and my back every now and then. It's a pain, but to me, it's just like a trick knee or a trick ankle; you just gotta shake it off, just move around a bit and it goes away.

———w———

After completing my probation, I did a year in communications, then got wheeled out to a pretty busy division. The radio was always hopping, so it was a fun place to work after spending a year answering phone calls. I was working with my regular partner when we got a call of a family dispute with some fighting going on. It was at some apartments on the north side of the street, so I pulled up on the south side.

There was a long driveway that led up to the apartment in question that went alongside of the building all the way to the back of the lot. As I was getting out of the car, I saw these three people: this man, this woman, and a little kid—maybe two or three years old—between them coming down the driveway toward us. I figured this was our disturbance because the adults were shouting at each other, and there was some kind of hustle and bustle going on between them. As I walked over toward them, it looked like they were arguing over the kid, like they were playing tug-of-war with him. They were almost shoulder to shoulder, just kind of fighting back and forth over the kid as they walked along. When I got about two-thirds of the way across the street, they stopped on the sidewalk at the end of the driveway. They hadn't spotted me, but I was watching them real close.

At that point, the guy pushed the kid away, grabbed the woman, and coldcocked her right in the face, which sent her right down to the sidewalk. When she hit, he reached down and pulled this big old fourteen-inch butcher knife out of the waistband of the baggy blue jeans he was wearing. To this day, I'm amazed that he didn't cut his dick off when he pulled that knife out of there. I don't know how he did that. That was a pretty good trick. He must have been a magician in a past life or something.

Anyway, this thing was going to shit in a hurry. She's down on the sidewalk, the kid is screaming, "Mommy! Mommy!" and the guy is standing over her with a huge butcher knife. Then it got worse. He jumped down on her and brought this knife over the top of his head like he was going to just plunge it into her chest. He had his knees on her arms, pinning her down on the sidewalk, getting ready to do her.

I started running as soon as I saw the knife, so I was pretty close when he jumped on her. I had my nightstick in my left hand—I hadn't even been out of the car long enough to put it in the ring on my belt. I didn't feel like I had time to draw my gun, so I just grabbed my stick with my right hand. It happened so fast I didn't even have time to grab it by the Uwara handle. I just took it and smacked the guy across the back of the neck and shoulders, just as hard as I could on a backstroke. I was aiming for just his neck, but I missed by a little and ended up hitting him right on the big vertebrae where the neck joins the torso. But I still caught him pretty good.

Now I go about six foot two, 225 pounds, and I hit him as hard as I could, but it didn't faze him much. But it did get his attention and get him to stop his attack on the lady. It also pissed him off. He jumped up real quick, spun around with the knife, and slashed me on the inside of my left forearm. Just like that, I was cut before I knew it. I felt the knife hit my arm, but I didn't even feel it slice me. In fact, I didn't know I was actually cut until I looked down afterwards and saw the blood.

As soon as the knife hit, I took a couple of steps back to put some distance between me and the guy, and I drew my gun. The guy was faceup on me, about five or six feet away. I didn't want to be cut again, so just as soon as I cleared leather, I fired my first round from the hip. It hit him in the lower abdomen. He was still standing there, so I decided to shoot him in the head because the first shot hadn't dropped him and I didn't want him to slash me again. So I brought my gun up, found my sight picture, put it square on his face, and popped him between the eyes with my second round. I squeezed it off just as soon as I got that sight picture on his face. So it was real quick—clear leather and "boom," first round in the gut, then continue up with the gun and "boom," second round in the face. Caught him right on his nose. Then he was down. I don't remember seeing him fall or anything, he was just lying there on the sidewalk.

As soon as he'd cut me, I felt something change. Everything came into clearer visual focus, and it seemed like time sped up. Then, when I fired, the rounds didn't sound loud at all. I saw the muzzle flashes real clearly, but the rounds didn't bother my ears at all. Not like they would if I fired my gun right now. I was also thinking how weird it all was as I was shooting. I was thinking this can't be happening. Like most cops, I'd pictured circumstances in which I might become involved in a shooting, and this wasn't one of them. As I was walking across the street, I was thinking that this guy was just going to let me put the handcuffs on him, and we'd sort things out. Then it went so sideways, so quickly, that I just couldn't believe it. I'd been on a lot of family disputes that were a lot more contentious when we arrived, and they turned out OK. This looked to be an easy one, and it just went to shit. I was thinking that this was just too weird. Guys shouldn't be pulling out knives to murder their wives in front of me, and when I try to stop them, they shouldn't hurt me. It was like things weren't adding up. There was something illogical going on. It was *Twilight Zone* stuff.

Once he was down, all that strange stuff receded, and I noticed that my side was getting wet. So I looked down and saw I was bleeding like a stuck pig from my left forearm, that I was standing in a pool of my own blood. It was really bleeding a lot. I started thinking, "Oh, man, this isn't good." The blood wasn't spurting out, so I knew he hadn't caught an artery. But it was coming out pretty good, like somebody had a hose on with a serious trickle coming out. I hollered to my partner at that point. Told him I was cut. He didn't know what the hell was going on because this had all happened so fast. He was on the radio putting us out at our location when it went down, so he didn't know why I fired the rounds. That's why I told him I was cut, to let him know why I just shot this guy.

He put out a help call and requested an ambulance. As we were waiting for the other units to show up, my partner went up and cuffed the guy. He wasn't moving at all, but we weren't going to take any chances. In fact, I thought he was dead. The woman must've thought so too because she was screaming, "Adios, mi hijo," and other stuff like that in Spanish. She had gotten up and grabbed her kid. Had her arms around him. Just standing there holding the kid and screaming stuff in Spanish as I was trying to figure out how to stop the bleeding.

I took a deep breath, told myself not to panic, that I was going to be OK. I felt myself to make sure that the knife hadn't hit me anywhere else. I looked at my shirt and didn't see any cuts besides the one on my sleeve. I had my vest on, so I was quite certain I wasn't cut on my torso. I didn't feel any pain anywhere besides my left arm. I figured from all that that I wasn't cut anyplace besides my arm, but I knew I was going to be in trouble if I just let the blood keep coming out. I had to get the bleeding stopped.

About then, Jan Nelson, one of my classmates from the academy, came rolling up with his partner. He grabbed a handkerchief or something and started some direct pressure on my arm with that. It didn't do shit to stop the bleeding. I knew that I couldn't let much more blood leak out of my body, so I pulled out my cord-cuff restrainer from my sap pocket, wrapped that around my forearm just above the gash, and cinched it down real tight. That stopped the bleeding. Once the bleeding stopped, it was like, OK, whatever happens from here, at least I'm not going to die. I knew I was going to make it. So I just relaxed a little bit and watched as more units and some supervisors arrived while we waited for the ambulance. After about three to five minutes, we got word that the ambulance was going to be delayed for some reason, so Jan and his partner tossed me in their car and took me to Presbyterian Hospital.

After I got to the hospital, one of the sergeants came in and told me that they had sent another supervisor to get my wife and bring her over to the hospital. I had been worried that she might hear about it from someone outside the PD, so knowing that the other sergeant was going to get her set my mind at ease. He could tell her what happened and explain to her that I was OK.

After they numbed my arm up a bit, the doctor took a good look at the wound. The long side of the knife blade had hit about the midpoint of my forearm, moving from the wrist toward the elbow. It dug in, all the way to the bone, then came out, leaving about a three-inch semicircle wound. It was a pretty clean cut, wasn't mangled at all. The best way I can describe it is to picture a turkey leg that you started to cut the meat off from the foot end, but you stop maybe halfway down. As long as the flap you just cut is laying flat on the bone, it looks like a thin semicircular cut, but once you flip the flap back, you've got a good hunk of meat exposed. That's what my arm looked like. Just a thin cut until the doctor laid the flap back to work on it. I looked over, and I could see bone and nerves and all the vessels in there. The doctor was amazed by the wound. He said it looked like a surgeon had gone around the nerves and blood vessels, except for that one big vein that had been cut open. He also said that the long sleeve of my shirt had probably prevented some serious damage. He said the thickness of the wool likely kept the blade from going a millimeter or two deeper. If that would've happened, it would have almost certainly cut some of the nerves leading to my hand, and I would have lost motion in a few fingers. It would also probably have snapped an artery, in which case there would have been a real good chance I would have bled out and died before they got me to the hospital.

It was pretty interesting watching the doctor work on my arm and having him explain all that stuff to me. As I was lying there, the ambulance showed up, and they wheeled the guy who cut me into the cubicle next to me. I couldn't believe he was alive. I knew I hit him real good with both rounds, one right between the eyes, plus he wasn't moving one bit when he was lying on the sidewalk. I figured he had to be dead, so I was curious about how badly he was hurt. They told me that he was hurt very badly, that he probably wasn't going to survive because his blood pressure was way down. He ended up surviving after a long hospital stay, so we all guessed wrong about him.

The supervisor who drove my wife and me home after they were done with me at the ER filled us in on what led up to the shooting. The guy I shot had almost killed somebody else at this party that was going on at the apartment we were sent to. He had gotten drunk and gone completely fucking bonkers at this party on the second floor of this apartment. He just went completely ape shit and pushed this other guy through a plate glass window. The other guy was damn near dead when he hit the deck down below.

None of this information got relayed to Communications Division and on to us because none of the people at the party spoke English— they were all El Salvadorans. Plus whoever called didn't communicate exactly what had happened, and the operator who took the call didn't get all the info. The caller just told the operator that Louise's husband, Joe—or whatever their names were—was on a rampage. So the operator just assumed it was a family dispute. So we didn't know this guy had just gone completely ape shit, violent bonkers before we got there.

After he shoved the other guy through the window, the guy I shot wanted to leave the party before the buddies of the guy he almost killed could kill him or the cops came to put him in jail. His wife wanted him to stay because she figured that he was safe with their friends at the party. So what I saw when I spotted them was him trying to drag her and their kid home, not a fight over the kid. Because the guy was unconscious back at the hospital, the sergeant couldn't tell me why he decided to try to kill his wife. I didn't care. I was just glad that I was able to stop him.

—◊◊◊—

I'd been on the job about five and a half years when we got a kidnapping call that came out as a kidnapping-neighborhood disturbance. When we got to the call, a teenage girl—probably about sixteen or seventeen—met us and told us that her child had been taken by a lady that lived in the house we had come up to. We asked the girl some questions, and she told us that the woman supposedly had some kind of mental impairment, that she sometimes baby-sat the child, but she had taken the child from the girl and told her she wasn't gonna give it back. She was really afraid. She kept saying that the lady was crazy, that she could kill the kid, that she was going to kill the kid.

We didn't really know what we had, so we started walking up to the house to see what the woman had to say about what was going on. As we were walking up the driveway to knock on the door, this female—I think she was in her late twenties—came out of the house. She came down the driveway toward us, and I started talking to her, just some nonsense chitchat, trying to make conversation with her, trying to figure out what was going on and what her attitude was. So we were standing about five feet from each other in the driveway, talking for a bit. I finally got to the point where I asked her, "Do you have this young lady's daughter?" She said, "Yeah." Then I told her, "You're going to have to give the child back. It's not your child." She replied, "No, I'm not. I'm not giving her back." I tried to explain the situation to her, but she just continued to say, "No, I'm not going to give the child back." Finally, I said, "Look, we're going to have to take you to jail if you don't give the child back."

When I said that, she pulled a box cutter out of her pocket. I already had my nightstick out, so I hit her arm with it, and she dropped the box cutter. Then she stumbled back, and before I could grab her, she made it to the front door. As she went through the doorway, I could see this little baby, this two-year-old child, standing just inside it. Then the lady shut the door and locked it. So now we had this lady who was extremely upset—much more so than when we were talking in the driveway—locked inside this house with the child. We had a real problem now.

I stayed at the front of the house, and my partner went around to the back to make sure that she didn't get out that way. As I was looking through the front window, I could see the woman standing in front of the little two-year-old, screaming at her. She was hysterical, and I was thinking, "Oh, this is not good." I was worried that she was going to hurt the child. Then she started dumping over furniture. The baby just stood there screaming—crying and screaming—while the lady was going ballistic. So I knocked on the window to get her attention, and she looked at me. I said to her, "Let us have the baby and we won't take you to jail." I mean, at that point I was willing to tell her anything to get that child out of there.

She said, "No." I kept telling her we wouldn't take her to jail if she gave us the kid, but she kept saying, "No." After a couple of minutes of this, she came to the door, opened it a little bit—just kind of flung it open—then took off running back toward the kitchen. Well, the baby was standing just inside the doorway—about six feet away from me—so I went in, grabbed her, and headed back out.

I radioed my partner and told him that I had the kid. So he came around front, and we started walking down the driveway. When we got about halfway down the driveway—maybe twenty-five feet from the front door—the lady came back to the front door with a knife in her hand. It was a big deboning knife—about thirteen inches total, with an eight-inch blade. Then she started shouting at us, "I'm gonna kill you! I'm gonna kill you!" She had the knife raised above her head, but she wasn't moving toward us. She was just standing in the doorway.

Both my partner and I drew our weapons at that point. I was still holding the kid, and I was thinking that if the lady started to come at us that I was going to shoot her. My partner and I yelled for her to put the knife down several times, and she finally lowered it from above her head and moved it down by the side of her leg. The child was still crying and screaming and wiggling around in my arms, so I decided to set her down. As I was bending over to set the kid down, the woman brought the knife back up over her head and threw it.

Next thing I knew, I felt this impact on the right side of my head. It felt like somebody had taken a brick and hit me with it or just punched me in the right side of the head as hard as they could. When the knife hit, I released the child. My gun fell out of my hand. I was stunned. I was feeling this dull pain with a lot of pressure on the right side of my head—not a real sharp pain like you think you'd have if you got cut or stabbed. It took me a couple of seconds to get my bearings, then I started looking around. I saw my gun on the ground, so I picked up my gun. I looked at the house, but the suspect had gone inside and shut the door, so I put my gun back in my holster. I knew the knife had hit me, so I started looking around on the ground for it.

I looked and looked, but I couldn't find it. Then I looked up at my partner. He looked at me and said, "Holy shit!!" I asked him, "Where's the knife?" He just repeated himself, "Holy shit!!" Then I noticed that he was looking a little bit off to my right side, so I raised my hand up, and I felt the knife sticking in my head. Then I said, "Holy shit!!"

My partner and I got on the radio and put out an assist the officer call. Then my partner told me to walk the rest of the way down the driveway and get next to the patrol car in case the lady came back out of the house. A citizen who was passing by came up the driveway and then helped me walk to the patrol car. I was thinking, "God, I hope this isn't it. I'm just twenty-five years old. I hope I'm not dying here in somebody's driveway at twenty-five." I mean, I could feel the knife, I knew I was stabbed in the head, and I wondered, "How far in did it go?" So I was real worried there for about ten or fifteen seconds, thinking it was all over for me, until I got back to the patrol car and sat down next to it.

My mom's a nurse, and she'd told me more than once—I don't know why—but she'd told me several times that if I ever got stabbed and had something stuck in me, don't yank it out. She told me that you never know what it has hit, what it hasn't hit, what kind of damage can be done if you pull it out. I knew not to try to take it out, so I sat there, and I held the knife to try to relieve the pressure I was feeling. It wasn't just from the fact that I had a knife sticking in my head. It was also from the way it was stuck in there. It turns out that the knife went into my head about seven-eighths of an inch, so the other almost twelve inches were just hanging down from my skull. With the pressure of the weight of the knife pulling down, it felt like someone was taking a crowbar and trying to pry my skull open. So I held the knife to kind of relieve a little bit of that pressure as I was sitting there by the patrol car.

After a little while, some other officers started to arrive. They just looked at me with amazement: like, "Oh, God!" Then one of the veteran officers, who'd been on about twenty, twenty-five years, came over and talked to me. He told me some stuff about how he'd been shot in Vietnam and that from his experience he could tell that I was going to be OK. He said, "You're still talking, you're awake, you'll be fine." As he was talking to me, this other officer came up, looked at me, and said, "I've got a first-aid kit in my car. We'll pull the knife out and bandage it up." I thought, "Oh, my God, no," and told the veteran officer, "Keep that guy away from me! Keep him away from me!" He told me, "Oh, yeah. Don't worry. We're not doing anything."

Then the ambulance got there. They got there even before Life-Flight could get off the pad. As they were working on me, the lady who'd stabbed me kept coming to the door—back and forth, back and forth. The scene still wasn't under control. We didn't know what other kind of weapons she had, whether she had a gun. The ambulance was still working on me, so the other officers decided to try to get the lady into custody next time she came to the door. Well, next time she came to the door, my partner and three or four other officers rushed her. She got the door partway closed and was bracing herself against this little half-wall right behind the door, trying to keep the officers from forcing the door open. As the officers were making some progress pushing the door back, they could see her arm coming around. She had another knife. My partner yelled, "Knife," and ended up shooting her through the door before she could stab this one officer who was closest to her. I heard that happen, and then they loaded me up into the ambulance and took me to the hospital.

When they brought me off the ambulance, there were about fifty officers waiting outside the hospital, all looking at me. Now I was still hurting pretty bad, but I wasn't thinking, "I'm hurt bad, I could die," or anything like that. I was thinking, "This is the most embarrassing thing I've ever been in." I mean, everyone there was staring at me, and I've got a knife in my head. I felt like *Friday the 13th* or something.

So the medical people got me into the emergency room, where they took some X rays. They couldn't get me into the CAT scan because the knife was sticking out. The ER doctors and a couple of the neurosurgeons who were there decided from the X rays that the knife hadn't penetrated into my brain. It went all the way through the skull, and later on, through angiograms and MRIs, they concluded it came one-sixteenth of an inch from going into the brain. But that day, they decided it was OK to remove the knife and that the best way to get it out was to simply pull it. So a bunch of people just braced my upper body, my head, my neck, and they pulled it out.

It actually hurt more when they pulled it out than when it went in. I was wide awake. The doctors didn't give me anything for the pain for thirty-six hours. They told me that medications like that could have a similar effect of hemorrhaging in the brain. They wanted to make sure I was awake and alert so they could keep track of my vital signs and everything.

I recovered just fine. Then, just over a year after I got stabbed in the head, I was working with a different partner when we got another call involving a nutcase with a knife. It came out as a family disturbance just before dusk on a Tuesday evening. Radio told us that the son was going crazy with a knife, threatening his family, threatening some neighbors, destroying the house he lived in.

Now I'd had some calls involving knives in the year since I got stabbed, but most of them turned out to be nothing. Most of the time, nobody had any weapon, and in the others it was just a knife on the kitchen table or something like that. But every time calls about knives dropped, I'd be thinking, "Holy Christ," on the way there because I knew that I could get hurt even if I kept my distance; twenty-five feet away from that woman meant nothing. She wasn't moving, and she still got me. So when I got that call about the son going crazy with the knife, I thought, "Oh, great." Just what I needed.

A one-man unit checked by with us. Then the three of us went to the scene. When we pulled up, there was a big group of people outside in the yard of the house where the call came from. We stopped one house away and got out. We could see that the windows in the house were all smashed and that the windows of the car parked out front were all smashed. As we walked up to the location, the guy's mother started yelling at us, "Shoot him! Shoot him! Shoot the son of a bitch!" When I heard that, I was thinking, "Lady, shut up. Come on, this is your kid here." So I told her that we'd handle it, and we continued up toward the house. As we went up, the guy came around the side of the house holding a three-foot-long machete. When I spotted him, I thought, "Great, here we go again."

So we drew our guns and kept our distance. We were behind a car about thirty feet from the guy, so we started talking to him. I said, "Hey, man, put down the machete." He just started cursing at us, using every word in the book. "Screw you, motherfucker. You want this? Come get it." Stuff like that. As he was carrying on, he was smashing stuff in the yard, so we asked for some more units to check by.

By now, the whole street was filled with people—families, kids, all in the street watching what was going on. As we were talking to him— I was doing most of the talking—he left the front yard and started walking down the street. Now, luckily for us, there were a lot of cars parked in the street, so we could keep some cars between us and the guy as we tried to contain him as best we could. While he walked down the middle of the street, we were walking through front yards next to the curb, keeping the parked cars between us. When we got three or four houses down, we ran out of cars. We were coming to a point now where we couldn't let him go any farther. There were people all over the place. He was going crazy, threatening to kill everybody, and telling us that if we came near him he was going to kill us.

When we ran out of cars, I was in the open, about twelve feet from him. I knew I was too close for safety—I mean, I knew from getting stabbed the year before that twice the distance wasn't safe—but I couldn't move farther away because I needed to be able to protect all the people that were milling around. I knew we couldn't let the guy go. Well, he stopped in the middle of the street, and I just kept my twelve-foot distance with my gun drawn while he held the machete in his right hand. My partner was about ten feet behind me, trying to keep the people back there away, and the officer from the one-man unit was in the street off to our left, trying to keep the guy from going back down the street where some other people were. I was closest, so I kept talking to him, repeatedly telling him to put the machete down. The officer from the one-man unit got on the radio and told them we needed a supervisor, we needed a TASER, we needed those other units we requested, stuff like that.

I could tell the guy was reaching his boiling point. The tone of his voice and his behavior became more aggressive. I wasn't gonna stand there for a substantial period of time twelve feet away from this guy holding a three-foot machete when I knew what a one-foot deboning knife did at twenty-five feet.

The next time I told the guy to put the machete down, he said, "You want this? You want this? Here you go. You got it." Then started to move toward me. When he took his second step, he drew the machete over his head. I wasn't gonna let what happened before happen again, so I fired at him. I saw him sort of dip after the first or second round, but he was still coming at me, so I kept shooting. The next thing I remember was seeing him on the ground a few feet in front of me.

I had heard from other officers who'd been in shootings that things slowed down for them, and they didn't remember how many rounds they fired. That's what happened to me. Everything slowed down when he started coming at me—then, when he hit the ground, everything went back to regular speed. I had no idea how many rounds I'd fired. I just kept shooting until he fell down, until he was no longer a threat. It turned out that I fired four rounds—all hits—but I had no clue how many rounds I was firing as I was shooting.

When he fell, the machete was still partially in his hand, so my partner ran up and kicked it out of his hand. Then the other units got there. A little while later, an ambulance showed up. By the time they got the guy to the hospital, he was DOA.

The investigators started showing up not too long after the ambulance took the guy away. Homicide came out. Internal Affairs, the DA's office, Civil Rights Division, they all came out, and I think almost everybody who came out to that scene had made the scene where I got stabbed. Nobody said anything about it, but a couple of guys just kind of looked at me like, "Good Lord, what is it with you and edged weapons."

—∿∿—

I was working morning watch as a training officer in February when I got a brand-new trainee fresh out of the academy. We worked a couple of shifts, and he seemed like a very good trainee. He was intelligent, had good common sense, would observe things. I took note that he was quick to notice things that were happening and that he paid attention to what was going on.

We were working an area that had a lot of criminal activity. A lot of prostitutes and pimps lived in the apartments there, so we had a lot of prostitution, a lot of narcotics activity, whatever. One night at about three in the morning, we spotted this Cadillac Eldorado that had no front plate and no current tabs on the back plate. The car was occupied by three males and one female. There were two people in front besides the driver—so three people in the front—and one person in the back. We'd been having a lot of Eldorados stolen in the area we were working. We'd find them up on milk crates, stripped, with their seats and whatnot gone. I told my partner that we should stop the car and check it out to see if it'd just been ripped off, so we did.

I told Jim to get the driver out of the car and pat him down, because when I ran the plate, it indicated that there were outstanding warrants associated with the car. It was late at night, so I wanted him to get the driver out and pat him down for our safety. After Jim got the driver out and patted him down, the guy got very belligerent and began to challenge Jim to the point where it became more than he could handle. I decided to intervene, so I went up to my partner and got the driver's license from him. I wanted to run the guy to see if he had any of the warrants that were associated with the car. After I got his license from Jim, I chatted with the driver and told him the reason we were stopping him. He started to get a little strong with me, so I explained to him that we just wanted to check on the status of the car, that we were just doing our job, and that if the status of the car was cool that he'd be on his way.

He calmed down somewhat at that point, but then I could see that something wasn't right. There was a lot of rubbernecking in the car. The people in the car looked very nervous. I said to myself, "You know, this isn't fitting exactly right," so we placed the driver to the back of the Cadillac. My partner stood behind him, and I started calling the other people out of the car from the right door. I got the two males out, patted them down, retrieved their licenses, clipped them to my tie, and sent them over with the driver at the back of the car. That left the female in the car. She seemed extremely nervous. She had a purse that she picked up, then set down. She was looking around, rubbernecking back as if she was thinking, "What do I do?"

When I told her to slide out of the car, the driver said, "No, bitch, you stay in the car!" I told the driver, "Be quiet, she's getting out of the car," then started to call her out again. At that point, the driver pushed past the other two guys and moved toward the open passenger door. I grabbed ahold of him from behind in an upper-body control hold, and we went down onto the ground. I was trying to choke him out, but I couldn't do it. It was cold out, and I was wearing what they call a Melton jacket, real thick, and the driver had on a crushed-velvet jacket with a big collar, so I couldn't get enough pressure to get him out. He was talking to me as we were fighting. At first, I couldn't make out what he was saying. Then he said something very distinctly. He said, "You don't know what you're doing. I'll make you have to kill me."

When I realized I wasn't going to be able to get him out, I called Jim over to have him help me with this guy. He came over to my right side, grabbed the guy's right arm, and helped me pull the guy's arm back to cuff him. As I was trying to get the cuffs on, the guy yelled, "Brothers, come on over and help me!" The other two guys started moving toward us, and at that point I told Jim, "Get on the radio! Jim, get on the radio!" Things were turning ugly, and I figured we needed additional units. We didn't have handheld radios back then, so Jim pulled his baton to push his way through the two guys in order to get to the radio.

As I was watching Jim strike out at the other two guys to get to the radio, I felt the driver tugging on my gun, trying to pull it from the holster. He was talking to me again, saying, "I'm gonna kill you, pig"— things like that. At that point, I felt my life was in danger, so I released him and pulled my gun out of my holster. But as I did, he grabbed onto it, so now we were in a life-and-death struggle over my gun. I heard some commotion over where my partner was. I couldn't see him any longer, but I could hear him screaming, "Officer needs assistance! Officer needs assistance!" calling on the radio to get us some help. I could also tell from the noises that he was fighting back and forth with the other two suspects.

As he was putting out the broadcast and fighting with the other two guys, I was still in this life-and-death struggle over my gun. At one point, the guy had his finger in my eye, trying to pull my eye out. He kept telling me, "Let go of the gun. Let go of the gun." No way was I going to let go of the gun. I just kept fighting. I was biting his hands to get him to release the gun, doing whatever I could. We were on the ground. Then we were up, then back down on the ground, just fighting over the gun. We ended up on the ground between the two cars. I managed to roll up underneath the Cadillac and break the driver's grip on the gun because he couldn't reach in between the bumper and the ground as far as I could. So now I had the gun, but my body was between me and the suspect because he was behind me, kind of holding me in a bear hug.

He kept trying to grab the gun. Then he said, in a real deliberate voice, "Get the bitch out of the car with the gun." Now I was trapped in this little space under the car with the suspect trying to grab the gun, and I was thinking that the female was gonna come up and just put the gun up to me and shoot me in the head. That's what went through my mind. I wanted to have some mobility, so I rolled back out from under the car to where the driver was on his back, and I was lying on my back on top of him. Now that I was out from underneath the car, the guy reached back up and grabbed the gun again. Then he started yelling, "Shoot the fucking pig, shoot him!"

I looked up and I saw the female appear above my head. As I watched her, she reached into her bra area and pulled out a gun. I know she did it real fast, but as I was watching, it went real slow. The driver was screaming, "Shoot him, shoot him!" When she got the gun out, the female pointed it at me. I started kicking at her, rolling around, thinking that way if she shoots, maybe she'll miss me and hit him. Then she fired—two, maybe three rounds. I could feel the pain in the right side of my upper chest. It was like maybe someone held up a cigarette and burnt me, but I just kept fighting. I knew I was hit, but I just kept on going.

Then the driver started yelling, "Come over here! Help me, brother! Get over here!" Stuff like that. Then one of the other guys came over and grabbed my legs. So now the driver and this other guy were holding me down, and the female was still standing above me holding this gun. I was yelling at her, "Don't do it! Don't do it!" My gun was pointed up at her, so she would jump back, then move in, then jump back again as my gun moved around as the driver pulled on it and I fought him. I was trying to shoot the female, but I couldn't squeeze off a shot because the driver had his hands on the cylinder of my revolver.

What happened next went real slow. The female reached down, put her gun right down into my abdomen, and pulled the trigger. I just blacked out. I don't know how long I was out, if it was a fraction of a second or what, but the next thing I knew, the driver was pushing me off of him like I was a dead weight. I realized that my gun was gone, so I jumped up.

The driver was still on the ground. He was sitting on his ass, holding my gun. He didn't have a good grip on it, but he was trying to manipulate it in his hands to get to where he could shoot me. At that point, I pulled my baton and started whaling back and forth at him with it. I don't know how it is that my baton stayed in the ring all the time we were fighting, but it did. At any rate, as I was swinging at him, he was trying to get away from me, scooting back on his butt. He managed to get far enough away from me to where he could point the gun right at me, so I threw my baton at him. As I threw it, I turned, sort of ducked down, and moved away from him to get behind the patrol car.

As I turned, he started cranking off rounds at me. He caught me in the left buttocks, and I don't know if it spun me around or what, but I went down over by the front of the car. Then I dove to the other side of the car to get away from him.

I found out later that my partner was in a fight of his own the whole time I was fighting. When he went to the car to put out the broadcast, one of the other suspects managed to take his baton away from him. As he was putting out the assistance call, the suspect was hitting him in the head with the baton. After Jim got the broadcast out, he pulled his pistol. The suspect grabbed it as Jim was bringing it up, so Jim was in the same struggle that I was in for his weapon. They wound up fighting up against the other side of the car that was parked in front of the Cadillac where I was fighting.

After the suspect who took my gun shot at me, he stood up and fired a round at my partner. It missed and hit the car. Then the guy went up to my partner, stuck the gun into his abdomen area, and pulled the trigger again. So my partner received one round dead center from my gun; then he went down.

At that point, I heard somebody say, "Let's get out of here!" I didn't know if it was the guy who shot me and my partner, or if it was one of the other suspects, but when I heard that, I came around the back of the squad car and stood up a little bit to try to look through the windows to see where they were at. When I did this, the driver started firing my gun again. I didn't know if he was firing at me, but after it was all over, there were bullet holes in the lights up on top of the police car. When I heard those shots, I just ducked back behind the car. A few seconds later, I heard the squeal of some tires.

At that time, I figured, "Hey, they've left," so I ran over to my partner, who was lying in the street in a fetal position. I said to him, "Jim, are you OK? Jim, are you OK?" He was moaning in that fetal position on the ground, but he didn't answer me. I could see blood all over his head. I didn't know that it was from the baton blows, and I thought that maybe they had shot him in the head. I told him to hang on. Then I went over to the police car and started pulling on the shotgun. I don't know why, but I couldn't get the shotgun out of the rack. I was just struggling with it. Then I went to grab the radio mike to put out a help call, but I couldn't find it. I thought to myself, "Where the hell is the radio?" I was pretty desperate now, and I realized I needed to get my composure. I told myself, "OK, you can't find the mike, start at the base where the cord is. Get the cord." So I reached down, grabbed the base of the mike cord, and went hand over hand looking for the mike. All I came up with was a couple of wires on the end. The cord had been severed in the middle someplace, and all there was was a couple of wires. It turns out that during the fight with Jim that the door closed on the wire, and one of the guys he was fighting ripped the mike off.

When I saw the mike was gone, my heart just sunk. I knew I was shot. I knew I was shot several times. It was getting difficult for me to breathe. I was starting to feel kind of faint. I knew I was in trouble. I didn't want to sit down, so I moved to the back of the police car and stood there, just kind of leaning against the car.

Then I heard some sirens in the distance. I was hoping they were coming to me. A little bit later, a car pulled up and two guys in uniforms got out. They were security guards. I immediately gave them some information, and they told me to sit down. So I kind of did what they said. A few seconds later, some police officers arrived. As soon as I saw some people I recognized, I gave them the information. I said, "Hey, the guys who shot us just left. They are in a Cadillac, a black Cadillac." The other officers broadcast that immediately. Then they started pumping me for additional information. I was giving it to them, and they were putting it out on the air.

After a while, an ambulance finally arrived. They went to my partner first. I kept asking them, "How's Jim? How's Jim?" They told me that he didn't look real good, and my heart sank again. Then they loaded us both up into the ambulance, and the next thing I knew, we were at the hospital.

I was having difficulty breathing, so they put a chest tube in me. The first thing that they did was cut my clothes off. Then I remember seeing the scalpel. They poked a hole right into my chest while I was still awake. I'm sure they numbed it first, but I remember watching the tube go into my chest and then, whoosh, blood just shooting out the other end. I just remember looking at that tube and then being able to breathe again. The next thing I remember was them stuffing another tube down my throat. As they were doing that, I started vomiting. I just leaned over the side of the table, and when I was finished, I lay back down.

Jim was on a table right next to me, and a friend of mine named Danny Schroenburger was standing there between us. I asked Danny, "How is Jim?" He told me that they were working on him now, but that he was going to be OK. Hearing that kind of put my mind at ease because I was really worried about my partner. Then they took me into X ray, brought me out, said they were gonna take me into surgery, and the next thing that I remember was waking up the next day.

When I woke up, it took a little while for things to start registering with me. I remember that I looked down at my abdominal area and saw a mess of meat on my stomach. That's what it looked like. They had just kind of loosely stitched together the incision they made over the contact shot, so I could see all this meat from my abdomen. When I saw that, I realized that I was alive. Then I saw Rob Johnson, the guy I had for officer survival in the academy, standing on my right side. He put his hand on my shoulder and said, "Don't worry, you did a good job." Then I remember Danny Schroenburger coming in and giving me a message that some guy had called to wish me luck. Then my wife came in, and everything was starting to register.

I don't remember too much after that except that I asked how my partner was doing. They told me that he was doing OK, that he was next door in the intensive-care unit we were in. I was really concerned about Jim because he was my responsibility. He was a probationer and I was the trainer. Here was somebody that was in my care, and he got shot with my gun. I assumed the responsibility for him getting shot because it was my fault. I knew it was.

There were things I could have done to prevent him from getting shot because I saw the warning signs and I didn't react to them. I was going to call for a backup unit as soon as I saw the guy was getting a little bit belligerent with Jim, but as I started to use the radio, I heard another car calling for assistance. So I thought about what I had—I figured that this is probably not gonna be a problem; maybe we'd just be kicking them loose, maybe just taking the driver to jail, no big deal. If I called for backup, all these units would be rolling down to me when there was this other assistance call. So I decided to let the other units go assist the guy who had already called for assistance. I shouldn't have done that. I should have put the call out. I needed the assistance. If we would have had a show of force with other officers, the situation never would have escalated into a shooting.

One other thing I could have done differently was handcuff the driver right away. He was very challenging. It would have been reasonable to put the handcuffs on him. If nothing turned up on the warrant check, we could have dusted him off and sent him on his way, or if we needed to, we could have called for a supervisor to the scene to explain to the guy why we did what we did. We could have dealt with that easily, but the driver needed to be neutralized. He needed to have handcuffs on him. I realized that at the time, and I didn't do it, so I could have done some things differently. I didn't, we got shot, and it's my fault. I decided that when I got back to work that I wouldn't make any more mistakes like that.

It took a few months for me to get back into shape and get back to work, but I made it back to my old slot as a training officer in the same division where the shooting went down. Same watch, same car, same everything. About three months after I got back to the field, I got a brand-new probationer from the academy. This particular officer had a background in law enforcement. He had worked for another agency, so I felt real comfortable with him.

We were out on patrol, real late in the shift, the sun was just starting to come up, when I spotted this Chevrolet. It was still dark out, and the guy didn't have his lights on. We were heading toward the guy, so I flashed the lights on the police car to get the guy to turn his lights on, but he didn't, and it seemed like he sped up to get away. I told my partner, "Say, something is wrong here. This guy is rabbiting on us, so be prepared." So I made the U-turn to get behind the guy, and he turned off the street and pulled into this subterranean parking area. I pulled in behind him, so now we were chasing this guy around the parking lot. We went around and around the lot several times. Then the guy turned back onto the street and took off. I figured the car was stolen, so I told my partner to get ready for a foot chase if the guy bails out. So now we're chasing this guy up the street, red lights and siren on. He went a few blocks, then hung a left and lost control of the car. It was fishtailing, then it jumped the curb and crashed into a building.

The car bounced back off the building and started to roll back a little bit. Then the door popped open, and the suspect fell out onto the pavement. I stopped the police car, and we jumped out to take him into custody, but he jumped up and started to run down the middle of the street. He got a good head start on us, because we were just in the process of getting out when he took off, so we jumped back into the car and started following him down the street. He made a right onto a side street, then a left into an alley. Then he ducked behind this one building. I told my partner to jump out and wait where he was while I circled around to the front of the building to pin the suspect between us. So he jumped out, I went to the front of the building, parked the car, put out a broadcast for more units to come to where we were, got my flashlight and drew my gun, then went to look for the suspect.

I went through some bushes, then spotted the suspect hiding under this car parked up against the building. I stopped about fifteen to eighteen feet from the car and told my partner to come to the front because I had the suspect. When Fred got up there, I started telling the suspect to put his hands where I could see them and for him to get out from under the car. As he was moving from under the car, Fred moved up to him, and the next thing I knew, the suspect and my partner were in a fight. Now this suspect was a real muscular guy, and Fred was small in stature, so I was sizing this up in my mind real quick: big suspect, little partner. What happened several months before flashed in my mind, and I thought, "No way is this going to happen again."

At that point, things started to slow down just like they did when I got shot. I knew I couldn't let the guy overpower my partner, so I ran up to the suspect and—"boom"—hit him over the head a couple of times with the butt of my gun. That knocked him down, but he reached up and grabbed my gun. I wasn't about to let this guy get my gun. I wasn't about to go through what happened before again, so I immediately pulled the trigger. I shot a hole through the suspect's hand and he let go. Then my partner jumped up and shouted, "I'm shot!" I wasn't sure what had happened, but the suspect was still struggling, so I had my hands full. I put my gun away and got the suspect handcuffed, then stood on top of him while I asked my partner where he was shot, how he was doing, this and that. I was really worried about him. I was thinking, "Oh, my God, here's another partner, another probationer, shot." The only shot I heard was mine, but the suspect hadn't been searched, so I thought maybe somehow he had shot Fred. Fred told me he was shot in the hand, so that put my mind at ease somewhat. Some other units showed up pretty soon after that; then an ambulance came and took the suspect away. Then another ambulance came and took my partner to the hospital.

I found out later that the suspect had raped a woman just before we spotted him. The car wasn't stolen. He was just trying to get away from the alley where he'd raped this woman. He was on parole for some other things, just out of the joint, so he was a real bad guy. The investigators also told me what had happened when I shot the guy. The bullet went through his hand, hit him in the head, ricocheted off his head, and lodged in my partner's hand. So that explained how my partner got shot. After it was all over, some of the guys gave me a hard time about it, kidding around. They said stuff like, "Hey, second probationer? You're kind of hard on rookies, aren't you, Carl?"

SWAT: Call-Outs to the Kill Zone

As previously noted, many of the individuals I interviewed were SWAT officers. The myriad sorts of operations that these officers are called upon to handle fall into two general categories: call-outs and preplanned operations. Call-outs happen when patrol officers, detectives, or officers working some other assignment find themselves in special-threat situations that crop up unexpectedly—almost always barricaded-suspect or hostage situations—and call for SWAT assistance to resolve the ongoing problem. Preplanned operations are those in which the SWAT team is brought in to handle some sort of high-risk operation from the start. The most common sort of pre-planned SWAT operation by far is the service of high-risk warrants, primarily search warrants for narcotics. Among the other sorts of preplanned activities that SWAT teams sometimes engage in are stakeouts and serving as the arrest team in sting operations that involve unusually dangerous individuals.

The stories in this section give the reader a sense of the sorts of circumstances in which SWAT officers shoot suspects during call-outs. They include shootings that happened during both barricade and hostage situations, shootings that occurred during long-lasting standoffs and those that happened soon after officers arrived on scene, shootings in which the officer I interviewed was the only SWAT officer to shoot and those in which others fired also, shootings in which the officers were just a few feet from suspects and those in which they were a considerable distance away, and—in a classic example of suicide-by-cop—one shooting in which the suspect clearly wanted to die. Together these stories show what happens and how SWAT cops think, feel, and react when they are called out to deal with situations that are beyond the ken of ordinary officers.

I'd been on the team about nine years when it happened. We were getting together for training up at the academy about 9:30 one morning when all the pagers started going off. Soon after, our lieutenant, Tab Bittner, rolled up and said, "Don't ask questions guys, I haven't got time to explain it. We need to head to Miner Street and Canyon Boulevard. We need to get up there as fast as we can." So we all geared up, and Bittner had all seventeen of us jump into the raid van—an oversized Ford. He wanted us together so he could brief us on the way so that we would all know what we had when we got there. I tell you, it was quite a sight, seventeen SWAT cops in one van. We were stacked up in there like cordwood.

As we drove, Bittner told us that the previous evening there had been a home invasion up in a little 'burb called Claremont Hills, a relatively affluent area surrounded by lower-income housing. A guy—all cracked-up—came into this house armed with a .22 pistol, confronted the father on the first floor, and demanded money. The mother and two children were upstairs in a bedroom when this happened. The father, who's an attorney, didn't have enough money to satisfy the guy, so he said, "I'll wait till the bank opens up in the morning and you'll get more for me." The mother barricaded the door in the bedroom, so the father stayed downstairs with this guy all night. The father couldn't call the cops because the guy was right on top of him, and the mother didn't have a phone in the upstairs bedroom.

Daytime came, and the bad guy told the father, "Go out and get me more money, you've got an hour. If you're not back in time, I'll kill 'em." Dad went out, and the first thing he did was go to the bank and withdraw two, three thousand dollars. Then he called the Northwest Police Department, which at the time patrolled the area. Northwest Police went, "Oh, shit," and called every available copper from the area and told them, "Get up there, get around this house, don't move on it, we'll call the county and get their SWAT team." That's when the phone call went out to our department and to us.

When we got there, Northwest had a staging area for us. I was one of two team leaders at that point, and it was my team's turn to be on containment, but Bittner for some reason wanted me on the assault. So I got together with Sammy, the leader of the team that had the assault that day, and told him I was working under him. Now all the homes up there are red brick, and the streets all wind around, so our biggest fear was that we were gonna surround the wrong house. So Ben, our sergeant, grabbed one of the first officers on the scene and said, "You need to show me the house. I want you to point this house out to me." So he walked out, and the guy kind of looked around for a second and said, "Shit! That's it right there," pointing one house over. And guess who was standing there in the window while they were looking? Shithead. And guess who was standing right out in the open? Ben in a set of BDUs and a plainclothes copper, going, "Duh!" There went the surprise.

Ben turned around, told us that the jig was up, and told us to get down to the house and surround it. The next thing we heard was radio traffic going crazy, cops on the perimeter telling us that our bad guy had run out the back door. At that point, I figured we were gonna be in a foot pursuit through the neighborhood with this idiot any second. We talked about that later, and almost every guy said that they thought that was what was going to happen. At any rate, Sammy and

Ben and I kind of looked at each other with looks that said, "Let's get the house. Let's secure the house first," so we took off on a dead run toward the house. My thinking was that I wanted to make sure that this guy couldn't get back in the house where he could threaten the family. So we bypassed the front door and went straight to the back door where he'd come out.

Our containment and our snipers were still moving into position when we ran into the house. Sammy and I were the first two through the door, and as we came through, I heard a male voice yelling at us, and I heard a woman screaming. That didn't click right off because we had been told the guy was gone. So I broke to the right, and Sammy broke to the left with a couple of other guys who were following us. They went into this area that was a kitchen with a breakfast nook, and I went into this little hallway that led to the living room area. When I got to a spot near this butler's pantry that was between the kitchen prep area and the living room–dining area, I heard guys yelling on the radio that the bad guy had gone back into the house. I said to myself, "Oh, fuck!"

I had one of the other guys, Cal Fuller, on my butt, and as I advanced down the hallway, he turned into the butler's pantry. A couple of more steps and I turned this corner and came to a common doorway between the kitchen, the butler's pantry, and the living room. There was an archway in front of me that led into the formal dining room, and I could see movement in there as I started to move into the area in front of the archway. What came into view as I got in the middle of the archway was a little boy, a little girl, a mom, and an asshole wearing a ski mask, who was holding the family in front of him and pointing his pistol at me.

I was about three feet away. I was so close that if I hadn't had to move out of the way of the gun, I could've reached out and grabbed for it. But I couldn't, so I just scooted right past him into the dining room. As soon as I saw that gun, I decided I was going to shoot the guy if I had the chance, so what I was hoping for when I broke into the dining room was that there would be a door leading back to where the guy was, so I could just move in behind him, put my gun up against his head, and drop him. Well, there was no door, so I hooked the wall and just spun around, hoping that he'd come around the corner, because if he came around the corner with all these people, there was no way he'd come around tight, and I'd be able to stick my gun right in his ear and take him out.

Now prior to this incident, I met a guy named Ron McCarthy, who had been an assistant unit commander with LAPD SWAT, and I'd had an opportunity to be involved in some training with him and pick up some of the philosophies that Ron and the other guys from Ron's squad have about dealing with hostage situations. His emphasis was to go hard and fast if the opportunity presents itself. Some other teams like to negotiate until the bad guy kills all the hostages, and they wait another week till he surrenders. They count that a success because they didn't shoot anybody. Ron's attitude, which I adopted, is, "Who cares about the bad guy?" The mission is to save the good guys, and you take the bad guys however they want to be taken.

So I was ready to shoot, but instead of coming around the corner toward me, the guy backed up. He backed up past the opening to the butler's pantry before Cal could get a shot on him. Then he backed up into a corner in the kitchen; had the woman and the two kids right in front of him. He was stuck in the kitchen because all the guys in the house had all his avenues of escape blocked. Cal and another guy were in the butler's pantry. Sammy was down behind a little serving-area counter on one side of the kitchen. We had a guy standing at the back door. We had two other guys down the hallway from me, and I was at the other end, so we had this guy pinned.

Sammy got on the radio and gave a synopsis of what was happening to the commanders. Lieutenant Bittner moved a sniper into position because the bad guy was exposed to a huge window, but he didn't have a shot because the window had an easterly exposure and he couldn't see through the glare of the morning sun. As I was listening to all this going on, I moved out of the dining room, back across the mouth of the archway and to a spot at the bottom of the stairs that headed to the second floor, which ran in between the butler's pantry and the hallway I'd originally come down when I ran into the bad guy.

I kept my right foot on the ground, put my left foot up on the second step, and positioned the gun against the vertical edge of the archway so that the front sight was lined up just off the edge of the kitchen doorway at the height of the bad guy's head, which was a good foot above the top of the mom's head. I braced the front of the weapon up in my hand in a comfortable position so I could hold that position for a long time, because I thought I might be there for a little bit. Then I just concentrated on the sights. I didn't say a word.

As I was standing there, the bad guy was screaming, "Get out of here! Get out of here." The woman was screaming, "Help! Help!" Sammy, the other team leader, gave an order to clear the house. He said, "Let's get out of here! Clear the house!" And I can remember thinking, "No fucking way." So I just held my position as the guy and the mother kept screaming. This went on for probably about a minute, minute and a half. Then the bad guy, as bad guys will do, started getting curious and tried to find out where everybody's at. Now he had on a blue ski mask, and as I was concentrating on the front sight, a blue blur came around the edge of the kitchen doorway at the height where the bad guy's head should be. When I saw that blue blur, I just popped two shots. Full-auto burst.

I shot that way because another thing that I got from training with Ron McCarthy was that in L.A. they fire two-round bursts with their MP-5s because if you're gonna have a flier, it'll be the third of a three-round burst that will go. So we had been training two-round bursts since we got MP-5s, and that's what I did. The bad guy was looking to his right, and the first one hit him just under his left eye, and the second one hit him just above it. He went down immediately.

Another thing that I got from my training with Ron McCarthy came into play here. During the advanced SWAT school I went to, Ron and another guy from LAPD SWAT named Al Preciado had explained the dynamics of a head shot with both rifle and pistol rounds. They had explained that when you shoot somebody with a pistol round like the ones in our .40-caliber MP-5s, it's not like shooting them with a rifle. There's no way to predict an immediate stop like you can get with a rifle shot to the medulla oblongata. Once a pistol round enters the body, there's no predicting where the hell it's gonna go. There's no direct line to this magical spot that's gonna turn 'em off.

Al told us that LAPD SWAT had had several capers where they took head shots on suspects who were holding guns and that about 50 percent of the time the suspects fired a round at the moment the bullet hit them. But he had also told us that whether suspects fire a round doesn't matter, because they had never had a hostage killed with a reaction shot. He said this was because when you fire a round into the head, the head moves, the gun follows the head, and if they fire a round, it will miss what they were aiming at. That's exactly what happened here. When I shot the guy, he had his gun pointed at the woman's head, had it right up against her temple. He fired a reflex shot, but it went three feet over her head and into the Sheetrock above the doorway.

At any rate, right after I fired my shots, there was half a second of dead silence as everybody else in the house came to terms with what just happened. Then I came off the step and followed our standard drill when you're going to go through an area where you might be exposed to another officer's gunfire. Our drill is to yell your name and "Coming through!" So I yelled, "Wilson, coming through!" stepped through into the kitchen, and straddled the guy. At about the same time I was moving into the kitchen, the little boy ran right into that butler's pantry and right into Cal Fuller. As Cal scooped him up, the kid was going, "Don't hurt me. Don't hurt me." Cal was just looking at him going, "I'm the police," as he took the kid out of the house. Mom and the daughter didn't waste any time getting out of that kitchen, either. They bolted right to the back door, where the guys there secured them, then hustled them out.

As this was going on, I was standing over the bad guy, getting ready to hammer him again because I couldn't find the gun. I was looking around, and I couldn't see the gun. I didn't have control of him. He was flopping around and there was a lot of blood. It was literally spraying around, so I really couldn't see everything. His hands were going under him as he flopped around. I couldn't see the gun, thought it might be under him, so I was getting ready to shoot him again. About then, Ben came charging through the door, spotted the gun, kicked it out of the way, and said, "We got it. We got it." Then Ben took my cuffs off my vest, cuffed the guy up, and we cleared the rest of the house.

We called for the paramedics, but they wouldn't come up right away, even after we told 'em, "OK, the house is secure." Firemen aren't stupid. They'll burn to death, but they ain't gonna get shot, so I had to get on the radio and request them again. I said, "We have a wounded suspect here; we need paramedics right now. Get 'em up here." They still wouldn't come up right away, but they finally did come up.

The guy was still flopping around when they arrived. I couldn't believe that he was still alive, because there was blood everywhere and brains smeared on the wall behind where he'd been standing. We also found one of the rounds. We were shooting Black Talons, and we found a slug sitting on the sill of the big window. It was just sitting there, and the jacket from it was on the floor, just peeled back. It looked like an advertisement for Black Talons. So he took one round that fragmented in his head and one that went through and through, taking a good bit of his brain with it.

As we were waiting for the paramedics, Lieutenant Bittner, our commander, came into the kitchen. He'd been involved with a fatal shooting a few years prior. He had killed a guy one-on-one, shot him three times with a 12-gauge, killed him deader than hell. The only time that I felt really any emotion on the thing was when he showed up. He came through the door, grabbed me by the shoulders, and said, "You did what you had to do." That was it. We kind of stood there, and we looked at each other for a minute. Then we shook that off and we went about our business.

—∿∿—

I was sitting at home with my family on a Saturday night when my pager went off. We'd just come back from eating some veggie burgers at my neighbor's house, and I was real tired. I was thinking of heading upstairs for bed, but the page put an end to that. The call came out as a barricaded subject with shots fired at officers. I got the address, asked my wife to make me a cup of coffee, and ran upstairs to get my SWAT gear.

When I got back downstairs, my wife met me at the front door with the coffee, I grabbed it, went out to the car, and turned the police radio on. As I was backing out, I heard a broadcast that the suspect was getting out of the car with a rifle. That struck me as kind of strange because barricaded subjects are usually in houses, not cars. Then someone broadcast that the suspect was walking around the car. When I heard that, I rolled my window down and told my wife, "Don't worry, honey, I'm not going to get a block away before I'll be making a U-turn to come back. They're gonna kill this guy." I figured that a guy who had already shot at some officers who was walking around in the open with a rifle was going to be shot pretty quick.

As I continued to the location, it was apparent from the broadcasts that patrol was in some kind of a standoff with this guy. I already had the information that he'd fired at officers, and I was kind of confused about why they were letting this guy walk around with a rifle after he'd already shot at some patrol cops. I was wondering, "Why aren't they shooting?" Then I heard one of the snipers report that he was en route to the location. I knew that he lived kind of close to that area, so I told him to go to another frequency. We both switched over, and I told him that when he got there that he needed to grab his rifle and get to high ground as quickly as possible. I told him not to worry about getting information, just get into a position to fire ASAP.

Both he and another sniper got there before I did, so I was the third SWAT officer to arrive. The atmosphere at the scene was very strange. There were police cars all over the place, with their emergency lights on, so many that I had to stop about three hundred yards down the street from where the gunman was. Police officers were all over the place, the news media was already there, and there must have been fifty spectators standing around where I pulled my car up.

A patrol officer came up to me as I was getting the rest of my SWAT gear out of my trunk, so I asked him what was going on. He explained to me that this guy had beaten the shit out of his girlfriend earlier in the day, then left. Sometime later, he called back and told her that he was going to come over and kill her. She called 9-1-1 and told the responding officers what was going on. They set up down the street to watch her house, and sure enough, the boyfriend pulls his car into her driveway a little while later. The patrol officers pulled in behind him, but he drove through the yard and back out onto the street. Patrol chased the guy until he rolled his car in this residential neighborhood and fired some shots into the windshield of the officers who were in the first car of the pursuit. None of them got hit by any bullets, but one of them did get glass shards in his eye and was on his way to the hospital. I asked the officer if he knew what kind of rifle the guy had, and he told me he wasn't sure but that he thought it was an AR-15. When he told me that, I was thinking that if that was the case, then all of these citizens back where I was were within the effective range of that gun and that all the cops in front of me were in danger too, even if they were standing behind their cars.

A K-9 officer arrived just as I finished getting geared up, so I told him to grab his dog and come with me. We moved up to a spot that was around a hundred yards from the guy. I knew that the two snipers were already there, and I wanted to find out where they were, but the radio was so busy that I figured it wouldn't do any good to try to raise them. So I asked one of the officers where we stopped if he knew where they were. He told me that the one named Jeff was lying in some bushes about forty yards ahead of us. Then I asked the officer to tell me exactly where the suspect was. He told me to look about twenty feet to the right of the car that was overturned at the head of all of the police cars.

I said, "OK," then I crouched down and went over to where Jeff was. I looked down toward the overturned car, and I could see this guy walking around with a rifle. He wasn't holding it in a shooting position. He was just holding it by the frame with one hand. He also had a handgun in the front of his waistband. After I spotted the guy, I asked Jeff, "Jeff, has this guy shot at people?" He said, "Yeah, he shot at a police car." I said, "You need to put him down. He's going to hurt somebody." He said, "OK, OK." Then I asked him, "Do you have a shot?" He said, "Well, I don't right now, but as he walks around, he comes back into my sight picture from time to time." I said, "The next time you see him, put him down."

Then I noticed about four officers behind the second car in the pursuit lineup. They were standing behind the open trunk lid, no more than twenty yards from the guy, so I decided to go up there and move them back because those guys were in a real vulnerable position. I was thinking that any time now I was going to hear the "BOOM!" of either Jeff or the other sniper's rifle. But I never did. So I got all the way up to the second car, and these officers were crouched down a bit behind the trunk lid, telling the guy to put his gun down. They were saying, "We can talk about this. Come on. There's no sense in anybody getting hurt. Put the gun down." Stuff like that.

The supervisors in my agency carry AR-15s in their cars, and one of them had given his rifle to one of the officers up where I was at. Why he did that, I have no idea, because the officer he gave it to didn't know how to use it. He told me, "I can't figure out how to work the sights on this gun." I said, "Jesus Christ!" and told him and the other officers that they were too close, that we needed to move the perimeter back and let the snipers contain the situation. I looked up, and the guy was standing right where Jeff had told me he had a clear view, and I couldn't understand why he wasn't shooting.

Then the officers I was with told me that Lieutenant Caldwell was up on the side of the car and that we needed to get him back, too. So I looked over there at Lieutenant Caldwell and saw that he was in an exposed position between the door and the car. I still hadn't heard a shot, so I decided to drop the guy. Then I thought, "Am I missing something here?" Then I decided, "No." I mean this guy has shot at a police car, he was walking around in front of me with an AR-15 in his hand, just casually cursing everybody out, saying shit like, "I may die tonight, but I'm taking you son of a bitches with me." He was armed, he'd already tried to kill some cops, he was making homicidal and suicidal statements, so from the back of the car I put my sights on him, and I said to myself, "I'm just going to take him out."

Before I pulled the trigger, I started wondering about my decision again. I said to myself, "Pete, maybe you're missing something here, because no one else is shooting. You just told Jeff to drop the guy, but he didn't. Maybe I'm missing something here. Don't shoot so quickly."

Then I told myself that the back of the car was not a good place to be thinking—that I needed to get some cover—so I moved around where Lieutenant Caldwell was because he at least had an engine in front of him. I told him to go to the back of the car and to move the officers back the next time the guy walked to where they would be out of his line of sight.

I told the guy to give up, but he just stood right there and didn't fucking move. As I was aiming my gun at him, I was thinking all sorts of stuff: "What's going on? He's already shot at the police, what if he starts shooting again? He's standing in somebody's driveway who doesn't even fucking know what's going on. What if the people inside the house come outside? What about all the citizens standing back where I left my car and all the officers in between?" They were all well within the effective range of his AR-15. I was also worried that the guy might run over to the next street, commandeer a car, and escape. Or that he might go into the house we were in front of and take a hostage. I was thinking all these things.

When I stopped myself from shooting him the first time, I started going through my mental check list: "What kind of gun did he have? What situation did we have? What happened before I got here? What justification do I have to shoot him when fifty other cops are standing around and they're not?" So I was running through this checklist again up at the car, but now I was also wondering if I should go back and get that cop's AR-15 or keep my MP-5. His weapon was superior to mine, but I decided to keep my MP-5 because I didn't know what the officer might have done to the gun when he was trying to figure out how to work it. Once I decided to keep my weapon, I thought about whether I should leave it on full automatic or click up to semi. I decided to leave it on full, thinking that if I ended up shooting the guy, I wanted to make sure that I killed him because I didn't want him thrashing around firing off shots with that rifle. I wasn't sure if the rifle was an AR or an M-16. If it was an M-16, the guy could dump a whole magazine in a few seconds on full auto and kill who knows how many people—me, other officers, citizens in nearby houses, citizens in passing cars.

So I just kept my gun on the guy as he wandered back and forth in front of me.

My MP-5 is sighted in for room distance—about twelve feet—because that's the range at which I anticipate a deadly encounter on warrants and hostage rescue situations. Because I knew that the twenty yards between me and the gunman would make my point of impact four to six inches higher than my point of aim, I was aiming a few inches above his belly button so that if I did shoot, I'd hit him in the center of his torso.

The guy wandered around for a few minutes, then turned away from me and threw something onto the car that was parked in the driveway of the house where this was taking place. I couldn't tell what he threw, but when he turned back to face me, he didn't have a gun in his waistband anymore, so I guessed that he'd just thrown his handgun onto the car. Then he walked over to the car and leaned against it. He was cussing, shouting at some other officers, "Get those goddamn lights off of me. I'm going to kill some people. You better get those fucking lights off me." So the officers who were shining their spotlights on him turned them off.

Then the guy got into sort of a relaxed posture up against the car there in the driveway and began to wrap his hand around the sling of the rifle, doing what we call *harnessing the sling*. When you harness a sling, what you're trying to do is bring a weapon into your body so that you can control it better when you fire. As he was harnessing the sling, he grabbed the back handle of the rifle, put his finger in the trigger well, and started to lower the gun.

When I saw him do that, I said to myself, "This has gone far enough." I wasn't going to let the guy kill me. I'd just come from lying in the living room with my kids and I wanted to go back. Dying was not an option for me, so I let go with a burst.

I thought that I fired four or five rounds, and it seemed like the guy stood there for a second or two, then fell to the ground. It turns out I was wrong on both counts. The investigation showed that I hit the guy with nine rounds, so I was way off there. My sense of time was also off, because when I saw the news video of the shooting the next day, it showed the guy going down as soon as I shot him. It was like he was standing there, then he went down real quick. That defied what I saw when I shot him, but the tape doesn't lie.

However long it really took for the guy to drop, I started walking up on him as soon as he hit the ground. I probably should have stayed behind the cover of the patrol car for a little longer and evaluated things before moving up, but I didn't. When I got up to him, I heard him kind of moan, and then he didn't make any more sounds or move at all. Another officer had gone up with me, so we rolled the guy over and handcuffed him behind his back. The EMS people came up, threw the guy on a stretcher, started doing chest compressions, and carted him off.

At that point, I realized that I had killed him and I said to myself, "Pete, you've been involved in another shooting." Then this strong sense that I didn't want to be left alone came over me. I don't know where that feeling came from, but I didn't want to be alone out there. Jeff, the sniper, had come up to where I was. I looked at him and said, "Jeff, don't leave me. Stay with me." He replied, "Don't worry. I'll stay with you." Then he said, "Let's go sit in my car." So we went and sat in his car and waited for the investigation to start.

I hadn't been on the SWAT team very long—maybe six months—when we got called up on a barricaded suspect holding a hostage at the Redwood Medical Center. We were down at the gym working out about nine in the morning when all our pagers started going off. The guy was a crack user with a $600-a-day habit, who bought a .25 automatic from a pawnshop that morning, went over to Redwood Hospital, walked into one of the offices, pulled the gun on a lady, and basically said, "You're my hostage and I'm gonna kill you."

When we got there, the patrol officers on the scene had already secured the area. They gave us the layout of the hospital, how to get in and around certain areas, showed us where the bad guy was, and all the different hallways leading up into the area. We asked about whether or not the ceiling in the area had crawl holes in it where you could go from room to room. We were also concerned about what to do to secure the area. You can't shut a whole hospital down. They can shut down certain portions, but you obviously have sick people, so there were a lot of people trying to get in and out of this place. The patrol officers that responded did a real good job of securing what they could and getting us all in the right places.

The guy was in a small room, maybe twelve by twelve feet, at the end of a long hallway that was basically in a T-design. The long hallway ended where the room was, then branched off to the left and right for a ways, then turned again around past the room. We had officers set up around the corner on one side of the door, and my partner, a guy named Alan Sholton, and I went to set up in the long hallway so that we could watch directly onto the door. We were in the X-ray department, so we took some of their lead plates and set them up about twenty-five or thirty feet in front of the door on the left side of the hallway and got down behind them. The door to the office was shut, so we couldn't see much, but we could see shadows moving back and forth through the crack underneath the door because the guy had the lights on inside.

I had an HK-91 .223, and I believe that Alan had an M-14 .308. We were a little concerned about those weapons because of the possibility of overpenetration if we had to shoot the guy. The biggest issue was all the oxygen in the hospital; what was gonna happen with that? We were wondering if we should get some guns that fired slower rounds, whether we should get some MP-5s. We felt good about the weapons we had if he came out, because the door was solid wood and the frame was metal, but if we had to make entry, it was a different story.

Alan and I would rotate positions about every ten minutes so that one of us would by lying down with his gun pointed around the side of the plates, and the other would be crouched down with his gun pointed over the plates. The negotiators would tell us what the suspect and the hostage were saying, and they would communicate with us from time to time about his state of mind. The guy had told the negotiators, "I don't want to hurt this lady. All I want you to do is do your job." That was his phrase, "All I want you to do is do your job. I want you to do your job right." The negotiators would say, "OK, you need to come out and talk to us," but he wouldn't. Then they asked, "Let us talk to her." When she got on the line, she said, "Get me out. I'm scared. He says he's gonna kill me." Things like that. Then he would get on the phone and say, "I don't want to hurt her. I just want you all to do your job."

He was pretty active, moving around a lot. He came to the door several times, and when he did that, we would call it on the radio, "He's standing by the door." Then, when the shadow would leave, "He's not by the door anymore. We don't know where he's at, but he's not by the door." All this time, the negotiators were still talking to him, and he would tell them, "I'm gonna come out, but I want you guys to do your job."

Then, about an hour to an hour and a half into it, the guy did something that really scared me. He opened the door, stuck his head out, looked around, and saw Alan and me down the hall. There's no way he could've missed us. We got eye contact with him. He had the gun in his right hand, holding it up in the air by the side of his head. The barrel was pointed straight up in the air, and then he turned it sideways like he was showing us, "I have a gun." He didn't say a word.

Just held the gun sideways so we could see the full view of it. When I saw that, my eyes probably got the size of silver dollars, and I called over the radio, "He's got a gun." Then the guy stepped out from behind the door.

As soon as he was in the open, he took off running toward Alan and me. As he started toward us, he started to move the gun down. He probably took a couple of steps when we started firing. I fired two rounds, but he was still coming. Now on television when you shoot somebody, they fall down, right? But this guy was still coming. I fired two more. When I fired that second time, the guy fell and slid along the floor. When he fell, some of his blood splattered and hit me and Alan. Alan had been up behind the plates, and I had been lying down, so when the guy fell, he slid right into me, face first.

The gun was still in his hand, off to the side, so I jerked back, got up, and pointed down at him with my rifle. Alan did the same thing, and we got on our radios, said, "Shots fired," and told the react team to come on around. The team came around, and I remember that Mike Church was the one who came up and kicked the gun away from the guy's hand. Then the guy tried to push himself off the ground, but Mike held him down. The guy was dead; he just didn't know it. It turns out our rounds blew his heart clean out of him, so he was DRT—dead right there—he just didn't know it. As Mike held him down, someone called for a doctor. Doctor came over, and the guy was still trying to push himself up. The doctor looked at him and said, "He's dead; he just doesn't know it yet." Within a minute or two minutes after that, the guy stopped moving.

Immediately after that, we set the weapons down, and somebody came up and took mine. I don't remember who it was. They also took Alan's gun, and then they shuttled us out of there. As we were leaving, my sergeant came over to us, and I said to him, "We had to kill him. We had to shoot him." That was all I could say: "We had to do this." He shook me, and he said, "It's all right. You did what you had to do. You did what you had to do." I mean, we gave him every opportunity to surrender. He could have come out and put his hands up, or even run at us without a gun, and it would've been different. But he didn't.

In fact, I was really surprised when he started running at us. When he started coming at me, I was like, "What?" because I thought he was gonna put the gun down. I thought he was showing it to us like he did to say, "Here's my gun," then he was gonna lay it down to show us, "OK, the weapon's out of the way now." Then he'd surrender. That's what we had totally expected because the lieutenant had come on the radio probably not two minutes before that with, "He's probably gonna come out, be ready for a surrender process." On all the other SWAT call-ups I was aware of, our negotiators had always done their jobs. The guys had always come out. Our team had never had any deadly confrontations, so I was basically in a state of shock when it happened. I was just in disbelief. I mean, I was like, "Wow." I was also afraid that I was gonna get hurt and that Alan was gonna get hurt.

When he started toward us, it was almost like it was in slow motion, and everything went into a tight focus. I had been trying to relax like I always do on call-ups because I want to be able to recall everything, to see everything, to make sure I get all my information accurately. This type of job is very stressful, and I feel like if I can relax, I can do a better job. If I can keep relaxed, I'll be more mentally alert and have a more accurate read of events occurring around me. When he made his move, my whole body just tensed up. I don't remember having any feeling from my chest down. Everything was focused forward to watch and react to my target. Talk about an adrenaline rush! Everything tightened up, and all my senses were directed forward at the man running at us with a gun. My vision was focused on his torso and the gun. I couldn't tell you what his left hand was doing. I have no idea. I was watching the gun. The gun was coming down in front of his chest area, and that's when I did my first shots.

I didn't hear a thing, not one thing. Alan had fired one round when I shot my first pair, but I didn't hear him shoot. He shot two more rounds when I fired the second time, but I didn't hear any of those rounds, either. We stopped shooting when he hit the floor and slid into me. Then I was on my feet standing over the guy. I don't even remember pushing myself up. All I know is the next thing I knew I was standing on two feet looking down at the guy. I don't know how I got there, whether I pushed up with my hands, or whether I pulled my knees up underneath. I don't know, but once I was up, I was hearing things again, because I could hear brass still clinking on the tile floor. Time had also returned to normal by then, because it had slowed down during the shooting. That started as soon as he started toward us. Even though I knew he was running at us, it looked like he was moving in slow motion. Damnedest thing I ever saw.

It turns out that it was a suicide-by-cop, that he wanted us to kill him. That's what he was talking about when he said, "I want you guys to do your job." The gun wasn't loaded, and he left a suicide note in his car, which he'd left in the hospital parking garage. I wasn't concerned much about the gun not being loaded. It bothered me, but I wasn't really that concerned because I didn't know that at the time I fired. It's not like he said, "Hey look. My gun is unloaded, and I'm gonna run down the hall, and I want you to kill me." None of that took place. We saw a gun. That's all I was concerned about. But I got mad when I heard about the suicide note. It said, "I don't have the balls to do this myself." I was really angry then because I realized that I had had to do somebody else's dirty work. I was mad because he was a chicken shit. He wasn't gonna do it himself. So this guy ruins somebody else's life because he doesn't want to live, because he was a crack head who didn't care about anything anymore. So he ruins somebody else's life rather than just go pop himself in the head, or go hang himself, or go stand out in the interstate and get run over. He didn't do something like that because he was too chicken shit to kill himself. That bothered me. I was mad. I wondered, "Why did he do this? Why did he put me in this position?"

SWAT: Preplanned Operations

As one might expect given the predominance of narcotics warrants among preplanned SWAT operations, most of the SWAT shootings that happened during preplanned operations occurred when officers I interviewed were serving narcotics search warrants. Consequently, all three of the shootings I have chosen to present in this section went down during the service of narcotics search warrants. We hear first from an officer whose story shows just how dangerous serving narcotics search warrants can be for the SWAT officers who do it—sometimes in unexpected ways.

—∿∿—

Our team went to serve this dope warrant at about eight o'clock one evening. We knew that the subject was highly violent and that he was trading guns for drugs. The house was a one-story house on a hillside in Brittany, where the garage enters into the basement, so when you pull in the driveway, you actually drop down to go onto the level with the basement. The front porch is above the driveway, about fifteen to eighteen feet up. We had the house under observation, and we saw him come home with two people. Our detectives who were up closer to the house told us that it looked like the guy went to the basement, so we figured that it was a good time because we were figuring most of the guns were probably upstairs on the main floor.

We knew the guy had a dog, and as we started to sneak up on the house, the dog started to bark. My ram men snuck up onto the porch while another guy went to the side of the porch and popped open the screen door. My two ram men were directly in front of me, approximately twelve to fourteen inches apart. I was on the first step, covering them through the middle with my HK-53, making sure they had a safe area to operate. The dog was barking. I was yelling, "Go, go, go!" Some other guys yelled, "County police!"

Meanwhile, unknown to us, the guy heard the dog barking, went over to his closet in the living room, pulled out a street sweeper—a short-barreled shotgun with a twenty-round drum magazine that's made for one purpose, and that's for shooting humans—and went to the door. That precise moment that he arrived at the door, my guys rammed it. From the time it took for the door to swing open, hit the wall, and come back, that's how quick the incident happened. It was over. In that time, the guy came up with his street sweeper, my ram men yelled, "Gun," and dropped the ram, and I fired two bursts on full auto—a three-round and a four-round burst. As I was shooting, the ram man on the left, a guy named Bob Jeffers, leaned back to get out of the way and lost his balance on the porch rail. He fell backward to the ground fifteen feet below, but as he was falling, his legs swung up in front of me, and I saw his pants leg jump as one of my .223 rounds went through his right leg, his left leg, then down range. Then the door swung back shut. The entire incident lasted maybe a second and a half, two seconds.

Even though it lasted just a split second—it was so quick—it seemed like it took forever. The entire thing was, like I said, real quick. Door swings open, door hits the wall, and comes back, but it seemed like everything happened slowed down to me. I mean, I can almost visualize every single little detail of what happened down to the point where I remember seeing pant legs pop as the round went through Bob's legs. It was definitely weird.

When the door swung open, my vision tunneled in on the threat. I knew I had people to the left, people to the right, but they were no longer in my vision. All I saw was the door frame and this guy with a street sweeper. I didn't even see his face. I saw the immediate area of the gun, his hands, and his chest. I didn't see Bob's legs until they came into the field of fire. I never saw them coming up, but when they hit the area I was tunneled in on, I saw them. Then I saw that right pants leg go up in the air and I knew I'd hit him.

After I stopped shooting, the other guys backed up off the porch while I held my ground for about forty-five seconds till all the other officers got behind cover and Bob was evacuated. After they evacuated him out, I then backed up, and we started yelling negotiations with the guys inside. The other two guys both came out and surrendered. Neither of them had any guns. We cuffed them and asked them some questions about what was going on inside the house. They told us that they had been on the main floor doing a thousand-dollar dope deal. When the dog started barking, the bad guy jumped up, looked outside, said, "Fuck! It's the cops!" and grabbed his gun. They told us that he was lying on the living room floor and assured us that nobody else was in the house. Between their statements and what the detectives had observed when they had the house under surveillance, we knew that they were probably telling us the truth.

We had to go back inside—A, to secure the house, and B, I knew that I'd hit the guy, and we needed to get him out because he was probably injured and needed first aid—so after about three or four minutes, we went back up onto the porch. When we got up to the door, the guy's dog was there. It was a pit bull who was obviously upset, and he was refusing to let us into the front door. We had to dispatch the dog, so I gave him a three-round burst through the chest. That stopped the dog and we went in. The guy was lying on the floor bleeding from the six rounds that I fired that hit him, one in the leg and the rest in the abdomen and chest. Fortunately for him, several of the rounds passed through the edge of the door as it was closing. It was a solid wooden door, one of the old types that was real heavy, so that slowed the rounds down before they hit him. That, and the fact that he was a very large biker guy—very fat, very large—saved his life. In fact, after we got him out to the hospital, that's what the doctors said. They said that they thought he was going to be dead on arrival from six .223 hits and that it was his layers of fat and the door slowing the rounds down that saved him.

Well, after we got him out and cleared the house, we found ninety-eight guns besides the street sweeper inside. He was trading guns for drugs. He had a big metal cabinet in his closet with thirty-eight guns in it, and I'd say about every three feet in the house we found a loaded weapon. He had AK-47s in two of the corners of the bedroom. He had .45s under the mattresses, .45s under his pillows. He had a gun in the refrigerator, guns in his shelves. Every seat cushion of the couch had a gun under it. It was like he was prepared for the worst-case scenario, and no matter where he would run in the house, he'd have access to a gun.

When we checked the street sweeper, we found out why he never got any rounds off when I shot him. He'd made a little mistake. He forgot to wind the magazine, which you have to do to get the rounds to feed. He even told the detectives that he had tried to pull the trigger, and when it didn't fire, he couldn't figure out what happened.

Where Bob is concerned, his worst injuries came when he hit the concrete driveway. He dislocated his right hip and broke one of his kneecaps. I only got him with one round. I think what happened was that he caught the last round. That's the only thing that can explain it, because the rounds were coming out too quick not to have had more go through his legs. So it must've been the last round. It went into the right side of the calf, exited the left side—missed his bones, muscles, and tendons—and then went into the left leg between the shin and the skin. It missed his bones. The doctor told him later that when he got a call that an officer was shot with a .223 round in the legs, he was anticipating having to amputate the leg because generally .223s shatter bone, just destroy it. He said it was a mystery how the round was able to pass through both legs and not spread out but instead go between the shinbone and the skin. He said he just doesn't know how it happened. Now, I always tease Bob that because he always wears a whole bunch of religious medals, there was an angel with him. Of course, the angel should've been a little quicker and got him completely out of the way. But still, he was lucky. Very lucky.

—◊◊◊—

I knew the odds that I would get into a shooting would increase once I came over to SWAT, but I didn't think it would occur so quickly. I'd been on the team for about two and a half years when we got an assignment to do a high-risk search warrant. Narcotics had hit the place—a single-family residence—before, and one of the guys there had supposedly stated that he was going to shoot it out if the police tried to hit him again. That's why we got the assignment. I was going to be point on the entry, so Robert—the team leader—and I did the workup on it: the drive-bys, the videotaping, getting all the information on the suspect, who's liable to be at the location with him, all that sort of stuff. Once we got the plan set up, we presented all the information to the rest of the detail, then went to execute the warrant.

It was about nine or ten at night, and we had some problems on the approach. First, after I and a few of the other guys had gotten out of the raid van, the armored vehicle pulled up right next to it, so the rest of the guys in the van had trouble getting out. Then, as we were making our approach to the front door, I heard this loud "BOOM!" Now we found out later that it was a damn basketball lying in the front yard that the armored vehicle had rolled over. But at the time, I didn't know that—I thought it was a gunshot—so I just had to trust that the guys behind me were engaging whatever it was. When we got up to the front door, we opened up the burglar bars, which were unlocked, but our MOBY man, who was supposed to breach the door, wasn't up there yet because he'd gotten tied up back at the van. Well, we were standing there for what seemed like a long time, counting off, waiting, when one of the other guys showed up with the Hallagan tool. I was thinking, "Jesus, is that all we got?" He hit the door with the Hallagan tool, but it stayed put. So I reached up, kicked the door, and it flew open.

The first thing I saw was a guy sitting on a couch that was directly in front of me. As I came through the door, he got off the couch. I saw him glance over at me, and I started hollering at him, "Police! Get down! Get down!" He ran around to the other side of the couch, then started running to my right, down this little bitty hallway toward an area that had two bedrooms with a bathroom in between. I followed him, probably ten feet behind, hollering at him, "Stop! Police! Police!" At that point, things started to move in a little bit of slow motion. I was thinking that I couldn't believe the guy was running. Given the statements we were told he'd made about how he was going to shoot it out if the cops hit his place again, I figured that he was probably going for a weapon in one of the back bedrooms, but I couldn't believe he was going to do something that stupid. The next thing I thought was, "Should I follow him?" There was a doorway to my left that opened into the kitchen, so if I'd needed to, I could've ducked into it and barricaded right there. That was my first instinct, to barricade right there, but I never lost my visual on the guy, so I stayed with him as he ducked into the bedroom to the left side of the hallway. Had he gone straight into the bathroom at the end of the hall, or had he gone to the right into the front bedroom, I'd have barricaded right there in that doorway, and it would've been a barricaded-suspect situation.

You can ask twenty of these guys on the team about what they'd do in that situation, and you might get twenty different opinions about it. So as the guy was running, I was thinking, "Do I follow him or do I stop?" If I would have lost sight of him at any point, I definitely would have barricaded up, but I never lost a visual on him, so I stuck with him.

When he ducked into that bedroom on the left, he stopped in front of this dresser that was against the wall that separated the bedroom from the hallway. I was still in the hallway, looking into the room, when I lost sight of his arms and his hands as he started to reach over the top of this dresser. At that point, time started to move really slow. I was still hollering at him, but I stopped advancing and held up in the hallway against the wall opposite the bedroom the guy was in. I was about five feet from the edge of the bedroom doorway that was closest to me, which put me about ten feet from the guy.

Because the guy was up near this dresser that was against the wall separating the bedroom from the hall, I was bladed off at a fairly steep angle to the doorway. So I was looking into the bedroom at this severe angle, hollering at the guy to freeze, waiting to see what he was going to come up with. I knew from my training that most likely he was going to come up with a weapon, but I didn't know whether it was going to be a knife, a gun, something else. I had no idea, but I couldn't believe he was reaching for something. I was actually thinking, "I can't believe this. Here I am sitting on him with the light from my shotgun on him. He knows that we're the police. He saw us coming in the door. The living room was so well lit that he has to know it was us. I'm yelling, 'Police!' I can't believe he's still going for a weapon with me right there on him."

Then the guy started turning to his right, pivoting toward me. As he turned, I was looking for his hands 'cause that's where the weapon was gonna be. So I was looking for those hands. When they came into view, I could see he was holding something black in one of them and that he had his other hand on top of the black object. At that point, I couldn't see anything but that black object in his hands—it was like everything else disappeared. Matter of fact, I couldn't even tell you which hand was on top of which. I just remember really concentrating on that black object he was holding. I couldn't see it clearly because it was dark in there; the only light in the bedroom was from the flashlight mounted on my weapon. At first, I thought he was holding a videocassette tape because I could see that the object was black and bulky. Then I realized that there was a hole at the end of the cassette. Now I knew the hole wasn't supposed to be there, so I realized at that point that he was holding some sort of gun and that the reason he had one hand on top of it was that he was trying to rack a round into it. At that point, I just instinctively shot where I was looking.

Now, like I said, my sense of time slowed way down when he started reaching over the dresser. So even though everything happened fast in real time, my mind was working real deliberately. It was like, "OK, he's reaching for something. I see his arms, but I don't see his hands. OK, here come his hands. There's something black in them. OK, that's a gun. Boom!"

When my gun went off, I saw this big cloud of smoke being lit up by the light on my weapon, like fog just rolled in. I thought, "Damn, where did all that come from?" We hadn't done any night fire with the shotguns—it had always been with the .223s, MP-5s, or pistols—so I wasn't used to seeing that big cloud of smoke, and it took me a few tenths of a second to realize that the smoke I was looking at had come from my gun. When it billowed up, I lost my visual of the guy's torso from about his shoulders down, but I could still see his upper shoulders and his head. I saw that he was moving away from me toward the corner of the bedroom, so I moved up closer to the doorway to try to get a better visual on what he was doing and stopped right near the bedroom doorjamb, peering into the bedroom at this steep angle to try to figure out what he was doing. It looked like he was trying to barricade back behind the far side of the dresser. I couldn't see his hands, I didn't know where the weapon was, so I started hollering at him, "Let me see your hands! Let me see your hands!" He didn't show his hands, so I fired again. The time between the first and second shots was about two seconds: a second for the smoke to clear, then another second for me to move up, get a bearing on where he was and what was going on, and then fire. So a lot went on in a short time.

Now after the second shot, he came up with his hands. Then I started hollering at him, "Get on the ground! Get on the ground!" When he got on the ground, my sense of time returned to normal, and the first thing I thought was, "OK, where's the gun?" I was sure what he had was a gun, but I couldn't see it anywhere, so I was wondering where it was. Then I spotted a piece of the handgrip on the floor by his foot, and that gave me a little peace of mind. At that point, I realized that I had a door to my left, so I called for support. Robert came up and covered the guy while I cleared the rest of the room. Then we went back to deal with this guy. We cuffed him and called for the paramedics to come up. And that was basically it so far as the shooting goes.

One thing that was kind of odd was that I didn't hear either of my rounds go off. In fact, I didn't hear anything from the time I went through the front door until after I fired that second round and the guy finally showed me his hands. After it was all over, Robert told me that he had been hollering at me to follow the guy when he took off running, the other guys were hollering at other suspects, the sirens were still going off outside, all the regular noises of a drug raid, but I never heard anything. It was like my ears just shut down when we made entry. Then, when the guy finally brought his hands up, it was like somebody flipped the switch back on and I could hear again.

It turned out that my first round hit the guy in his hands. That probably saved his life because the weapon he was holding took the bulk of the shotgun blast. I hit what I was aiming at because, like I said, I was looking at his hands and I just instinctively fired where I was looking. Then, when he moved away from me and tried to get behind the dresser, he increased the angle between us, which decreased the space in the doorway that I had to shoot through. The bulk of the blast from my second round hit the doorjamb opposite of where I was standing. We found one of the shotgun wads in the hallway past the door, we could see where part of the doorjamb was torn out, and we could see that some of the pellets had gone out the window of the bathroom at the end of the hallway. We figured that what happened with the second round is that when it hit the door, the pattern expanded real quickly, so even though I was no more than six feet from him, he only caught a few of the pellets from that second blast. So he lived even though I shot him at close range with two rounds of 00-buck.

About three years after I killed this guy who pulled a knife on me, we went to serve a warrant on this guy who'd been selling sawed-off shotguns to one of our undercover officers. We hit the place about ten-thirty on a Thursday night. It was a little one-bedroom house, so there wasn't much to it.

We were stacked up in the driveway because the porch was made of wood, and we were worried that if we tried to sneak up onto it that the people inside would hear us. I was point. Two other officers did a break and rake on this window on the other side of the house, and a third officer deployed a flash-bang into the house. The ram team breached the front door, and I entered into the living room. It was empty, so I went into the kitchen, which was to my left. It was empty too, but as I was moving through it, I could hear some noise coming from the bedroom, which was attached directly to the kitchen.

As I stepped through the doorway and into the bedroom, my attention was drawn to some commotion in this bathroom that was to my left, but I caught some movement in my peripheral vision off to my right. As I shifted my attention that way, I saw this guy pulling a shotgun down off this wall rack and turning to his right, toward me. The bedroom was only about eight by nine feet—we're talking real small—so he was only maybe two yards from me. When I first saw him, the barrel of the shotgun was pointed up at about a forty-five-degree angle. As the guy completed his turn, he lowered the barrel and brought the stock up to his shoulder, so that the shotgun was pointed right at me.

As I was watching the shotgun come around on me, my mind went into this mode of incredibly clear thinking, just like it did in my first shooting. I knew I could get shot. I knew it would probably hurt like crap because I was really close and it was a 12-gauge, but I wasn't scared. It was weird—just really clear, cold, calculating thinking. I knew that the possibility existed for me to get shot and die, and I knew I needed to protect myself from that, but I wasn't scared.

I was focused on the gun, and the first thing I saw on it was the adjustable choke mounted on the end of the barrel. I said to myself, "Look at the action." So I followed the barrel down to the action, and that's when I saw that it was a Remington. I actually thought, "That's a Remington 1100." Then I said to myself, "See whether his finger is on the trigger." So I went to his hand. I saw the finger on the trigger, and I thought, "This is going to hurt like hell, but you gotta keep going." So I was thinking that I was going to get shot, but I was also thinking, "Sidestep the barrel and try to give yourself some more time." So I started to sidestep as I brought my gun up. Then I thought, "Here we go again," looked through the sights of my MP-5, and fired.

As I started to pull the trigger, I was thinking, "How do I need to shoot this guy?" It was really weird. I wanted to keep the rounds on center mass, and I'd trained to fire two-round bursts, but this guy had a friggin' shotgun at point-blank range on me. I was thinking, "Do I just need to hose him till he goes down, or do I need to give him two-shot burst, two-shot burst, two-shot burst?" I knew I couldn't control the MP-5 on full auto—especially trying to move sideways—and I was worried about misses because of the other officers on the scene. So all that was going through my mind as I started pulling the trigger, and I thought, "No auto. Two-shot bursts." I ended up firing two two-shot bursts, and the guy went down in a heap onto a pile of clothes on the floor. He didn't get a round off.

I thought he was dead because I saw his T-shirt jump in my sights when I fired.

I didn't see the bullets hitting, but I saw the shirt jumping as they hit. I thought I'd hit him center mass because all I could see in my sights was T-shirt—like deer hunting with a high-powered scope and all you can see is fur—but I was wrong. It turned out that I discharged one round early as I was bringing my MP-5 up. That one caught him in his right knee. The next two rounds—the rounds I saw hit his shirt—caught him in the upper-right quadrant of his chest, and the fourth one went over his shoulder and into the wall. The bullets that hit him in the chest severed his brachial nerve, severed his brachial artery, and broke his shoulder.

As he laid there on the pile of clothing, I covered down on him because I wasn't sure that he was dead. His arm was lying between his legs. His fingers were slightly off his gun. There was blood running down his arm and blood all over the front of this shirt. He was bleeding real bad.

One of the first things I thought of while I was standing there covering the guy was that the media's going to crucify me on this deal. My agency hadn't had a shooting between my first one and this one, and I thought the press was absolutely going to toast me, because they sure tried to the first time. I was sure they were going to have a field day with this. Fortunately, it never happened. This one was a lot easier for them to understand, I think. The bad guy points a gun at a cop; the cop shoots the bad guy. The first one they looked at from the perspective of TV drama. You know, T. J. Hooker never shot a guy with a knife in the back. John Wayne would never shoot anybody who had a knife in the back.

As I was thinking about the press crucifying me, Bill—the team leader—stepped in behind me. He looked at the kid and me. I told him, "I still got guys behind me!" because my back was now to the bathroom door, where I heard the people when I first stepped in the bedroom. I could still hear them moving around in there, and I thought, "God, do they have guns too?" Bill was standing there, looking at me, so I yelled at him, "Behind me, behind me!" Then he turned, went to the bathroom, stepped in there, and got the two people who were in there.

As Bill was taking care of the other two guys, the guy I shot kind of swiveled and looked up at me with these big pancake eyes. Then the guy looked down at his arm. He couldn't move it. It was just laying there, and he said, "Man, help me. Don't let me bleed to death!" I told him, "Don't worry, there will be some guys here in a minute to help you. Just don't touch the gun again." He said, "Don't worry, I won't." He was the nicest kid, turned out he was seventeen. He was like, "Yes, sir. No sir. I apologize. I'm sorry." Just apologizing all over himself like some kid you would run into on the street who realized he had done something wrong and was trying to make amends for it. As I was looking down at him—looking him straight in the face—I thought, "That kid's not a threat anymore. He's just some innocent kid." That same type of thought went through my mind in my first shooting. When I looked at that first guy and realized he was dead, it was just like total innocence, like a baby. Like this guy can't hurt anyone ever again, so he's completely innocent. I don't know how to explain it, but that's the way I felt in my first shooting, and that's what I felt in this second one. Even though the guy had just tried to kill me, once the threat was gone, he was just some innocent kid lying there.

When Bill came out of the bathroom, we called the medics up, two guys on our team who were EMT-trained. Before they got there, Chuck—one of the other guys on our team—stepped into the room, and I told him to get the shotgun because it was laying at the guy's feet. So Chuck took the shotgun and moved it far away from the guy. Then the medics came in and dragged the kid up on the bed. One of the medics—Frank—found the entry wounds on the guy's chest and put the pressure on them right away because the blood was coming up like a fountain, like a water fountain just bubbling straight up. No break in the stream, no nothing, just a straight fountain coming up out of his shirt. That was the first time I saw where I had hit the guy.

When Frank started working on the guy, I said, "Has everybody got this?" One of them said, "Yeah, we've got it." And I said, "OK, I'm out of here," and I left. I was thinking, "He's going to die, and I don't want to watch it." I was thinking that even before the medics got there. I was looking at this guy, thinking, "He's hit hard. That's an artery hit, and I don't want to sit here and watch this guy die."

So I left the room, walked outside, sat down on the porch, took my helmet off, and started bawling. After a little while, some of the guys came up to me and told me that I needed to move because the ambulance was going to arrive in a minute. So I got up off the porch. The main thing that I was thinking about then was that I did not want to go through killing someone again.

The FBI case agent on this deal was a woman named Sally Ranch, who'd been in a shooting herself and did a lot of peer counseling for the feds. We had worked undercover together, so I'd known her for quite a while. As I was walking away from the porch, she came up to me, asked me how I was doing, and gave me a hug. I said, "I'm fine. I just don't want him to die."

She went, "But you're OK?"

And I said, "I'm OK."

I don't remember how she put what she said next, but it was something like, "You know you did what you're supposed to do."

I said, "I know that, Sally. I don't have a problem with what I did, but I don't want the guy to die." After that, I was OK. I quit crying.

It turned out that the kid made it. He didn't fight the charges. He just stood up and pled guilty to attempted assault and some other stuff. One of the other charges had a mandatory five-year sentence, and that's what he got. The guy did the five years and came out.

Extended Action

As previously noted, most police shootings are rather short affairs in that the involved officers typically fire a small number of rounds in a few seconds or less. Each of the several shootings presented to this point fit this pattern. In fact, the largest number of shots fired by any officer was the nine fired in a single burst by the SWAT officer who killed the angry, AR-15-armed boyfriend; and the longest time between the first and final shot was the several seconds that elapsed in the case of the patrol officer who helped kill the shotgun-wielding murder suspect.

The stories in this section deal with a different, less frequent, sort of shooting: those in which officers are actively engaged with suspects for an extended period of time. Like police shootings in general, more involved cases come in many shapes and sizes: the locations and circumstances in which they occur, the armaments and actions of suspects involved, how the police respond to the threat posed by suspects, and many other things can all vary substantially. This section presents a set of four stories that show what can occur in these more protracted shootings and how officers experience them. We hear from a SWAT officer whose team was ambushed when they attempted to serve a high-risk warrant, an officer whose day in court turned into a bloodbath when a gunman started shooting the place up, an officer who found himself in the middle of a wild shoot-out when a trio of robbers invaded the bank where he worked an off-duty security job, and a SWAT officer who was one of more than a dozen teammates who traded shots with a barricaded suspect over the course of a several-hours-long gun battle. Among the many things we learn from these officers is that Hollywood isn't *always* all wet when it comes to their wild portrayals of police shootings.

We went to serve a warrant about eight o'clock one morning. It was something we had been working on for days because these guys we were after were bad news. It was a huge operation that involved several other investigative units and the hitting of three different locations by our office: two simultaneously and then a third immediately thereafter.

We were going after some suspects who had robbed the jewelry department of a major department store of over $300,000 worth of estate jewelry. They had done it in broad daylight with high-powered rifles—a CAR-style weapon and an AK-47-style weapon with a drum magazine—as well as pistols. It was a very aggressive, takedown-style robbery. The same crew was also wanted for a couple of other very aggressive daylight robberies in the county. We knew the guys we were going after were the right suspects because one of the investigative units had actually purchased a piece of this estate jewelry from them.

The people who were planning the operation assigned my team to the house where they thought the jewelry was being kept. They sent another team to the place where they thought the ringleader was hiding out. I was a little bit disappointed when I heard that my team wasn't going after the main guy because I wanted to be involved in the takedown.

Our plan was to make a dynamic entry on the house we'd been assigned—basically get in there as quickly as possible so that whoever was in there could not destroy the evidence. There was a lot of discussion about this—a little before, a lot afterward—as to whether we should serve the warrant dynamically or whether we should just surround the place and call for the people inside to surrender. The investigators thought that the suspects might be able to destroy some of the jewelry if we got into a prolonged standoff, but some of us didn't think that was a realistic concern. I guess they thought the suspects could somehow flush a-third-of-a-million worth of jewelry down the toilet. I don't know. But anyway, they didn't want the jewels to be lost or destroyed or anything like that, so the decision was made that we were going to take this place dynamically.

The house we were going after was in a residential neighborhood, with houses close by on either side. It had a garage that had been converted into a living area with a sliding glass door that ran perpendicular to the street, facing the side of the house next door. Our plan was to make entry through the sliding door with an eight-man entry team after a perimeter team and a canine officer had set up outside. We drove up in a few vehicles—the van I was in and then a couple of other vehicles—and everybody kind of scurried to their positions. I was the number-two guy in the entry stick.

As we walked up the driveway toward the glass sliding door, I noticed that there were kids' toys all around. There was Big Wheel and other toys that would belong to kids from maybe three to five years old. As the number-two guy on the stick, one of my functions was to deploy a flash-bang prior to entry. The toys meant that I had to be extra cautious about where I put the flash-bang. I had to make sure I didn't throw it in some baby's crib, or bed, or something. So I was very cognizant of my responsibility as I took up my position next to the door.

There was a vertical blind with a bedsheet attached to it on the inside of the sliding door, so when the breacher broke the glass out, I had to move the blind and the sheet aside in order to deploy the flash-bang. I stuck the muzzle of my MP-5 into the doorway, moved the curtain material out of the way, and took a pretty good solid peek in—more than I normally would—because of my concern about children. Then I dropped the flash-bang right inside the doorway. As soon as it hit the ground, I heard a "pop," which confused me, because it wasn't supposed to go off immediately. At the same time I heard the "pop," something hit me in the right side of my upper lip—right in my mustache—and it stung.

My mind was going very fast, and I thought, "The fucking flash-bang didn't go off right, and something blew up and some kind of flack hit me in the face." Then the flash-bang went off properly, and I started thinking really, really fast: "OK, if that was the flash-bang going off properly, what was that little pop before that?" Just when I started coming up with the answer, I heard another "pop" just as a bullet came through the wall right in front of me. It missed me by inches. At that point, I realized what was going on: the pops were rounds going off, and I knew that we were under fire. Somebody inside was shooting at us.

When that second round came through, what I saw was the explosive opening of a bullet hole in the doorjamb, literally a foot or so in front of me. It happened in kind of a slow motion, as I watched the fragments of wood coming off the jamb. Not super slow, but slower than it was actually happening. Then I saw some other rounds coming out in that same explosive way. I found out later that some of the other guys in the stick couldn't believe what was happening. One of them told me that he saw my ghost leaving my body as I was standing there; another said he couldn't believe that I wasn't going down because he saw bullets just flying right by my head. At any rate, it was pretty weird watching those bullet holes appearing in slow motion.

At first, I was surprised when I realized that we were being shot at. Then I got pretty pissed and started returning fire with my MP-5 through the opening in the glass and through the doorjamb. I took three or four bursts of five or six rounds each. As I was firing, the number-one guy in the stick stepped back and started returning fire into the target house also. As I was firing, I heard several more "pops" from inside. Then there was a transition to some very aggressive "BOOM, BOOM, BOOMs." The investigators told us after it was all over that there were two suspects shooting at us—the main suspect, who was supposed to be at the other location, and his girlfriend—and that two guns had been fired at us—a pistol and an AK-47. From that, we figured that what had happened is that one of them started shooting the pistol at us, then the other one grabbed the AK-47. It was like a whole new world when that thing started up.

The whole entry stick started to back away from the door as the suspects continued to fire through the door and the jamb. We kind of slid around to the left to the front of the house. There were three palm trees out there, and most of the entry element ended up in that area. The rest of the guys backed down the driveway and got on the other side of this four-foot fence that separated the yard of the target house from the sidewalk. Those of us at the palm trees started firing into the converted garage–bedroom area. We didn't have a specific target; we were just putting suppression fire into the area.

I could hear the guns going off inside the house, and at first it sounded like rounds were hitting the palm trees where I was positioned. I remember thinking, "My God, they're shooting at the palm trees." Then I ran my MP-5 dry, so I changed magazines and shot some more into the wall. As I was returning fire from that second magazine, I realized that the people inside weren't shooting at the palm trees. They were shooting out where we had been when the gunfight started, so their rounds were going parallel to the road and into the house next door. The reason I could tell that's what was happening was because there was a big old yucca plant between the door and the house next door, and rounds were just slicing through it. It looked like Edward Scissorhands was trimming that thing. It was really an awesome sight to sit there and watch that thing disintegrate because it was happening in slow motion. Shit was flying everywhere. It was an incredible experience.

Then our team leader started calling for us to fall back to the rally point, which was the van that we had parked in the street. He was right beside me, and he started shooting some suppressive fire from his shotgun. The barrel was right next to my head, and he was shooting slugs. That was the loudest thing in the whole shoot-out. Up to that point, the sound of the rounds had been muted. But that shotgun put out some definite noise.

I don't know exactly what the team leader was thinking when he called for us to fall back to the rally point, because we had a pretty good position of cover right where we were. Rounds were still coming from the house, and I was not ready to leave that position at the trees. It wasn't that I was afraid. I felt very comfortable and very calm. I just didn't think we were ready to go back because we didn't have containment on the left side of this place because all of our containment people had run up the right side just prior to us getting in this gunfight. So I was sure that nobody had gotten around the far side of the building to provide containment on the east side of this house. I was trying to tell the team leader that we needed to make sure we had containment on the east side and that we were not ready to go back, but I didn't get all that out. What I said was like, "Have we got somebody on the side?" Then there was a lull. The suspect quit firing.

I put my gun on safe, climbed over the four-foot wall separating the yard from the sidewalk, and headed for the rally point. As I was moving to the van, another slow-motion episode happened. Somebody had thrown a flash-bang up to the front of the house, and it detonated right by the front door. I watched it, plain as day, go off and fly into the air, coming our way. We were clear out in the street at that point, so I was like forty feet away, and this thing almost hit me. It came that far, flying at chest to head level—whoosh—and I just calmly sidestepped it. I was thinking, "Jesus, I've never seen one of those fly before." After that happened, I got back to a position behind the van. Then I helped throw some more ordnance, a couple of flash-bangs and sting balls and whatever else we had there to try and distract the suspect from continuing to fire at anybody. Then we started putting chemical agents in the place.

We still had people who were unaccounted for, people who were actually between the target house and the house to the west. There was a fence between the two houses, a big six-foot-tall block fence that belonged to the people in the target house, and we had one of our SWAT officers and a canine officer trapped on the walkway between the target house and the fence. We were looking for people to go around there and check on these officers, so I volunteered to go with a sergeant who was gonna try to pull these guys out of there.

As we were looking for a way to get to these people, I realized that if we went around the house next door to the west, we'd be able to double back and get to those officers. A few of us went that way and found the gate into the yard of the house was locked. So I climbed over a garbage can, got inside the fence, got the gate opened up, and off we went. The canine officer had been extricated by that point, and one of our snipers was talking with her. I told him I was gonna go up and find the other guy because we still had one not accounted for. So I ran up to the wall and found the missing officer—he was trapped just on the other side of the wall from me.

I could see him. He knew I was there. I put my gun over the top of the wall and said, "I'll cover you. Come on over." He said, "I want more cover." Apparently, he wasn't ready to move with just me providing cover. A short time later, the sniper who had been back with the canine officer came up to my position; then another guy came up there right after that. With three guys with weapons covering his move, the trapped SWAT officer came over the wall. It went off without a hitch, except that one of the flash-bangs he had hooked to his body got caught up on the top of the wall as he was scrambling over. It pulled free from the pin as he dropped down onto our side, then fell to the ground right beside us. When it went off, it blew all sorts of shit into the air.

After we calmed down from that, we went back around the house to where the raid van was parked. There was still a lot of activity going on, and one of the guys at the van was throwing gas into the house, so I made myself useful and covered him. As I was doing that, I noticed that one of the gas grenades he threw got stuck between the vertical blinds and the sheet at the glass sliding door and caught the sheet on fire. I broadcast that the house had caught on fire and advised that we were going to need the fire department to respond. But it was too dangerous for them to come up and put the fire out, so we just let it burn.

Two people had came out of the house while I was in the back— the main suspect's mother and her boyfriend. They had told one of the other guys that the suspect and his girlfriend were still inside, so we knew there were two people in the house as it burned. We finally got some fire fighting equipment close by, and the firefighters eventually said, "OK, there's no way anybody in that house could still be alive," then went up and put the fire out. They didn't find any bodies in the rubble, but in the subsequent investigation the detectives found the charred remains of the suspect and his girlfriend. They were in a corner of the house near where the shoot-out went down. She had a contact pistol wound to the back of the head, and he had a contact pistol wound to the temple. So at some point, he killed her and then he killed himself.

One thing that was interesting about what happened is that I was really calm throughout most of the incident. In fact, a sense of calm and comfort settled in within the first few seconds, right after I started putting rounds back into the house. Returning fire was sort of a defining moment for me because I'd never been in a shooting before, so I didn't know how I was going to react. I had always thought that if I was shot at, I would not run, I would not panic, I would not drop my gun or fall on the ground in fear. I had always thought I would return fire. And that was what I did. So after I started shooting back, I started feeling comfortable with the situation. From that point on, it was obvious to me that I wasn't going to be afraid, that I wasn't going to run away, that I was going to do what I was supposed to do. It felt good. There was a rush associated with that.

I was in my uniform at the courthouse waiting to testify in a robbery–stolen auto case when the shooting happened. The courthouse is set up with a lobby in the middle of each floor, courtrooms arrayed around the lobby, and a hallway that goes completely around on the outside of the courtrooms on each floor. I was standing in the lobby of the second floor, waiting to testify, when I heard a bunch of gunshots—at least five—go off in the courtroom next to me. I didn't know if they were playing a tape for evidence or what, but I started walking toward the courtroom, and people started coming out.

They were saying, "He's shooting everybody! He's shooting everybody!" Now the doors to the courtroom have a thin panel of Plexiglas in the wood, so I looked through the Plexiglas and spotted a woman slumped in a chair at one of the tables in front of the judge's bench. It was obvious that she'd been shot, and it was obvious that she was dead. I also saw two men laying on the ground next to the table, yelling, "He ran into the hallway! He ran into the hallway!" The courtroom is set up with doors on either side of the judge's bench that lead to the outside hallway that runs around the courtrooms, and I could see one of the doors closing.

So I pulled my weapon out, went back to the courtroom I was gonna testify in, ran through it, and went out the door on the left of the judge's bench that would put me near the corner of the outside hallway. When I got into the hallway, I spotted an older guy with gray hair who was wearing glasses. He had on a blue blazer with brown or tan pants, and he was holding a gun in his left hand. He was dressed similar to what our bailiffs wear, and because bailiffs are usually retired police officers or sheriff's deputies, my first impression was that he was a bailiff. He looked scared, and I asked him, "Are you OK?" or "Is everything all right?"—some type of statement to that effect—then I turned my head to look down this long hallway that goes for about sixty yards. Just as I turned back, I heard a gunshot. I saw a flash, and I could almost feel the bullet or the report go above my head. Obviously, at that point, I realized that this was the guy who had done the shooting.

Then the guy turned and went around the corner, and I—just out of reaction—went back into the courtroom and took cover. There was silence for a while. All I could hear was people running around in panic. There were a lot of people in the courthouse, and there was a lot of confusion going on. Then I heard more shooting on the other side of the floor, so I walked out of the courtroom and into the lobby. While I was standing there, Jack Sierra—a sergeant in my department—approached me and asked me what was going on. I told him that I confronted the guy, that he's an older white male, that he's got gray hair, this and that. As we were conversing, I heard this door around the corner come flying open. It was like someone had just flung open a door, slamming it up against a wall. Right after that, I heard some more gunfire, and Jack moved away from me a little bit. A second or two later, the guy came around the corner, firing more rounds.

Now there's an escalator right there that he could have gone down to try to escape, but he didn't take it. Instead he looked right at me—I guess because I was in my uniform and Jack was in plainclothes—and then started running toward me. As I looked at him, I could see a gun in each of his hands. So there I was in the hallway, with this guy running at me, firing two guns.

I brought my weapon up and I fired.

Jack fired just a split second before me. His round struck the suspect in the lower left side, which caused the guy to kind of spin and fall at the same time. I saw my first round hit him in the head. I fired a second round, but I didn't see where it hit. Then the guy went down, lying on his stomach and his chest. I could see that he had dropped one of the guns and that he was trying to get up. I started yelling at him, "Stay down! Stay down! Stay down!" But he didn't. He started to get up by pushing up with his hands. He got as far as his hands and knees, then he started to pick his hands off the floor. At that point, I fired another round, and he dropped the gun. Then I went up to handcuff him.

As I was handcuffing him, he asked me, "Did I kill the bitch?" I guessed that he was referring to the woman I'd seen in the courtroom, but I didn't say anything at that point. After I got the cuffs on him, he started to complain to me that the cuffs were too tight. I thought—maybe even out loud—"Why is this man worried about how tight the handcuffs are when he's bleeding from the head and the chest?"

It was total chaos in this courthouse. There was a report of another gunman on the plaza level, so I asked the guy, "Who's with you? Is anybody with you?" He responded, "No, I came alone. I took the bus here. There's nobody else with me." I couldn't believe what had just happened, so when I heard the report that there was another gunman, I thought that maybe the situation wasn't over. I'd thought to myself, "My God, what is going on here?" But once he said he was by himself, I took heart in that. I kind of believed him. Shortly after our brief conversation, the medics showed up and took him away.

The whole thing had lasted five, maybe ten, minutes from the time I first heard the gunshots to the time the medics took him away. I couldn't believe what was going on, especially when the guy first shot at me. It was the ultimate surprise because I always thought that if somebody was going to try to kill me, it would be a gangster, a biker, someone like that. So it was a total shock when this older white male who looked like my father shot at me. It was total amazement: "Oh, my gosh, *you're* the bad guy!"

Then, when he came around the corner shooting at us, I couldn't believe that it was still going on. There were a lot of other officers all over the courthouse, so I just couldn't believe that this thing started on one side, and this guy managed to go almost all the way around the floor; that nobody had put this guy down, killed him, or taken him into custody. I just could not believe it went on as long as it did. I even said to myself, "I can't believe this. This has got to stop."

I had tunnel vision, and things started to slow down as he came at us. I was so focused on him that I didn't even know that another officer, Mike Ball, was in the hallway shooting along with Jack and me. I also didn't know that when the guy turned the corner, he shot a security guard who was standing in this little indentation in the hallway off to my left. Shot him in the leg. I mean, the hallway was only about twenty-five feet wide, and I didn't know these guys were there. When the suspect came around the corner, it was like my brain fixed on what I needed to do, so all I saw was him.

I was looking down the barrel of my gun through the sights when I fired my first round. I saw him spinning. I heard Jack shoot, but it was like my shot was just an instant after his. It was like, "Bang, bang," real fast. My .45 didn't feel like it would when I'd shoot at the range. I didn't feel the recoil, and I even said to myself, "My gosh, this isn't like it is on the range!" It was weird. I was concentrated on the suspect, and it felt like a popgun going off in slow motion. After Jack's first round, I didn't hear any of the other shots he and Mike fired. I could hear my own, but they were muffled, like somebody put a pillow over the gun.

Like I said, I saw my first round hit the guy in the head. It caught him kind of above and behind his right ear. I could see the flesh separate, and I could see the blood splatter when the round impacted. I didn't see my other two rounds hit him, but I found out later that the second round hit him in the upper chest, and the round I fired as he was trying to get up hit him in the hand he was holding the gun in, separating one of his fingers from his hand. That's what he was talking about when he complained about the cuffs being too tight; his hand hurt because he was missing a finger. I don't remember where all of Mike and Jack's rounds hit, but all total, we shot the guy nine times: three by me, three by Jack, and three by Mike.

Before we stopped him, the guy shot five people. He was in court for a divorce proceeding, and he just went nuts. He pulled two .38s out of his briefcase and started shooting. He had a lot of ammunition that he'd stuffed in his pockets, and he reloaded a couple of times after he got out of the courtroom. In fact, he reloaded right after my first confrontation with him where he shot at me. The woman I'd seen at the table was his wife. So he killed his wife, shot his attorney, shot her attorney, shot the security guard, and shot a bailiff. He also shot at the judge, but he didn't hit him. He also shot at another police officer at some point but missed him. So all together, he fired on at least seven people besides Jack and me, wounded four, and killed one before we were able to stop him.

The key thing about my shooting is that the North Hollywood bank robbery happened one week prior to it. The morning of the shooting, I saw the video of that incident for the first time. I had heard what had happened, but I was still shocked as I watched those two guys with body armor and automatic weapons shooting it out with the LAPD for such a long time. It sent a shiver down my spine because I was getting ready to go to my extra job, working security at a bank, as I watched it. I double-checked all my equipment, made sure my pistol was loaded, topped off my magazines, and headed to work.

I got to the bank at 7:15 and just did the usual stuff. At a quarter to nine, an armored car pulled up. I thought that was kind of unusual because they usually come over after the bank opens. The armored car left at about five minutes until nine. I know the car times because I was watching it. Nine o'clock I opened the doors. I was getting really sleepy, really bored, and I said to myself, "What a boring job this is." I actually remember myself saying that. Then, at 9:10, I saw three masked figures with assault rifles run through the foyer of the bank. They were wearing all black, including their ski masks.

I was located adjacent to the front door in a little hallway that branches off the front door before the floor opens up into the lobby. When I saw the figures run in, I had some weird thoughts. The first thing I thought of was SWAT for some reason, like maybe the team was doing a practice raid. Then Halloween even came into my mind. Maybe they were trick-or-treaters. It was just disbelief. Those thoughts lasted like a hundredth of a second, because by the time I had them, I already had my gun up. As soon as all that weird stuff passed through my head, I moved closer to them because I wanted to reduce the advantage they had with their long guns. I remember seeing these two girls sitting behind these two desks that were dead smack right in the middle of the lobby, and I thought, "Oh, God. They're going to get hit." I had to think of a way to draw the robbers' fire, so when I got about fifteen feet away from them, I shouted, "We're being robbed!" and went to shoot the first guy. I was scared, but I felt that I had to stop them before anything happened to the people inside the bank.

When I squeezed the trigger, my gun malfunctioned. I heard this loud "CLICK" that echoed through the hall, so I did the tap, rack, and shoot drill to clear the weapon. I watched the ejected round come out, and by the time I came back up with my gun, I had eye-to-eye contact with the third guy through the door. He raised his weapon, and I got off my first round. I fired that first round center mass, but nothing happened. When he didn't go down after that center mass hit, I thought that he might be wearing body armor. I moved down to his legs with one round and then back up to his face with at least two more. He dropped like a rock. As soon as he dropped, I stopped firing at him.

By that time, all hell had broken loose. When I opened up on the third guy, guy number one and guy number two started shooting at me with their AR-15s. I didn't know it at the time, but the number-four guy, who was on the outside with the getaway car, also started shooting at me through the glass with a 9-millimeter pistol at about the same time. So as I was shooting at the third guy, I heard a lot of gunfire and watched the walls exploding by me as the rounds from the other three guys were hitting the Sheetrock.

It was kind of strange, but once they started shooting, I wasn't scared anymore because all of a sudden I felt like I had a duty to protect the people in the bank. I really can't explain it, but I was thinking about those people and about what I had to do to take out the bad guys. I felt I had a duty to eliminate the threat they posed to those people. So I stood my ground, exchanging shots with the two guys in the bank for a few seconds. Then their rounds started getting closer to me, and I retreated back into the hallway. A few seconds later, I came back out and tried to take them on again. When I got back to engage the guys inside the bank, the guy I shot was gone, but the other two guys inside the bank were still shooting at me. Their gunfire was real intense. Then I ran out of ammunition and retreated back into the hallway again.

In the back of the hallway, there's a door that leads to the back of the bank that I wanted to go through to get out of the bad guys' line of sight and sneak around on them. The door is always locked, so I went to open it with the key I had, but my hand was shaking so bad I couldn't get it in there. As I was doing that, the number-one guy apparently figured that I was out of bullets, and he came almost all the way into the hallway to get me. I peered around the corner, and what I saw is the thing I remember the most out of the whole bank robbery: the number-one guy firing at me with his AR-15. I remember it because I saw these star-shaped bursts of fire and the heat vapors coming at me. Then, as soon as I pulled my head back, I saw the Sheetrock explode in front of my face where my head had been.

The rounds were penetrating through the wall at the corner there, and I thought I was going to die. I saw my whole life pass before me. Then, for some reason, I got real angry. When that happened, I started thinking about my new girlfriend, how I'd hate to lose her because I'd just met her. I also thought about my dad because I'm real close to him. I don't know what it was. He just came to mind. I also thought about the rest of my family. I could almost see their faces, but that was not connected to anything.

I could still see the bullets popping into the hallway, but I reloaded and shot back. The gunfire from the guy was so intense that I just stuck my hand around the corner and just started spraying. When I stopped shooting, there was silence, and I peered around the corner. Nobody was there. I didn't want to walk into an ambush if the guys were still in the bank, so I went back to that back door and managed to open it. It leads behind the teller lines, so I scanned and checked the area and went into the teller booths. Nobody was there. Then I jumped over the teller booth into the main lobby. I didn't see anybody. Then I ran over to one of the desks in the middle of the lobby, ducked under it, and called 9-1-1.

A little while later, everybody started reemerging from underneath their desks and whatnot. Then I went outside to look around, and I saw a security guard. He was dressed in black, and I almost shot him. As I was pointing my gun at him, he said, "No! No! No! I'm a security guard." I saw his hands were clear and that he was with the Westside Mall Security. After that, I went back inside the bank and collapsed. My right leg gave out from under me. I thought I'd got shot, because they say sometimes you don't feel the one that hits you, so I started feeling myself, looking for bullet holes.

I found some pieces of glass and brick embedded in my skin, plus one bullet fragment in my arm that hit me when I first engaged the guys. It came from whoever was shooting through the wall, and I remember that it stung when it hit. That was the only part of the whole thing that happened in real time. Everything else from the time they came in to when it was all over was in slow motion. I was amazed at the speed and the intensity of that little piece that hit my right arm.

After I finished checking myself, I sat down in a chair and called my family because I didn't want the media to make them think that I was severely injured. After that, the cavalry arrived, including my brother, who is also an officer. When he got there, I was on the verge of tears. I don't know what the tears were for, though. I was ready to explode, but I didn't know what for. I don't know if it was relief, fear, or what.

A while later, the homicide investigators showed up. They told me they understood that I needed my attorney there before they talked to me. When my attorney showed up, we walked the crime scene with the investigators, but I don't really remember any of it. They told me afterwards that there was a big old pool of blood where I shot the guy, but I don't remember that. I just remember walking through broken glass. I also remember that there were a lot of people congratulating me, saying things like, "Good job!" but I was just numb. It was a real hollow feeling.

After we walked through the crime scene, the investigators took photos of me. Then we walked outside, and I was greeted by this entire parking lot full of media people. They were shouting questions at me, and my hollow feeling turned to anger because I felt like they were making a circus out of what happened. I felt like the situation belonged to me; they were intruding. What happened was very personal to me. Those people didn't know what I went through, and I was very angry at them. I just ignored them, got in a squad car, and went to the hospital.

It happened in August. It was warm, really warm, and it was a long call-out. A patrol unit had gone to do an eviction, and the suspect confronted the deputies with a rifle. They thought better of it, made the right decision and backed out, then called for the tactical unit, which was us. The suspect was a meth-head who had a lot of weapons, had threatened people before, and had been arrested several times for weapons and narcotics. It ended up being a long, protracted incident—seventeen or eighteen hours in all.

The location was a large warehouse area, maybe twenty or thirty thousand feet. I had recently moved from entry team leader back to shooting the long rifle, so I was in a containment position most of the time. We surrounded the place and tried to talk to the guy for quite some time, but he never responded. After several hours, there was an initial confrontation, when a team of deputies breached one of the entry doors and the guy shot out at them. He was firing an SKS, and one of the deputies got hit, took a piece of jacketing in his wrist. It eventually needed to be surgically removed, but at the time he didn't even report it. It was no big deal. He let it slide.

My partner and I were behind a short block wall adjacent to a bunch of large tanks made of quarter-inch steel plate that were empty at the time. One of the rounds the guy fired at the deputies who tried to breach the door penetrated one of those tanks. I remember seeing the hole and thinking that we probably needed to utilize some better cover.

Anyway, the entry team retreated, and we fired a lot of gas into the place. We kept trying to contact the guy, but we got no response. Then another team went up to breach some of the other exterior doors, just to give alternate entry and exit points. The guy fired a couple of more rounds when they pulled one of the doors, but nobody was injured or anything. After that, there was no more contact for quite some time, so the decision was made to make entry.

Because it was such a large area, they used several different entry points and several different clearing teams. There was an office area, but the bulk of the area was an open warehouse with large, floor-to-ceiling metal storage racks. The teams cleared the open areas using the dog; then they cleared the office area. That left a bathroom that was at the end of this narrow hallway. We hadn't found him yet, so everybody was thinking he was probably in there. I was outside, and the guys inside said, "OK, what we're going to do is we're going to stake out the bathroom and set up some containment, and we're going to attempt to get him to come out."

So a team went down this hallway and tried to breach the bathroom door. The guy fired through the door with his SKS and wounded two of them. One of them took a shot in the shoulder, through and through. The other one took a shot to the wrist. Some of the other guys laid down suppressive fire, and the team ended up having to back out.

Once we got the wounded deputies out, we said, "OK, let's think about this for a while." We tried the bullhorn some more, tried to call the guy, but no response. Then the decision was made to fire some gas into the bathroom. They saturated this bathroom area, which was fairly small, but didn't get a response, just some more gunfire. Some of the guys returned fire in hopes that maybe they would be able to keep him down and stop him from firing out. Then there was another lull, and that's when I came inside. The guys inside said, "Hey, why don't you go over there and take this position opposite the door. We want some experienced guys in there." So I took a position directly in line with the doorway, about twenty-five feet from it, along with two other guys, one to my right and one to my left. We all had CAR-16s—eleven-and-a-half-inch-barrel M-16s—and there were three or four rows of racks between us and the door, so we really had a limited window where we could shoot if the guy came out. I was behind some tires. One of the guys had a shield, and the other one was behind an old engine block, so we had fairly good cover. It wasn't great cover, but it was good enough for the time.

After we got into position, they decided to shoot in some hot gas, which is tear gas dispersed by smoke, which is caused by the burning pyrotechnic material. So they end up shooting a hot-gas grenade into this bathroom. One of the by-products of hot gas is that it can catch stuff on fire, and apparently that's what happened in the bathroom. He started screaming and yelling, then he came running out with a .45. He was firing it, so we shot him.

There was so much smoke in the hallway that I heard him shooting before I saw anything. I eventually saw the weapon as the guy moved forward, and it was pointed pretty much in our direction as he was firing. When he came out of the smoke, that's when I had a shot, and I took it. I had a small area to shoot through with all the racks, but I had a pretty good target. So I shot and I guess everybody else did. I really didn't hear anything. The short-barrel M-16 is very loud, it's deafening, but I don't remember hearing it. That's one of the things that really struck me about the shooting, because in that contained environment it should have been even louder. I don't remember ringing in my ears, and I would expect there would be some ringing, because it would definitely have been high decibels with all of us firing, but I don't recall it. But then again, I didn't hear a whole lot of anything. I knew that I shot, and I don't remember the people next to me shooting, but I really wasn't paying attention.

At the time, I didn't know how many rounds I'd shot. I assumed it was only four or five rounds, but it ended up being fourteen. I thought that was pretty significant. I'm a firearms trainer, and I teach officers to be aware of the number of rounds they fire, and I didn't have a clue.

At any rate, I stopped shooting when the guy dropped out of sight, but there was still some gunfire going on because there were several other deputies at different angles who still had a shot at him as he was going down. After the shooting stopped, I heard him screaming and yelling. Someone said that he was down, that he had no weapon, so some of the guys approached him with shields. He struggled and fought with the guys when they first got to him. I thought that was amazing, because there was blood all over the place. I realize that a little blood goes a long way, but it looked like an awful lot to me. But they finally got him under control and dragged him away from the hallway. Then our paramedics tended to him.

He didn't make it. It turned out that he had taken something like forty different hits. This is the funny part. Well, not funny, but interesting. Of the maybe forty rounds total that hit him, most were 9 millimeters from the MP-5s the guys off to the sides were firing, but none of them were terminal wounds. The terminal wounds were from the .223s. There were only, like, four terminal wounds, and they were all .223 wounds. I'm assuming they came from my weapon because I had the best shot at him. The other two guys with M-16s weren't 100 percent sure if they even hit the guy. I'm pretty sure I got some hits because I had a good sight picture on my first few rounds. He was pretty much coming out directly at me. Because he was in a three-foot-wide hallway, he didn't have much room for movement, so it was pretty much a channelized shot. That's why I feel pretty sure that I hit him with my first few rounds.

My other rounds went into the steel racks because I lost that little window that I initially had to shoot through when he made it out of the hallway and did finally move a little sideways. And that's the other thing besides not hearing things that really struck me. You see all these movie shoot-outs with sparks flying everywhere, and I'd always thought that was bogus. Well, sparks were flying everywhere from bullets hitting these metal racks. That was one of the most significant things about the shooting that I remember. I was thinking, "Boy, there are sparks. It isn't a bunch of garbage that they have in the movies." I mean, this was real and there were sparks flying everywhere. The lighting wasn't great in there, and a lot of the guys besides me were trying to shoot through racks and hitting metal. All these years, I'd been thinking the sparks in the movies was a bunch of crap, that it's just Hollywood hype and special effects, but it was for real.

Three from the Busy Cop

The last section of the previous chapter focused on one of the more active officers I interviewed, presenting several of the more than two dozen close encounters in which he has been involved during his quarter century of big-city police work when he didn't shoot. This section also focuses on this busy cop, presenting his accounts of all three of the situations in which he did pull the trigger—the first of which occurred when he was working an off-duty security job while still a rookie, the second of which happened during his stint in Narcotics, and the third of which took place during one of the hundreds of SWAT missions in which he has participated over the years. Taken together, these three shootings show how it is that an officer who almost always manages to resolve exceptionally dangerous situations without firing any shots handles those situations in which he has no choice but to pull the trigger.

—∽∽—

My first shooting happened when I was still pretty new to the job. I was working an off-duty job at a Jack in the Box near downtown from 10:00 at night until 2:00 in the morning. I'd spent several months on patrol, then got sent to work a 2:00 P.M. to 10:00 P.M. shift at the jail, so I'd go right from the jail to the Jack in the Box. The Jack in the Box was in a high-crime area—lots of prostitution, lots of drugs, stolen cars, and whatnot—so they hired cops to work security from 10:00 P.M. until they closed at 2:00 A.M. Nothing much happened for the first hour and a half. Then, at about 11:30, I happened to walk outside and heard a lot of sirens. I was thinking that it was either the fire department responding to a multialarm call or a police chase. Why else would there be that many sirens?

I was standing out there listening and sort of reminiscing about when I was on patrol driving a squad car. The sirens kept winding through the neighborhood a little ways away, so I figured it must be a car chase. It sounded like it was going in two or three different directions, when, all of a sudden, the sirens started getting louder and louder. I walked out to the intersection and looked down Pine Street. The chase was heading my way, so I just stood there and watched. Now Pine comes into First and it dead-ends. So if they kept coming, they were going to have to go left or right at the T-intersection where I was standing.

When they got closer, I could see that patrol was chasing this red pickup truck. It tried to make a right but lost it and hit this telephone pole. Two of the police cars come screeching up to a halt. I took off running up behind them 'cause I was thinking the driver was going to bail out and run. I was real young, and I liked to chase people when they ran. I always kind of got a kick out of it, just to see if I could catch them. Anyway, the driver bailed out just as I was getting up to one of the squad cars. He came swinging out, looking a little disoriented or intoxicated, I wasn't sure which. He was a big, barrel-chested Mexican guy with a scruffy beard. Looked to be about forty or so. As he finished swinging around toward us, I saw he had a pistol in his hand, a big six-inch blue steel revolver. That surprised the heck out of me because I was thinking that he would run. When the door came open,

I was fully expecting to see some tennis shoes running off into the darkness, not some guy with a gun.

I was about a car length away from him. I had positioned myself on the right front quarter panel of one of the patrol cars. It was a one-man unit, and the driver was positioned on the other side. The other car was a two-man unit. They stayed behind their doors, lit the guy up with a Q-beam, and started shouting for him to get out of the truck. Because they had the Q-beam on the guy, we could see him clearly. Some other units were starting to pull up when the guy started to swing his gun in our direction. I was thinking that this guy needs to be shot, that I needed to shoot this guy. I had my sights lined up on the center of his chest, and I was in the process of pulling the trigger when I heard a gunshot go off to my left—it sounded like a shotgun blast. I fired one shot, then heard two other pistol rounds go off almost simultaneously, and the guy went down.

It happened real fast. Milliseconds. I saw my muzzle flash, started looking for my front sight—I was thinking I needed to get back on target in case I needed to fire a second round—but by the time I found my front sight, he was already out of sight. One of the other officers started screaming, "He's down, he's down, I got him!" I could see his body laying underneath the driver's side of the truck, so I went up to the passenger side to see if there was anybody else in there. There wasn't, so then we all kind of positioned ourselves in a semicircle around the guy to make sure that he was, in fact, down. He was bleeding profusely, so we figured he was no longer a threat. In fact, it was pretty obvious that he was dead.

Then I just sort of started backing away from the guy. I really didn't want to look at him. Plus I was thinking that I was a rookie officer, not even on duty, not even supposed to be involved in this crap. I was worried that maybe I was going to get in trouble—not for shooting the guy, because I had ample cause to shoot him—but because I might have violated some department policy by getting involved. At one point, I even thought that maybe I should just go back into Jack in the Box and act like nothing happened. But I knew I couldn't do that, so I just stuck around talking to the other guys, waiting for a supervisor to show up. We were talking about what had just happened, and then one of the guys asked me who I was and what I was doing there. I'd never met any of these guys because they worked a different beat. Everybody started laughing when I told them that I was a rookie working an extra job at the Jack in the Box. They thought it was pretty funny.

When the sergeant got there, I told him what I did. He thought how I got involved was pretty funny, too. Then the homicide detectives started showing up. They told me I had to go downtown and give a statement. I was really scared because I was still worried that I might get in trouble for getting involved, but when I gave my statement to the senior homicide detectives downtown, they thought it was comical how I got involved. Because of their response, I figured that there wasn't any problem with what I did, and that gave me a big sense of relief. I bounced it off my attorney when he showed up, and he told me not to worry about it. Several other people I talked to said the same thing. All those responses gave me a sense that I wasn't in any trouble, that what I did was OK.

The investigation determined that the guy I shot was a three-time loser. He had a substantial load of marijuana in the bed of the pickup; I don't remember how much, but it was all bricked up. A lot of pot. I guess he just didn't want to go back to prison.

The next guy I shot was a dope dealer, too. I was working Narcotics at the time. We went to serve a warrant on this apartment where the guys inside were known to be armed constantly. Every time the informant went over there, the guys came to the door with shotguns or pistols on them. They always pointed them at the informant. We got our briefing, went out, made our plan, and went to the staging area to stand by for the informant to go in and make a final attempt to buy dope. That way, he could tell us who all was in there, a last-minute update while surveillance was watching. He came back, told us what was up, and we went to go do it. The location was part of a four-plex apartment. It was an upstairs unit with one or two bedrooms. We didn't have a floor plan because the crooks would never let the informant past the front door. We knew the general floor plan of four-plexes in this area, and by looking at the windows and sewer vent pipes and things like that we had the general idea of where the different rooms were, but not the specifics. We knew there was at least two people inside, but not much more than that.

I was the point man on the entry team, and our plan was for me to slide to one side when I got to the top of the stairs, so the guys working the two-man ram could breach the door. They'd then step aside, and I'd be the first one through the door. The guys behind me would follow me in, and the ram guys would bring up the rear. We were moving up the stairs, whispering, walking slowly, trying not to be detected. But when we got right to the top, this older fat guy who didn't fit the description of any of the suspects came walking out on us. He turned out to be a taxicab driver who was in there scoring dope. Well, one of the breaching guys let go of his side of the ram and grabbed the cab-driver and pulled him out of the way. As he was doing this, I heard him yell, "Shotgun! Shotgun!" While it was probably not the best idea in the world, I just continued on like a normal entry 'cause the door was open. I entered the room, and the rest of the guys followed me in.

As I went in, I saw a guy running across the room away from me. He had something in his hands. The room was real dark, no lights on, so I couldn't get a real good look at the guy. But he was about twelve feet away when I spotted him, heading toward the kitchen. I kept moving along the wall perpendicular to the guy and screamed, "Police!" The guy started to spin around on me. I saw that what he was holding was a shotgun, so I fired.

The muzzle blast from my shotgun blinded me for a split second, and when I got my sight back, the guy was no longer there. I started scanning the room, looking for him, and I spotted a clump on the floor on the other side of the room. As I had come into the room initially, I had noticed someone else off to the left of the guy I ended up shooting. I thought that he might have a gun too, so I scanned left and saw him lying on the ground. Then I started scanning the rest of the room, looking for other suspects. One other guy from the team stepped in with me and started screaming, "Who shot, who shot?!" I said, "I did, I shot the guy over there." I pointed at him and started screaming, "He's got a shotgun! He's got a shotgun!" because he had fallen into the darkness, and I really couldn't see what he was doing at this point. I didn't know if I hit him, or if he was repositioning himself to return fire, I didn't know.

I positioned myself around to another part of the room, thinking that if this guy jumped up, I didn't want to be standing in the same place that he last saw me. As I positioned myself around to another part of the room, I was covering down on the clump and shouting directions. The other guys were flowing into the room now, so one of them went over and checked the guy to my left. He immediately hand-cuffed the guy and spotted a pistol underneath a nearby couch. Then he started working his way around the couch to the area where the suspect I shot was lying. I was continuing to cover down on the darkened blob over there when I started to hear him moan and groan. It sounded like he was hurt, but I wasn't sure that he wasn't bluffing. When the other officer got there, he prodded him a few times with his foot. As he was doing this, he told me that he didn't see a gun. I told him it was there, that I saw him holding a shotgun. He replied that he didn't see it. Then the guy I shot really started to moan and groan, almost screaming from pain.

I was worried that some of the guys might relax prematurely, so I kept saying the guy I shot had a gun. The officer over by the suspect I shot told one of the other guys to move over and cover down on the suspect. When this officer did so, the first one holstered his weapon, reached down with both hands, and rolled the guy over. He saw that the guy was bleeding pretty bad from a chest wound and that the shotgun had been lying right under the guy. He said, "OK, I see it, I see it. It's here, I got it." At that point, I felt somewhat safer, but I was still concerned about the possibility of additional suspects in the location. Some of the other officers went ahead and cuffed the guy. Then someone got on the radio and told dispatch we'd had an officer-involved shooting, that all officers were OK, but that we needed an ambulance for the suspect. After that, we continued to clear the rest of the location. We found a third suspect back in the kitchen hiding, but no one else.

We cuffed the third guy up, brought him into the living room, and stood by for the ambulance to help the guy I shot. He was still moaning and groaning. I really didn't think the guy was going to make it. It was an upper-right torso shot. He had a sucking chest wound, and blood was oozing out of his chest like nobody's business. He had a thick leather jacket on, it was wintertime, so we just bound the leather jacket up to make it a tight fit and cut down on the bleeding a little bit. Then just told the guy to hang on, that the ambulance was coming. He ended up surviving, but I still don't understand how. A full load of 00-buck from twelve feet away, I couldn't believe the guy made it.

While we were waiting for the ambulance, we started chatting about the deal. The other guys were saying they couldn't believe how fast it all happened. In fact, the third guy in the stack kept telling me, "Man, that gun went off so fast. You were no sooner in that room and, 'boom,' the shotgun went off." But it didn't seem fast to me at all. It seemed like forever. Like slow motion.

When I first went into the room and saw him moving away from me, I was just thinking, "Does he have a gun, does he have a gun? It looks like he's got a gun but I'm not sure." I mean, the ram guy said he had a shotgun, but I wasn't sure. As I moved away from the doorway and down that wall, I was aiming my shotgun at him. I took my finger from an index position and put it on the trigger, intending to shoot the guy if he did anything other than just continue to run away. I decided that if he spun around and I could confirm that what he was holding was a weapon, or if he did anything else in a threatening manner, I was going to shoot him. Well, when he spun around, I could see the perfect silhouette of a shotgun. Even though there wasn't much light in the room, I could clearly see the shotgun and both his hands against the white Sheetrock wall on the other side of the room from me. I could tell the shotgun had a pistol grip on it, that it was sawed off. I could see everything about it. He had his right hand back on the trigger and his left hand up on the foregrip. As he continued to bring it around, I was thinking, "That's a shotgun. Yeah, that's definitely a shotgun!" I thought that two or three times in probably less then a tenth of a second. Then I told myself, "Shoot! Shoot, damn it!" It just seemed like forever before my shotgun went off.

When the round went off, it sounded real soft, like a pop. It didn't hurt my ears at all. That seemed odd because I know that if I was standing on the range and fired a shotgun without ear protection, it would hurt my ears. I was in an enclosed room, so it should have been even louder and hurt even more. But it didn't.

Another thing that was weird was before I shot the guy, I was thinking that I couldn't believe what was happening. I couldn't believe this guy was turning on me with a gun. I mean, here is this whole Narcotics raid team in our raid jackets and whatnot, he's got to know that we are the police. Later on, I thought that maybe he didn't know we were cops. Maybe he thought we were drug dealers trying to rip him off. But at the time, I was thinking, "Why? Is this guy crazy? What's he doing? I've got the drop on him. He's running away from me, and now he's going to stop and engage me?" I just couldn't believe he was doing something that stupid.

I had similar thoughts when I was waiting for the ambulance. I was standing over him, looking down on him while some of the other guys lit him up with flashlights. He looked like he was a young kid. I was wondering if he was going to die. I was also thinking, "You stupid idiot, you did it to yourself." Because he looked so young, I was hoping he wouldn't die. But I still thought he was a stupid idiot for making me shoot him.

The last guy I shot also did something pretty stupid. I was working SWAT, and we got a call-up that came out of a home invasion robbery that went bad. These guys had done a series of capers in cahoots with another guy who provided home care for invalids. The caregiver would find wealthy elderly folk, and the other guys would go in and rob them. In this case, patrol got a call about a robbery at this one residence. When they got there, they surrounded the place. Well, the three robbers started running around inside, freaking out because the police were outside. While this was going on, the victim crawled out a window and escaped. Then two of the other crooks decide to surrender. The third crook, the worst, the leader of the gang, refused to give up. His last words to the other two before they surrendered were something to the effect that he was going to climb into the attic with his gun, that he was never going to surrender, that the cops were going to have to kill him, that he was going to take some cops with him, stuff like that. So the other two guys walked out, gave up to patrol, and told them what the third guy had said. By the time we got there, the standoff had been going on for thirty minutes to an hour.

So we set up and tried to talk the guy out. We tried the bullhorn, tried to call him on the phone, all that stuff. We got no response. After about four hours of this, the commander decided we needed to go in and get the guy. We decided not to use gas first because we didn't want to ruin the victim's house. It was a very large house, so we'd have to put oodles and oodles of gas in there to have any effect. Also, if the suspect was in the attic like he said, the ventilation would probably just send it out before it had any effect on the guy. We also didn't want to use gas because the masks would make it more difficult to operate in this big house; we were likely going to have to be in there for a long time, and those masks can get real uncomfortable.

My squad had the assault that day, so we did a covert entry from the door the suspects had gone in because that was the easiest point for us to sneak up to and not be observed from the house. I put Paul Riker at point and had Matt Johnson covering him. As team leader, I was in the third position, with Skip Patterson working rear guard. Then I pulled about four or five other team members to supplement my squad in order to hold a presence in each room as we cleared the house. Anyway, the clearing was pretty much uneventful. We'd clear a room, stop, leave one of the other guys in there, then move on to the next room.

We were working our way to the attic, because that's where the suspect's buddies told us he said he was going to be. But he could easily be anyplace in the house, so we wanted to clear everything before going into the attic. That way, we'd have a secure base for going up.

The house had two attic entries, one that we found fairly quickly. It had one of those spring doors with a ladder on it that you pull down. We just left it up, posted somebody on it, and went on with the clearance. After a while, we found the other attic entry, put somebody on it, and then finished clearing the house. It took us about an hour and a half to do all the rooms. We'd clear a room, stop, do a secondary search, put somebody in to hold it, then we'd go on again. After finishing off all the rooms, we felt confident that the living area was clear and that the suspect was, in fact, in the attic.

At that point, we stopped and took a break. We geared down for a little while to cool off. It was pretty hot in there because we had cut off the electricity when we were trying to talk him out, and we left it off because we wanted to be able to hear him walking around if he was moving while we were inside. We didn't want any AC noise to mask any movements. We also got a little something to eat because we'd been out since the wee hours of the morning. Nobody had eaten since the afternoon before, so we ordered in some breakfast. We were down a good forty-five minutes.

We just relaxed for a little while, kind of critiqued our initial clearing a little bit, but mostly just relaxed for a little while because we had been going real intense, real real intense, for an hour and a half to two hours. Even though we thought he was likely in the attic, we thought he could be downstairs. The downstairs clearing was intense because, based on what the other two guys had told us, we figured that if we found him downstairs, we were going to draw some fire. We knew that clearing the attic was going to be even more intense if we had to go up there, if he didn't give up, so we just took it easy for a while and had some breakfast.

When we got through eating, we knew it was time to get back to business. My team and I drew up a detailed plan for how we wanted to clear the attic. Then I went over and discussed it with two other team leaders, who were holding other areas in the house to see what they thought of the plan. They pretty much concurred, so we went to work.

First, we pulled open both attic doors, one at a time, just to see if we got any reaction. Then we gave some voice commands. You know, "Give up!" and all that. We got no reaction, so we flooded the attic with pole-mounted lights, one opening at a time. Then we stopped and tried some more voice commands. Then we pushed up the big pole-mounted mirrors to look around from below. It was a real large attic with blown insulation throughout. Lots of obstructions too. A lot of cross braces, a lot of air-conditioning ducts, a lot of piping, hot water heaters, stuff like that. It was also real cluttered with boxes and storage stuff. We inched up the ladders, moving more lights up and looking around with the mirrors. Once we cleared from both openings as much as we could with the mirrors, I used the SWAT-cam to make sure we hadn't missed anything. All along, we gave voice commands. Just worked real methodical, step-by-step, trying to get a reaction from him at some point.

We never got any response, so we had to go into the attic. I stayed at the foot of the ladder and sent my point and cover guys up the ladder back-to-back, one step at a time, pistols in front of them. That way, they could cover each other. It was a real small opening, and they didn't feel comfortable taking shields up there. We had talked about using shields, but they didn't feel like they could maneuver well on the rickety ladder with the added bulk. I was a little concerned that they didn't want to use shields, but I didn't want to force them. My thinking was that the shields would only protect them from one angle of fire, but they were going into a 360-degree threat area. If I made them use shields and they took a round from an unprotected angle, I'd feel bad because I told them to use the shields. They were experienced guys, so I decided that if they felt more comfortable going up without shields, I was going to let them.

As they were going up the ladder, I was fully expecting to hear gunfire. I even thought that I might be watching one of them die pretty soon. I was pretty nervous. Pretty nervous. I was shaking a little bit. I was really worried about Paul and Matt. I thought that one of them might take a head shot as soon as they poked their heads above the entrance, that I might possibly see one of their heads explode right above me. I was also really busy mentally, trying to make sure I'd covered all the possibilities; running back over everything in my mind to make sure that I hadn't forgotten anything.

Fortunately, they got up with no problems. I went up behind them, and the three of us took up positions in a sort of semicircle facing the big part of the attic. Then I had the guys at the other opening reposition their lights a little bit, so we could see different areas of the attic a little bit better. Both Paul and Matt spotted areas that they thought the suspect might be hiding in. They both identified large mounds of blown insulation that were big enough for a body to be underneath. I figured he could be almost anywhere, with all the obstructions up there, but I was especially concerned about those insulation piles. When I looked at the mound Matt had spotted, I saw the tip of a boot sticking out. I figured that was him, but I was also worried because that's an old trick we used to pull in training. We'd take some shoes and place them so that just the tips were sticking out to sucker the guys searching into a trap. So I was concerned that the shoes could be a trap, and I was still concerned with the rest of the attic.

I decided to address the insulation mound with the shoe sticking out first. I told my rear guard to come up and cover our backside when we moved toward the pile with the shoe. It was about thirty feet away from the opening, almost at the other side of the attic. We moved up to within about fifteen or twenty feet from the mound. From there, it definitely looked like someone was hiding under that pile. We stopped so that if the guy's feet were twelve o'clock, I was in the two o'clock position, Matt was at straight-up twelve, and Paul was at about eleven o'clock. We all had our weapons with the lights on pointed at the mound.

Matt started to try voice contact. We knew the suspect's name was Larry, so Matt was trying to talk to the guy. He said stuff like, "Come on, Larry, give it up. Give it up, Larry. We see you there. We know you're there. Come on, nobody's hurt. Just show us your hands, OK?" No response. So now I started thinking that maybe the guy's dead. Maybe he covered himself up and shot himself. Some of the things we've heard about him in our intelligence portion of the operation indicated that he might be suicidal. Matt just kept trying to get the guy to respond, "Come on, Larry, give it up, man," and so forth. This went on for about forty-two, forty-three seconds. We found the time out later when we listened to the audiotapes we keep of our SWAT operations.

Then, all of a sudden, the mound moved and the guy popped up holding a shiny, semiautomatic pistol in his right hand. It looked to be a .40 or a .45. I wasn't sure, but I could tell it was bigger than a 9 millimeter. The light was glistening off it. I could tell it was a stainless, because it wasn't shiny enough to be chrome. When he popped up, it surprised the hell out of me. I had relaxed a little bit because I figured he was going to give up. I mean, he didn't have anywhere to go and he knew we were the SWAT team. In fact, that was the first time in all my years in SWAT that when I had the drop on a guy like that, he didn't give up. They always gave up. I never had one stand and fight. I couldn't believe it was happening.

Even though I had relaxed a little bit, I was on my weapon. I had my M-16 shouldered, with the barrel aimed right at the mound where I thought his torso would be. As he came up, all I had to do was raise my sight picture a little bit and I was right on him.

All three of us fired at the same time. I could hear Paul and Matt's rounds going off, but it wasn't that loud. That kind of gunfire in that closed-in environment—especially my M-16, with no ear protection on—should have hurt my ears tremendously. But I never felt any pain sensation in my ears. It should have been really, really loud, but it was pretty soft.

I couldn't tell if the suspect fired, because it was fairly dark right where we were, and the muzzle blasts from my weapon got in the way of my seeing. But in between the blasts, I could still see him there. He was sort of flopping around a little bit. I was on semiauto, riding the dot on my optical sights, just cranking rounds off at the guy's chest. I was going to shoot until I didn't see him anymore, but he never disappeared from view. After a few rounds, I still saw him in my sights. Something told me this guy's got to be done; there's no way he could still be a threat. I knew Paul and Matt were shooting, too, and we were all too close to be missing. Even if the guy was wearing body armor, I figured he had to be done; the .223 rounds from my gun would punch right through. So even though he was still in my sights, which I'd normally take to mean he still presented a threat, I just quit shooting.

When I stopped firing, I realized what was going on. The guy was propped up by one of the rafter boards. He was over near one of the eaves, so there wasn't much room overhead. When he sat up and pointed the gun at us, our shots knocked his upper body sideways a little bit to where his shoulder was sort of wedged against one of the rafters. It was holding him up, so he couldn't fall back. That's why he was still in my sight picture. He couldn't go down. When we quit shooting, there was nothing to hold him against the rafter, and he fell back down into the insulation.

Paul and Matt stopped shooting just about the same time I did. I think Paul was the last to stop, because it turned out he ended up firing the most rounds. He fired ten. I thought I fired three or four, but it turned out I fired six. Matt fired five. All twenty-one rounds hit the guy. Because I was off to his right side a little bit, my rounds caught him on his right side. Some of them hit his right arm first, tore it up quite a bit before passing into his chest. Matt stacked his rounds on top of each other, right in the guy's ten-ring. Paul's rounds were spread out a bit more on the left side of the guy's body.

I saw how bad the guy was shot up when I moved up to check him out. When he fell back into the insulation, his hands disappeared from view, and I didn't see the gun anywhere. I could tell he was still alive because he was moving one of his arms a little bit and his body was kind of twitching and rolling a little. I also heard him moan once or twice. I told Paul and Matt to stand by and cover me. I moved from the two o'clock position I'd been in to about four or five o'clock. That way, if he was still a threat, I'd be coming at him from a different angle than the one he'd first seen me at. When I approached him, I could see just how badly he was shot. I saw lots of blood, lung matter, and things like that all over the place.

He was still moving a little bit, and Paul said, "Watch him, watch him. He's moving, he's moving." I was being real careful checking him out because his hands were hidden and I couldn't see the gun. I wanted to find that gun, so I reached down into the insulation and started scooping around for it. No pistol, but I found his right hand. It had a glove on it. Then I noticed some bone coming out of his arm where some of my rounds hit on their way to his torso. Then I swooped down again and found his other hand. It was gloved, too. But still no weapon. I scooped around a little bit more looking for the gun. As I moved a little insulation aside, I saw a huge gaping hole in the center of his chest where Matt had stacked his rounds.

When I saw that, I knew the guy wasn't going to make it. In fact, I was amazed that he was still alive. Because he was so shot up, I wasn't worried about the gun anymore. I started thinking about all the procedural stuff we needed to do. The guy was definitely down. He was clearly no longer a threat. We just needed to protect the scene and make some notifications. I had gotten on the radio after the initial gunfire and told the CP that shots had been fired, that the suspect was down, that all officers were OK. They said that's clear, and then I told them to stand by, that we still needed to secure the guy. So after I was done checking him out, I got back on the radio and told them we needed an ambulance, we needed a paramedic to come up and check on the suspect. I also told them to get Homicide rolling. I sent both Matt and Paul downstairs to gear down and relax, but I stayed right there because I wanted to make sure that the scene wasn't tampered with. The EMTs came up, looked at how badly he was shot up, took his pulse, didn't find one, and said he was DOA.

Then the supervisors came up. I ran it down to them real quick. They didn't go up to his body and really look around; they just kind of studied at a distance as I described to them what happened. One or two of the other team leaders also came up and once again at a distance looked things over while I described where we were and what happened. They asked me if I needed anything, and when I told them no, they took off.

About fifteen minutes or so later, Homicide showed up. I gave the detectives a quick rundown and then left to head downtown to give my statement. After they had done all their photos and other prep work, they rolled the guy over and found the gun lying underneath him. They couldn't determine if he got any rounds off at us. The gun had been fired recently, it had rounds in the clip and one in the chamber, but they couldn't tell whether he fired it up in the attic. They never found any casings, but they could have been lost in all that insulation. I don't even think they found all of our brass. So we'll never know if he shot at us.

But I remember wondering about that while I was up in the attic by myself after the other SWAT guys left and I was waiting for Homicide to show up. I went over the whole thing in my mind several times, just playing it back over and over. I could see that gun coming up, me just riding the dot as I fired, the whole thing. I still couldn't believe the guy did what he did. I just couldn't believe he did something that stupid. He was in such a compromising position. The only thing I could figure is that it was suicide-by-cop. I was thinking that he was hoping we'd miss him in the search and that he'd get away later but that if we found him, he wasn't going back to jail.

So I was thinking about a lot of stuff up there in the attic, waiting for Homicide to show up. It was kind of eerie, knowing that I had just helped kill this guy. I was just standing there thinking all this stuff, my weapon at a low ready, his body lying over there. It was a little weird. Just me and him up in that attic.

Same Shooting, Different Views

As the foregoing story indicates, both of the other SWAT officers in the attic with the busy cop also shot the suicidal robber. This section presents their stories and thereby provides the reader with the second look in this book at how different officers experience the same shooting incident.

—∿∿—

I was working the number-two position on Randy's team, so I was covering the point man as we cleared the house, room by room. It was pretty much a regular deal, no different from any of the other deliberate clearings I'd done over the years, so I don't recall any particular thoughts I had as we moved along. But I do remember being a bit apprehensive as Matt and I got ready to go into that attic. Adrenaline started pumping a little bit 'cause I knew that the guy had to be up there. Even though we had mirrored it and we used the SWAT-cam to look around, we didn't spot him, so it was still dangerous. The guy had said that he wasn't gonna be taken alive, so I was thinking that he might start shooting as we went up there. Since I didn't want me or Matt to get shot in the head, we were real careful.

After we did the pole-cam, Matt and I popped ourselves up real quick a time or two—did a couple of quick peeks into the attic—then we eased on up. We worked our way up the stairs back-to-back. Matt was looking one way. I was looking the other. That way, we had a visual on the whole attic—kind of 180 degrees one way, and 180 the other. Randy was below us, looking through the pole-cam and kind of directing us. I felt pretty good because I had Matt behind me, and with the light on my gun I had a good view of my part of the attic. But I was still a little bit nervous.

Once we got all the way up, Matt and I just sort of scanned the two sides of the attic until Randy got up there. Then we started looking around real thoroughly. I saw some insulation stacked up in my half, so I eased over that direction a bit. Then I heard the other guys say, "He's over here."

I said, "Are you sure?"

They said, "Yeah, we see his boots, and the insulation's moving." So, in other words, they could see him breathing.

So I turned around.

I could see a pile of insulation over near the eaves, and I could see the guy's feet in front of it. I knew that he was underneath there 'cause I could see the insulation rising and falling as he breathed. Then we eased ourselves into positions closer to where he was—Randy up around his right side, me down around his right foot, and Matt kind of off of his left foot—and at that point I relaxed, 'cause I figured he was gonna give up. I felt real confident because everything was in our favor: there were three of us, we all had light-mounted weapons so we had the light in our favor, plus we had all our training. It was the three of us against one; we had the advantage. So I thought, "He's gonna give up." But he didn't.

Matt started giving the commands, but the guy didn't react. Then he just popped up. All I remember seeing at that point was the gun. Before he popped up, I could see Randy and Matt off to my side, but when he came up, my field of vision shrunk to about two feet, and all I saw was the gun. I saw the barrel, then the frame, then I saw a hand holding it. And then, for just a millisecond—at least I think it happened then, but it might have happened right after it was over—I thought, "That looks like Randy's .45." Randy carries a .45 Smith & Wesson stainless, and the gun the guy had looked just like it. As it turned out, the guy's gun *was* a Smith & Wesson stainless. But it was a 10 millimeter, not a .45. Still, it did look just like Randy's gun.

Like I said, I don't remember whether I had the thought about Randy's gun in that blurb of time or if I thought of it immediately after the shooting was over, but I identified the gun right away. And that's when I started shooting. I didn't make a conscious decision; I just reacted to the gun. It was like, "Here it is, time to shoot." I don't remember how many times I pulled the trigger or how long I was firing, but it turns out I got off ten rounds in about a second and a half. Then it was over.

A lot happened in that second and a half. The first thing I remember is firing toward that gun. Then, for a split second, I could see the guy's head. I had this thought—but just like the thought about the gun, I don't remember if I thought it then or if I thought it later—"He's still wearing a mask." Then he disappeared, and I think I held up for just a millisecond, like I was gonna get back on target, and then something kicked up in front of my face. I didn't know what it was, but I fired at that also. Then I stopped when I didn't see any more movement.

Later on, I found out it was his foot that had popped up after his face disappeared, 'cause it turns out that I put a round through the bottom of his foot, and that's the only way I could have done that. He fell over backwards when the first rounds hit him, and I guess his foot just came up as a natural reaction to that. I just saw the movement after that millisecond of hesitation, and I thought he was still in combat with us. So I just kept firing even though I didn't recognize what it was that flashed in front of me.

I never used my sights. I knew I had 'em lined up on him, but I was point shooting. I never saw the flash of my gun as I was firing because I had the light on and Matt and Randy had their lights on, so it was quite bright up there. The way I saw what I saw was kinda different though, because I don't remember any motion. It was more like blurbs of vision, like snapshots: there's the gun. Then there he is. Then he's gone. Then there's something in front of me. Then it's gone. And it was over. It was so fast, but as I remember, later on it seemed like it came, "Pop, pop, pop, pop." I saw this, I saw this, I saw this, I saw this, and then it was over.

Also I didn't really hear any of the rounds go off. All I could hear was little pops. In fact, I didn't even know Randy and Matt were shooting. I should have heard 'em, especially the M-16. I mean Randy fired several times, and if I'd been on the firing line, I'd have been deaf from all that noise. But all I heard was some pops.

Once we quit firing, things returned to normal. I started talking to Randy, and I started to look around and breathe again. Breathe and scan, to check and see if Matt had been shooting or if he was shot. Then I looked over to Randy to see if he'd been shooting or was shot. So it was just a matter of looking around and talking, and things got back to normal.

Randy wanted to approach the guy, and I told him to be careful because I couldn't see the gun. I could just barely see his face sticking up, and I even thought about shooting him again, just to make sure he didn't pop up again. I wasn't sure if we'd hit him or not, 'cause I couldn't see him, and I didn't want him to try to kill us again. So we had a little conversation about being careful as we approached him. When Randy got there, it was clear the guy was DOA. From there, we just notified the CP about what happened and waited for Homicide to show up.

I was a little bit concerned until they got there and did their investigation because we couldn't see the gun when we moved up on the guy. We kind of looked initially, but we didn't want to disturb the scene, so we stopped. Then I said to myself, "That was a gun, wasn't it?" I mean, we had blasted him and then the gun disappeared. I wasn't really worried that I made a mistake, but I always second-guess myself. I knew it was a gun. I mean, I identified it in my head. It looked just like Randy's gun, but then, it wasn't there. Homicide found it kind of underneath him. I guess it fell out of his hand, and then he fell back on top of it. I knew it was up there somewhere. But my initial thought when we couldn't find it was, "Gosh, I hope that was a gun."

I know Randy was a little bit nervous about sending Paul and me up into that attic. But I wasn't worried. When I first heard the guy wasn't gonna give up, that he planned to take a couple of us with him, I figured it wasn't going to be any different than any other barricaded-subject call-up. Just same ole, same ole. In fact, I was looking forward to going in to find him. It's like a hunt-or-be-hunted type of deal. You need to think of what he's doing, think like he's thinking, listen carefully, and pay attention to your nose. A lot of times when we go into a room where suspects are hiding, I can smell these guys. Their adrenaline's going, they're sweating, so if you're paying attention, you can smell 'em. You know what each room in the location smells like, and all of a sudden you go in, and something smells different. Well, the guy's probably in there. You gotta think of all the potential hiding places, because by the time SWAT gets there, the bad guys have usually had a lot of time to hide. Now in this case, we knew the guy was around six foot, 230, so we could rule out some of the smaller places—like tiny cupboards—but we still had to look at all the potential threats. So my mind was not on fear at all. That was the last thing in it. It was on all my training, all my intuition, just doing my job and thinking, "Where is this son of a bitch? Where's he at?"

Because we had cleared the rest of the house, I knew he had to be in the attic. We did all the stuff with lights, mirrors, the SWAT-cam. We didn't spot him, so up we went. I was facing the stairs, and Paul—my cover man at the time—was up against my back, and we started coming up real easy. I had a Beretta with a light mount on it, a 92F. Paul had his .40-cal. H&K. We couldn't take shoulder weapons up because it was so tight in that entrance. So up we went, Paul and me back-to-back.

Because we'd gotten a good look around with the mirrors and that SWAT-cam, we had a pretty good idea of what to expect. My main concern was the AC unit up there, because we couldn't get a view of all four sides from down below. I was also concerned that he might be buried under some of the blown-in insulation. I looked around when our heads cleared the opening and spotted a lump that didn't fit with the rest of the insulation. I don't know if it was my hunting background or what, but it just didn't look right. So I leaned over above Paul, still keeping eyes on the lump and said, "Paul, I got a lump over here." He said, "Well, I got a lump too." So now I was thinking maybe I could be wrong about the guy being there. I took a quick peek over at what Paul spotted. You couldn't fit a tennis shoe in that lump. So I told him, "My lump is better than your lump." He turned, looked at my lump, and said something like, "Oh, you're right." Then I looked at my lump more carefully, and I saw this black tennis shoe sticking out of the insulation. We found him.

Randy came up about then, and he sent Sam, the rear guard, to get some more lights and a shield. The three of us moved up on the lump. I was almost straight in line with the bottom of the shoe, Paul was off to my right a bit, and Randy was a little bit further to my left. We all had our guns pointed at the lump, Paul and I with our pistols, and Randy with his M-16. We all had lights on our weapons, so we had the lump lit up pretty good. I looked to Randy, Randy nodded to me, and I start talking to the guy. "Larry, we know you're under the insulation. We can see you." Stuff like that. We've learned over the years that when some of these guys hide, they think they're invisible. Just like an ostrich sticking it's head in the sand. Unless you tell them exactly where they're at, what they're doing, what they're wearing, they won't respond, because they just tell themselves that we don't really see them. So I was trying to let Larry know that we knew exactly where he was: "We see you. We need to see your hands." That type stuff. But I got no response. Nothing at all. I didn't like the fact that he wasn't responding. The jig was up. It was over. He had no place to go. He had to know I wasn't by myself up there. He must've heard us whispering and stuff. He had no advantage if he came up shooting. I was thinking that we had him but still was concerned that he was not reacting. So I started talking again. "Larry, we need to see your hands."

I saw the insulation move a little bit. Then, all of a sudden—like a vampire in an old, cheap B movie coming up out of the coffin—Larry sat straight up. When he sat up, he punched out with his right hand this big stainless steel semiautomatic pistol. The barrel looked as big as a basketball hoop. When he popped up, my vision went "voomp," focused in on that barrel. I could see the guy behind the gun, but he looked sort of fuzzy, while the gun was in crystal-clear focus. It was like a photo where the foreground is clear and the background is blurry. When I got that focus, it was like a flag dropped in my mind, a green light went on, some signal telling me, "Threat, threat, threat! It's time to shoot!" I don't remember making a decision to pull the trigger. I just reacted. I was shooting.

I didn't even know that Randy and Paul were shooting until I stopped and heard a couple more rounds go off. The guy fell back into the insulation, then everything stopped, the three of us just looking, waiting, waiting for something to happen. Nothing happened, no movement in the insulation, so we moved up a little bit. Real carefully. When we got closer, I could see him doing the old death rattle. But all I was thinking about was the gun; where's that gun? I wanted to know where that gun was. I didn't care that he was death rattling. That doesn't mean he couldn't come back up and shoot. When Randy brushed some insulation away, I could see that his rounds had just disintegrated the guy's right arm. It was laying almost like a snake, with bone sticking out. His torso was peppered. Holes everywhere. I could tell the guy was on his last legs. He did the death twitch and rattle a little bit more. Then, maybe five, ten seconds later, he shut down.

The shooting part of it went real quick. Before I fired, it seemed like it took a long time for my gun to go off. I knew I needed to shoot when that flag dropped in my mind, but it seemed like that first trigger pull went real slow. My mind was saying, "Hurry, hurry, go, go, go!" I know it takes about a half a second to react to something you see, but it sure felt a lot longer than that for that first round to go off. After that first round though, the rest came real fast: "Boom, boom, boom, boom, boom!" and it was over. It happened so fast, in fact, that I didn't even know I'd fired five rounds. I thought I shot three, maybe four rounds, so I was surprised when I counted the rounds in my gun afterwards and found fifteen in my twenty-round magazine. Another thing that was weird was that the gunfire wasn't loud at all. Just popping. It sounded pretty soft when I was shooting. Then, when I stopped, I just assumed the other two rounds I heard were from Paul because they didn't sound like the M-16. I figured Randy wasn't shooting because that M-16 puts out a good loud sound, and it was just, "Pop, pop." That's all I could hear. Plus my ears weren't ringing at all afterwards. So that was sort of interesting.

But the thing I remember most is how fast the shooting happened once I got the first round off. I started shooting, then—just like that—it was over.

—∾—

The closing words of the officer we just heard from—while quite compelling—are somewhat misleading. Shootings aren't really "over" for officers when they cease firing, for after the smoke clears, officers have to deal with the consequences of their actions. And this, as noted at the outset of the book, can be a difficult process. This is the topic of the final chapter, which completes our trip *Into the Kill Zone.*

CHAPTER FIVE

When the Smoke Clears

T he men and women who shared their stories with me had a variety of responses in the wake of their shootings. Some experienced no problems, a few viewed what happened in a positive light, but most endured at least some sort of psychological, emotional, or physical discomfort at some point, and some suffered extremely severe negative reactions, such as depression and suicidal despair.

The previous chapter provided a glimpse of the sorts of negative reactions that officers can experience in the immediate aftermath of shootings. The remorse of the new mother who shot an unarmed robber, the tears shed by the SWAT officer who shot the gun-toting arms merchant, and the worry about whether he'd done the right thing expressed by the rookie whose shooting led to a riot, all demonstrate the sorts of short-term discomfort that officers can feel. How officers react immediately following shootings is only part of the picture, however, for it can take quite some time for the personal repercussions of these violent events to play themselves out. And officers' responses following shootings involve more than just reactions to the incident in which they fired.

Police shootings are social events that engender reactions among various individuals and entities besides the people involved directly in them. Both the agency that employs the officer and other elements of the criminal justice system mobilize to investigate the shooting in order to establish whether the officer's use of deadly force conformed with law and department policy. Police shootings almost always generate some sort of press coverage because the personal drama of individuals locked in poten-tially mortal combat and the social drama of the clash between state authority and individual liberty that they involve make them inherently newsworthy. Shootings also generate a good deal of interest among the peers and supervisors of the involved offi-cers, so it is not uncommon for other officers to seek shooters out to hear from the horse's mouth what happened and to offer commentary on the incident.

In a similar vein, officers' parents, spouses, children, other relatives, boyfriends-girlfriends, and other close acquaintances can be curious and concerned about what transpired. On the opposite side of the personal-interest coin, the friends and family of suspects (as well as suspects themselves, if they survive) can become part of the post-shooting landscape through a variety of means, such as seeking officers out, court appearances, or simple chance encounters. Finally, because shootings are public spec-tacles, members of the public at large sometimes get into the act.

The ways the justice system, the press, officers' families, and other third parties react to shooting incidents can exert their own effects on officers following shootings. Support can buoy officers, for example, and a lack of it can leave them floundering. Similarly, positive comments can build officers up, and negative ones can drag them down. And so on. Because the social reactions spawned by shootings can affect offi-cers, it is not possible to understand officers' experiences in the wake of shootings apart from the reactions that others have to them. Knowing this, I spent a good deal of time talking to the officers I interviewed about their post-shooting reactions, how various third parties responded to their shootings, and the intersection between the two.

The officers I interviewed went through a variety of experiences following their shootings and had a broad range of post-shooting reactions—from extreme delight that they had survived a potentially fatal event to abject despair that they had killed someone. Within this range, there was a strong tendency for officers to suffer some notable short-term disruption, which dissipated markedly as time passed. The stories in this chapter present a representative slice of how officers are treated and how they react in the wake of shootings.

Most of them come from officers we have already heard from, but some are fresh voices. Readers will be able to link some of the stories in this chapter with those in the last, as it is apparent in some cases that a particular story here comes from a particu-lar officer that we heard from there. In order to protect officers' privacy, however, there is no clear link between most of the stories in this chapter and those in previous ones. Another step that I sometimes took to protect officers' identity was to break their post-shooting stories into pieces and place them in different sections of the chapter. So the post-shooting experiences of single officers are sometimes spread across multiple sections of the chapter.

In sum, this chapter is structured to provide maximum insight into what happens to police officers following shootings, while protecting the privacy of the men and women who so graciously shared their experiences with me. The stories begin with a section that focuses on officers' experiences with the way the justice system deals with officer-involved shootings.

Lawyers, Guns, and Justice

One of the first social reactions to officer-involved shootings is an official investigation into the incident, which begins as soon as the scene has been secured. These investigations—conducted by detectives from the officer's own department, other police agencies, or both—are major undertakings that follow the same basic protocols that are involved in the investigation of major crimes. The detectives collect physical evidence, obtain statements from relevant parties (including the involved officers), and undertake the numerous other investigative steps they would take in any significant case. The information that is developed during these investigations is then used in a pair of formal inquiries that consider the appropriateness of the shots that officers fired.

First, the police department that employs the officer who fired conducts an inquiry to determine whether the shots were within the scope of department policy on the use of deadly force. Some departments have supervisory or command officers make individual determinations about the shooting, whereas others convene special panels (known generically as *shooting review boards*) to pass collective judgment on the officers who fired. Whatever protocol an agency employs, nearly all shootings are found to be "within policy," so officers are rarely disciplined by their departments for shooting someone.

The second review is a criminal inquiry to determine the legality of officers' actions vis-à-vis state law regarding the use of deadly force by police officers. These inquiries are generally handled by the prosecutor's office in the county in which the shooting occurred and often include a grand jury or coroner's inquest. Whatever procedures a given jurisdiction might employ to review the legality of shootings, criminal inquiries nearly always find that the police acted within the scope of the relevant law, so officers rarely face criminal charges for the actions they take during shooting incidents.

Whatever local legal authorities decide about whether a given shooting was within the bounds of state law, federal authorities have the power to conduct a separate criminal inquiry to examine whether the officers who fired violated federal civil rights laws that govern police conduct. Unlike the legal review of officer-involved shootings that occurs at the local level, however, federal criminal inquiries are not routine. The federal government opens formal probes in just a small fraction of the police shootings that occur in the nation each year. These queries almost always clear the involved officer(s), so federal prosecutions in the wake of police shootings are extremely rare.[1]

Even though officers are rarely administratively sanctioned, prosecuted, or punished for shooting someone, the prospect that they might be looms large in many officers' minds. And there is one other sort of inquiry that makes many officers wary: civil litigation. Suspects who survive their wounds and the estates of dead ones can file civil lawsuits asserting that the shooting was not justified and demanding damages for the injuries they suffered. Such suits can be filed in federal court, state court, or both and can level a variety of allegations against police officers and their departments. There is no national database on these sorts of lawsuits, so it is not possible to say with any precision how frequently suits are filed in the wake of shootings. What is known is that they are filed frequently enough to support a cottage industry of lawyers and expert witnesses who specialize in litigation against police officers and departments.[2]

The final piece of the justice system's response to police shootings pertains only to cases in which suspects survive the incident. When suspects survive their wounds, prosecutors will review the incident to determine what criminal charges should be brought against them. In a case in which the police shoot an armed robber who fired upon officers while fleeing the scene of the crime, for example, the suspect might be charged with both attempted murder for attacking officers and robbery for the initial crime. Unless the suspect pleads guilty (or in the rare case in which the suspect is not charged with any crimes), a criminal trial ensues, during which the shooting officer usually testifies as a witness for the prosecution.

The previous chapter included a bit of information about the investigations that follow shootings (in the form of officers' reports about things such as handing their guns over to supervisors and heading to the Homicide office to give their statements to detectives) and the concern that officers can feel about the inquiries that follow (for example, the rookie who was worried that the gun the suspect used to shoot at him and his partner had gone missing). The stories in this section flesh out the picture of shooting investigations, the various inquiries that can follow, and how officers respond as these aspects of the social reaction to their shootings are played out.

And they do much more. They also show how factors besides post-shooting inquiries can play critical roles in framing officers' experiences and reactions in the wake of shootings. Most prominent among these factors are race and religion.

Police officers, like all people everywhere, tend to draw upon what ever religious faith they have during trying times, especially those involving injury or death. Thus do many officers call upon their religious faith to help them deal with their shootings. But religion can cut both ways in the wake of shootings. Because all faiths have some variant of the biblical admonition that we should not harm other humans, religious officers must make peace with what they did in terms of the teachings of their faith about the sanctity of human life.

Where race goes, the previously discussed historical tensions between the police and minority communities over the use of deadly force can translate into a source of personal difficulty for officers who shoot black suspects because they may be accused of having shot based on racial animus.

This chapter contains several stories that provide the reader with some notion of how race can become an issue following shootings and the sorts of responses officers can have to it. But the stories do more than that; they also shed light on the role that race plays in deadly force decision making, as well as police perspectives on the role that race plays in law enforcement more generally. Stories that touch on race are interspersed throughout many of the sections of this chapter. They begin in this first one for the simple reason that racial concerns often arise during the investigations and inquiries that follow shootings.

—⁘—

The supervisors took our guns from us at the scene, then put us in a room, and cleaned us up a little bit because we had some blood on us. I think the first thing I did was take my gun belts off, then I took my T-shirt off, and I got some tears in my eyes. I was scared. The fear started right after I stopped shooting. I was worried for two reasons. First of all, I'd never killed anybody before, never shot anybody before, and I was thinking, "God, I lost my job." I wasn't sure how the administration was going to react because officers in my department hadn't killed anybody in a long time, and the last one was a bad shooting.

The other reason I was scared was that this was a black guy. I was worried that all the black people were gonna say was, "White cop kills black man." That went through my mind. It didn't matter that he had a gun; just, "White cop kills black man." So I was worried that there would be some community outcry and that I would be accused of shooting someone who didn't need to be shot. I was worried that the department would use me as a scapegoat, that I would lose my job for political reasons. I was also scared for my family because I was worried about what people were gonna think of them. I live in this diverse neighborhood, and my kids were going to the elementary school there. I was really worried about a racial issue coming out of the shooting, and I wondered what would happen to my kids in school if it did. I was probably more worried about them than I was me.

Everything worked out. The department's review came back that we'd done exactly what we were supposed to do, and there were never any problems on the racial angle. But I was sure worried about that stuff for a while.

—⁘—

I never really had a problem with shooting the guy—I mean he was holding a gun, trying to chamber a round when I shot him—but I was a little worried at first about how the department was going to handle it. The department has a reputation for dropping guys over shootings, and one of our snipers had shot a guy just a few weeks before my shooting, so I was worried that the investigation was going to uncover some technicality, like the date or the address typed on the warrant was wrong, and that the city was gonna use that as an excuse to try to distance itself from me. Some of this came from the fact that some of our supervisors were real indifferent after the shooting. It was like, "Oh, we had a shooting. There could be some liability. We don't want to know anything about it, don't want to have to testify." So I had some concerns about that kind of stuff early on. Then I went to the grand jury. They asked me a few questions, and I told 'em what happened. They came back four hours later and told me they didn't have any problems with the shooting. At that point, I felt like it was over, and my concerns about the city disappeared.

The one other thing I did feel was some regret that the guy I shot was injured, but he made the choice to go for his gun. I would've rather taken him down without him being injured, but I also look at it that he didn't die, that he didn't make me kill him. I don't know for sure that I would have felt any different if I had killed the guy, but I'd rather not kill someone. I think that's because of my religious upbringing, the "thou shalt not kill" type stuff. So if I got a choice between killing and not killing somebody, I don't want to kill 'em. If I have a choice between hurting somebody and not hurting 'em, I don't want to hurt 'em. But at the same time, I'm not gonna be hurting, so I did what I had to do. But I wish it hadn't happened.

―――∿―――

The guy I shot robbed a bank and pointed a gun at me as he was trying to get away, but I was still a little fearful of the legal stuff with the grand jury. I knew that I had done the right thing, but I didn't know what to expect in a grand jury. I didn't want to lose my job because the grand jury decided I wasn't justified in shooting. I had thoughts that this could ruin my career. I guess I was just worried somebody there might have the thought that this was not justified. I just had that fear. It turns out I didn't even have to go in and testify. They "no billed" me without me having to go in and talk. Got there with my attorney, sat there for twenty to thirty minutes, then the DA came out and said there was no need for me to go in. I guess it helped that there were a lot of people who saw what happened. They didn't need to have me tell it.

I felt really relieved when I got the no bill. That thought and fear of legal problems went away. Now I still had in my mind that there could be a civil problem. People can always sue. But I was like, "I got this no bill here, and I know it's right and everybody else knows it's right, and if there was gonna come a civil suit, I could handle it. I can go through that if I have to." But I knew I was gonna keep my job.

―⁓―

I was worried about getting sued. I wasn't so much concerned about the criminal part of it. I knew we were clear there. I mean, he shot the two of us. It's just that I'd heard a lot of horror stories coming out of California, where officers get sued after they shoot some guy who shoots them. I realized this wasn't California, but it still put me on edge, wondering if I was going to have to go through the civil stuff, wondering what happens if the judge favors this guy I shot. But all those thoughts ended when the criminal case got rolling. The guy had hired a pretty good law firm to handle his case, but they sent this first-year attorney, fresh out of law school, to handle some pretrial, look-at-the-evidence-type hearing. Well, the guy ended up confessing on the stand, and his attorney didn't stop him. The DA couldn't believe it. She was like, "So you intentionally shot Officers Dotson and Morales?" He replied, "Yeah, I shot them. I wanted to get away from them. I was going to kill their ass if they didn't let me go." So out the door went the civil process, and I breathed a sigh of relief. We never got sued, and I wondered what happened to that first-year lawyer. After he screwed that up, I'm sure he got fired.

―⁓―

The only thing that bothered me about the whole deal was the guy's trial. First off, I couldn't believe it when I got the subpoena. I figured the guy was dead. Turns out that the round I put in his abdomen didn't do too much damage, but the one that I hit him in the face with did. It entered alongside his nose, hit the bone at the base of his eye, ricocheted upward, ricocheted back down off of the frontal part of his skull, stayed under the skin, and went around and lodged alongside his spinal cord. He was paralyzed and comatose for about six weeks afterward, blood pressure up and down, real bad condition. They really didn't expect him to survive, and then he pulled through. He decided not to plead guilty, so we had to go to trial.

Initially, he was charged with aggravated assault for what he did before we got there and then attempted murder on a police officer for attacking me, but they reduced that one to an aggravated assault with great bodily injury. That really pissed me off, because he was sure as hell trying to kill me when I shot him. Then his wife got up to testify, and she lied through her teeth. She perjured herself and said that he never attempted to attack her with a knife, that he never cut any police officers, that he was a good man who held a job, and all sorts of other baloney. I couldn't believe what I was hearing. I was steamed. It was like so many other family disputes where the couple is all in love again the day after some horrendous melee. She went on about what a great father he was, how he might have had a beer or two that night, but he never even had a knife in his hand. I couldn't believe it.

Then the prosecuting attorney called me up and just had me stand in front of the judge's bench, right at the dead center of the courtroom, with her sitting in the witness box and asked me to roll up my left sleeve, so I rolled up my sleeve and showed off my scar. It was still pretty gruesome looking at that time, with some stitches hanging out and stuff. The prosecutor said that she'd like to have a photo taken of my arm and put it into evidence so that the record would reflect that there was indeed a knife at the location. The defense attorney then said, "We'll stipulate to that," and asked for a recess to speak with his client. So the prosecutor brought all that bullshit to a grinding halt.

The guy got convicted on both counts and ended up serving two or three years hard time, then got out for good behavior. I didn't really have any ill feeling toward the guy. He got convicted and went to prison for what he did, so he paid for it—not enough, but he did pay. I was much more angry at his wife for lying on the stand. When I heard her lying up there, I thought to myself, "I should have just let him fucking stab you." I was so pissed off. I didn't give up part of my arm and almost bleed to death so she could get up in court and tell a bunch of lies.

———

The suspect's lawyer really pissed me off. I was one of the first witnesses to testify in the preliminary hearing, and he just opened up on me. "Isn't it true that you are an abusive police officer? Isn't it true that you don't like blacks?"

Apparently, he was trying to get me to say, "Yeah, that's me. I don't like blacks, and I beat the shit out of people every day." I thought, "What's wrong with you? Do I look stupid?" I mean, do prejudiced people actually answer correctly to these questions? If I were a prejudiced person, why would I admit it in court? It was just a dumb question. And then on top of it being a dumb question and me thinking, "Would a prejudiced person answer that truthfully?" I was offended. I'm not a prejudiced person. My partner the night of the shooting was Mexican. My partner after that was black. I judge people on the single basis of their behavior, not by the tone of their skin or whatever. So that offended me, the lawyer insinuating that I was prejudiced. I wanted to answer him by saying, "You're right, I am prejudiced. Toward criminals like your client and toward fucking assholes like you." I really wanted to say that. I had to bite my tongue big time.

—◊◊◊—

We beat the shit out of the guy after we finally got the gun away from him, so bad that both his eyes were swollen almost shut. Then, when some of the other officers showed up a few minutes later, he got his ass kicked some more. One officer in particular really thumped him. He came up, rolled the guy over onto his back, and stomped on the guy's chest about three times. I mean, he stomped the shit out of him.

This became a very delicate thing in court because his attorney tried to use it to turn the tables, to put me on trial instead of the state putting his client on trial. He didn't ask me about the facial injuries, just about the stomping. I guess the suspect thought it was me who kicked him. The officer who did it is Hispanic, but he looks a little like me. I guess that when the guy looked up through the slits in his swollen eyes, that he mistook the other officer for me.

So his attorney asked me if I had done the kicking, and I said, "No." Then he asked me if my partner had done it, and I said, "No." He never asked about any other officers, so I didn't lie. He just never asked me the right question. After I gave my testimony, I was standing off by myself in the foyer outside the judge's office, and one of the people who works at the courthouse came up to me and—in a voice nobody else could hear—said, "Buddy, given what he did, I'd have kicked the shit out of him too."

—◊◊◊—

The criminal trial didn't go the way we wanted it to. He was there all cleaned up, as crooks will be, in a suit, with his attorney. His hand, minus the fingers I shot off, was still wrapped up. My testimony was very short. Nothing outstanding about it. The prosecutor asked, "Were you there?"

"Yep."

"Did you shoot him?"

"Yep."

"Did he have a gun when you shot him?"

"Yep."

"Did you feel threatened?"

"Yep."

"Thank you very much, have a nice day."

No cross.

They ended up convicting him of one count of burglary first, for breaking into the house, but in terms of me, they only convicted him of a third degree assault, the lowest-level misdemeanor assault under state statute. The prosecution was going for first degree assault, which includes attempted murder, because the crook pointed the shotgun at me. His testimony was that he was only trying to scare me when he pointed the shotgun at me. The jury bought that, that he wasn't trying to hurt anybody, that he just wanted to scare me. They also convicted him of third degree assault for firing at the other officer before I got there. I guess the jury figured they had a male Annie Oakley in front of them, that he was just trying to shoot the gun out of the copper's hand with a shotgun at thirty yards.

The judge went goofy when the verdict came back. He told the jury it was one of the worst decisions he'd ever heard and hammered the guy in sentencing. The guy was on parole at the time, and the judge hammered him on the parole and gave him everything he could on the burglary and the two third degree assaults. The guy deserved a lot more than he got, but, hey, you win some, you lose some. I shot part of his hand off, he went to prison, and I figure that every time he goes to tie his shoes, he's gonna remember me.

———∾∾∾———

The second guy I shot during my rookie year had robbed a bunch of people with an Uzi at this drug-den-type apartment building, shot one of the robbery victims, and pointed his gun at me and two other officers. He lived, and when it came time to charge him, the prosecutor's office didn't file on him for pointing the gun at us. They didn't issue that because we didn't get hurt. That ticked me off. I was like, "OK, you're telling me I have to get hurt before you'll do anything?" Then I found out that the victims couldn't care less about what happened. All they wanted was their money back. The homicide detectives had to bribe them to cooperate. They had to say, "Hey, if you want your money back, you gotta meet us downtown."

I thought, "You know, isn't this something? Here I am out there trying to help these people, trying to get this guy off the street, and the victims don't care, and the prosecutor's office won't do anything." They wound up issuing a charge for flourishing a weapon; that was all they issued on him for pointing his weapon at us. They also issued maybe five counts of robbery first, and they issued one assault first for shooting the guy in the leg.

So they did wind up issuing something on him, but it was just that I'd been through the ringer, been in this pretty tense situation, and here you got this desk jockey sitting there, saying, "Well, you know you're not hurt, so we're not gonna issue any kind of assault on you." I just wanted to say, "Hey, you take the fucking gun, and you go out there and go through this shit that I just went through, and we'll see what we're gonna issue for you, and we'll see how irate you're gonna be." But I came to find out that that's pretty much the norm down there at our district attorney's office, that they don't want to do anything. They try to say how great they are by saying, "We win 98 percent of the cases that we take to trial." Well, when you issue on 2 percent of the cases that are brought to you, it's probably really easy to get a 98 percent conviction rate. Before I came on the job, I always thought the prosecuting attorney's office and the police department would work together. But I've come to see that that's not the case.

Problems with the Press

Given the newsroom dictum that "if it bleeds it leads" and the role the press has historically played in monitoring government activities in the United States, it is not surprising that the news media find deadly encounters between citizens and police officers compelling targets for coverage. But all shootings are not created equal, so the nature of the coverage that the fourth estate devotes to them can vary considerably. The scope can range from short blurbs or brief spots in local papers or on local broadcast stations to repeated and in-depth stories in national media outlets. The tone of coverage can also vary, from high praise for "hero cops," who save innocents from the clutches of criminals, to vitriolic condemnation of "trigger-happy" officers, who "shoot first and ask questions later."

There is an old adage about media coverage of the police that goes something like this: cops read about their failures on the front page and their successes in the "law and order" column of the local section—if they make the paper at all. Given the tendency of the press to stress police problems, it is the negative stories of shootings that tend to get more media play. As a consequence, it is a widely held belief in law enforcement circles that the press is just waiting to dump on officers who shoot people. The press practice of playing up negative stories, together with the trepidation it generates among the police, creates a climate in which officers who shoot can have strong reactions to the manner in which the press treats what they have done. The stories in this section focus on these twin issues: the coverage the fourth estate gives to police shootings and the sorts of reactions that the involved officers have to it.

—◊—

The press just had a field day with me. One of the newspaper head-lines read, "POLICE OFFICER MURDERER," in big two-inch print, then underneath it in small print, "Family of Victim Says." All sorts of other ridiculous statements from the family appeared in that paper. Plus the picture they showed of the guy was his boot camp photo, where he was standing in front of the American flag in his greens. That wasn't the guy I shot. The guy that I shot had a tattoo with a skull and crossbones on his chest. He had big, bushed-out, wigged-out hair. He was dirty, a real scumbag. So the family and the press coverage pissed me off. They were talking about what a fine young man he was, but the truth was that he'd been in trouble ever since he was old enough to be in trouble, that he'd tried to stab some people, and that he pulled a knife on me.

—◊—

Some stuff about the way the press reported the incident kind of both-ered me. The first day, it was on the front page of both local papers. The second day, the bigger paper had a big half-page article that had diagrams of the scene and pictures of me and the suspect side by side, right next to each other. They had a stock photo from an interview that I had done about six months prior that they just threw in the paper without asking me if it was OK. It wasn't a good picture, and putting it right next to the suspect really pissed me off, because I could just see people reading the damn caption underneath the pictures, turn-ing the page and not knowing which one was the crook and which one was the cop. I mean, the picture was so bad that from the looks of it I thought that people were probably going to think that I was the crook. That really bothered me, being associated with a hoodlum that way.

—◊—

There was never, ever any doubt that this was a good shooting. The only thing that ever came up was that some liberals—a bunch of attorneys—were flapping their gums in the press, questioning why the guy was shot nine times. My response to them was that they shouldn't question me or the other officers because they weren't there. They didn't know how fast it happened. When the guy came at us, it was split seconds that we made our decisions and did what we did. It wasn't like, "OK, he's coming out in the hallway. OK, he's got two guns. Oh, he just shot a security guard. Oh, he's pointing a gun at John. I'd better make my decision about what to do." It wasn't like that. It was, "Here he comes. Boom, boom, boom, boom, boom, boom, boom, boom—a brief pause—then boom," and it was over. I think three seconds total from the time I saw him till I fired my last shot. I don't think the people who questioned what we did ever really sat down and thought that it happened like that.

Maybe the best way to describe it is like a car accident: you're driving down the street one day, and, "Wham!" someone hits you. I mean, I didn't even know what was happening, then it was over. But the critics don't bother to get the facts before spouting off.

—〰—

The press always plays up the racial angle on police shootings around here, and that used to affect my thinking about things. I remember this one time before my shooting, a black guy took a shot at me and my partner and then took off running. When we caught up with him, he was walking toward some citizens with his rifle. I told him several times to drop the gun, but he just kept moving. I was about twenty feet behind him when he turned to go into this apartment complex. I yelled, "This is the last time I'm gonna tell you to put the gun down. If I have to shoot you in the back, I'll shoot you in the back. I don't want to shoot you in the back, but I'm gonna shoot you in the back right now!" As soon as I said that, he threw the rifle down.

The whole time I was telling him I was going to shoot him, I was thinking, "They'll crucify me on the news tomorrow if I shoot this black guy in the back." That was all it was gonna be: "White cop shoots black man in the back." That was gonna be the extent of the story because that's just what the press preys off of.

The racial thing even came up with my buddies after my shooting. I grew up in a very diverse area, so I've got a lot of black friends and Mexican friends from where I grew up. After my shooting, one of my

Mexican buddies said, "Tell me the guy was white, because if not, I'm gonna have to go to the news station and tell 'em you're not a racist white cop." That issue even crossed my mind. I thought, "God, that sucked. I had to shoot and kill somebody, but thank God it was a white guy."

That thought should've never gone through my mind, and it wouldn't now. Now I just ignore the media for the most part, because the press always changes the facts to make stories cater to their views. The one thing I do look for is stories about officers getting hurt, because I want to learn from what happened. But I've noticed lately that when officers are killed and I see it on TV, I get really depressed for three to four days. It usually takes me a few days to pull out of it and get dialed back in. So I've found that the less newspapers I read, the less news I watch, the happier I am.

Psychological Services

Most police departments across the country are aware that officers can experience negative reactions in the immediate aftermath of shootings. Consequently, it has become commonplace for law enforcement agencies to give officers who have been involved in shootings a short paid leave to gather their thoughts and to send them to mental health professionals (MHPs) for an evaluation prior to their return to duty. Many large departments maintain in-house psychological-services units that can conduct this checkup, whereas other departments contract post-shooting mental health services to outside sources.

Whatever their affiliation, MHPs who debrief officers in the wake of shootings have a tough job, because several factors conspire against successful counseling sessions. Police officers are notoriously insular and suspicious of outsiders. They also tend to distrust police administrators and are fearful that their supervisors are "out to get them" (or are at least willing to sell them out if it will benefit them).[3] Unless an MHP has a solid reputation among the rank and file as a stand-up professional, officers sent to them for duty fitness evaluations will likely withhold information out of fear that any hint that they are having difficulties will get back to their superiors, who, in turn, will punish them. Indeed many of the officers I interviewed told me that they had lied to the MHP about how they were doing for this very reason.

Conversely, many officers had high praise for the MHPs to whom they were sent. The stories that follow include tales of both positive and negative encounters with MHPs, starting with a visit to a clinician who has the reputation of being one of the best police psychologists in the business.

The first few days after the shooting, I had this sense of sadness. I knew that what I did had to be done, but still I had taken somebody's life. It's mandatory in our department to go see someone down at psychological services after a shooting, so about three or four days after, I went to see Dr. Steadly.

He asked me general questions; then he asked me how I felt about the shooting. I told him I felt bad for taking somebody's life. Then he asked me to put what happened in some perspective. He asked me what alternatives I had. I told him it was either me or the guy. Then he asked me if I would give up certain things to bring him back. Would I give an arm? A leg? I said, "Well, no. I wouldn't."

Then he said, "Look at what you just said. It's not like you shot some ninety-year-old lady pushing a grocery cart who has just won the Citizen of the Year award and was just standing there. The guy was trying to kill you." He told me to look at the situation, to look at the facts. When I did that, it helped.

The first few days afterward, I had this sense of elation. I was pretty satisfied with the fact that I was just involved in a very high-profile operation where I reacted in the way I was supposed to. I was placed in a situation where I could've gotten shot, and I was very satisfied that I reverted to my training and that it had helped me get through the situation without getting shot. None of the good guys got hurt. We did exactly what we planned to do, what we were trained to do, so I was very elated.

Before I could go back to work, however, I had to see the department's psychological-services people. The guy that I met with wanted to know what my feelings were. I basically ran the scenario down for him and expressed my satisfaction with the way it went. He asked me, "What do you know about the guy you shot?"

I said, "I don't know really anything about him other than the information that was given to me by the case agent."

He asked, "Does he have kids?"

I said, "I don't know."

He asked, "Well, does that concern you that he might have kids and that you might've destroyed his family and his life?"

I said, "No. Not at all."

He said, "That doesn't bother you at all?"

I said, "No. Not at all."

Then he said, "Well, what if he has a family? What about their feelings?"

I said, "I have a family too, four kids and a young baby, so I'm not thinking about that at all."

He said, "OK, we'll be giving you your release. You can go back to work."

I said, "All right. Thanks." And I left.

When I was in there, I felt like, "Why in the world is he asking me this stuff?" I was never really angry about anything that happened about the shooting, but if I was a little pissed at anybody through the whole deal, it would've been this guy, because he asked me those questions.

The PD sent me to the fit-for-duty interview that they send everyone who kills someone to. It was really strange. First, when I got in the elevator to go up to the guy's office, two beautiful women got on with me—really hot, maybe sixteen or seventeen. They got off with me, and we all went into the same small waiting room. The room was set up so you have to flip a switch to tell this doctor that you're there. I flipped my switch, and then these two chicks went and flipped another switch. I didn't want to stare at them because we were in a shrink's office, but I couldn't help but look at them. Then it hit me that they were transvestites. It made me feel a little uncomfortable, like the PD thought like maybe I was messed up and confused like guys who want to be girls. I was thinking, "Oh, my God, what's going on here?" I found out later that the guy I was going to see shares an office with someone who does pre- and postop counseling for transsexuals, so that's the answer to my question.

Then, when the wait was over and I went in to see the guy who worked for the PD, the first thing I noticed about him was that his glasses were falling off his head because the temple going back to his right ear was missing. He was a younger guy—not some doddering old Sigmund Freud—probably about my age. There were boxes and other stuff piled up to the ceiling all over the place. His sofa was all tattered. It had foam and some other stuff sticking out of the cushions, all messed up.

When I saw all this, I asked him, "Gee, are you moving out of this office, or did you just move in?" He replied, "Neither. Why?" And I thought, "Oh, man, this is going to be a circus sideshow. This is the guy who's going to certify me as being fit for duty?"

When we talked about the shooting, he was cool about it, but it was just a joke. It struck me that anybody who had any wits at all could pass that interview because it's obvious what the answers to the questions are supposed to be. I think the only way someone might fail is if they were just a raving lunatic. The guy might be able to pick that up. I felt like it was a waste of my time and a waste of the city's time. If there really was some officer who needed help after a shooting, who shouldn't go back to work, I don't think this guy would be able to catch it. I don't know. Maybe I was just so OK with what happened that he was just kind of being real mellow about it. I don't know how successful he is in his practice or what the city's standards are to hire someone like that. But I talked to other officers who had to go see this guy, and they said the same thing, that it was a strange experience. And these guys didn't even get to see any transvestites.

Then, about a year and a half later, I got in another fatal shooting, and the PD sent me back to see the same guy. He wasn't wearing his one-armed glasses, so I asked him, "Hey, you got contacts on?" He replied, "Yeah, how'd you know that?" I told him not to worry about it. His furniture was still all in tatters, but most of the boxes were gone, and there were no transvestites to be seen. So it was a little bit better, but it was still pretty bizarre.

—◊◊◊—

I had to go talk to the department psychologist because the guy I shot died. They make everyone who's in a fatal shooting go talk to the shrink before going back to work. It was no big deal, pretty much just a matter-of-fact thing, but he did bring up a couple of neat points about talking to other people about it. He said that a lot of people were going to ask questions about the shooting and want to talk with me about it. He said to go ahead and talk with other policemen if I wanted but that I might want to think about handling it different when I was around people who aren't police officers because they don't think like me; they probably wouldn't understand it in the same terms cops do. So he said it's up to me, go ahead and talk to noncops if I wanted, and then he gave me a suggestion about how to deal with questions if I didn't want to talk. He said I should just say, "Hey, you know how every once in a while you have a bad day at work and you don't really like to talk about it, you would just as soon forget it? I'm sure you've had days like that. Well, that was one of the worst days I've ever had at work." He said that people usually understand that.

The other thing he talked about had to do with my son, who was five at the time. He asked me if I had told my son about it. I told him that I hadn't because I felt like he was too young. He asked me if I thought that later on some other kids who heard about the shooting might tell him about it. I told him that was possible. Then he asked me if I thought he'd rather hear it from me. I said that I guess he would but that I still wondered if he was old enough to understand. The doc replied that he should be able to if I explained it to him in the right way. Then he encouraged me to tell my boy when I got home.

So I did. I went and I told him about it. Just the basics. It went pretty well. The only question on his mind was he wanted to know if the man that I killed had a son. I sure wasn't expecting that. I was kind of curious why he wondered that. But I didn't ask him about it. I just told him that I didn't know but that I didn't think the guy had kids. Then I asked him if he had a problem with anything I told him. He said, "No, Daddy. I don't have a problem with it," and that was it.

Family Matters

As demonstrated by the preceding story, the personal impact of shootings does not stop with the officers who pull the trigger. Shootings also have ramifications for the families of the involved officers. Those close to officers can be strong, uncertain, and fearful as they watch and participate in the post-shooting process. They can be supportive, indifferent, and even antagonistic toward officers as they try to make sense of what has and is happening. And these various responses can, in turn, affect officers' adjustment as they traverse the post-shooting landscape.

The stories in this section address the twin issues of how officers' loved ones reacted following shootings and how these reactions played themselves out in the lives of the involved officers. One thing that stands out is the key role that intimate partners can play in officers' post-shooting adjustment—for both the good and the ill. Some partners provided officers a safe harbor for working things out, whereas others were a thorn in their side. For the most part, the difficulties that officers experience in this connection stem from their spouses' fears about the dangers of police work, fears that are brought painfully close to home by shootings. Such was the case for the wives in the initial stories that follow.

—✳—

My wife took it much harder than I did. She was pretty upset for a while. A day or two after the shooting, the gravity of what had happened hit her. She'd never really thought about me getting hurt or killed at work; then she answered the door one night, and it's this sergeant telling her that her husband just capped a guy who stabbed him. She said that prior to the shooting she understood on an intellectual level that something bad could happen, but she never worried about it. Then, when this happened, it made her realize deep down just how real the danger was. So the shooting gave her cause to think about what I do for a living more carefully and in much more detail than she really wanted to.

—⁓—

The shooting made me take my job a little bit more seriously. I've always taken it seriously, but the shooting pushed me to an even higher level. I played college baseball, and it's the fine little things that make the difference on the diamond. I think the same thing applies here in SWAT; it's the little things that make the difference, and the shooting just reinforced that. I realized that if I'd been a fraction of a second slower, the guy could have gotten a round off at me, so I started paying even more attention to what I do when I train, and I spent even more time on job-related stuff.

This didn't make my wife too happy. I wasn't a cop when we got married, and she's reminded me more than once that she didn't marry a police officer. But this detail is a little bit more than just the job—here, I've got all these guys who depend on me for their lives—so I feel that I always need to be at the top of my game. I know that I put a little more into it than my wife would like, especially my spare time. For example, I just now got a good computer at the house. It's better than the ones at work, which can't run a lot of the software I like to use, so I do a lot of my work stuff on the home computer. That's time she wishes I'd spend playing with the kids and things like that. And the time stuff is on top of the general concern she has about my safety. If I left police work tomorrow, she wouldn't blink an eye; she'd be happy. She's not too thrilled about me doing this job, but I don't know if any wife would be.

—⁓—

My family was real supportive, all but one sister-in-law, that is. She was nineteen or twenty at the time, really into the liberal scene. We were having a family dinner a short time after the shooting, when she asked me if I minded talking about it. I said no, so we started talking about it. I was being real mellow about it, just describing what happened. When I mentioned how I shot the guy five times, she went off. "Five times! Five times! Why did you shoot him five times? Isn't that pretty excessive? Didn't the first one kill him?" and all this other stuff. Just went on and on about how I shot too much. That just set me off. We went around and around and around. It led to a big argument about police brutality and the whole business. But what set me off was her saying it was excessive when she wasn't there.

But that was awhile back. We get along now. We just don't talk about the police. I'm very interested in what she is doing. She's a great kid. She's going to law school, and she actually went down to Mexico to help out with the Chiapas deal. She went down there and was almost put in prison. I mean, she's a great kid but she's just—let's just say our values are different.

Talking to my dad about what happened, I learned some stuff about him that I'd always wondered about. He was a captain of a fighter squadron in Korea, but when I was growing up, he never talked about any combat he'd been in. Us kids would ask him about his time in the military, but he only talked about things he did in training with his buddies and some of the fun things they did in their deployment. I never understood why he wouldn't talk about combat, but I found out after my first shooting. I was going through some tough times, and he told me that he'd gone through some tough times, too.

He told me that one day they scrambled his squadron for ground support of some troops who were pinned down. As they were running out to their planes, he was given the coordinates. They jumped in their planes, went to the coordinates, and dropped their bombs. Later on, they learned that the guy who had written down the coordinates had them wrong, and they had bombed and killed three of their own soldiers. He told me that they sent his squadron to counseling and that they were told to deal with it by putting it in a vault, shutting the door, and locking it. They were told, "Don't bring it out. Don't do anything. Keep it locked in that vault and don't think about it." That's what he told me that they told him, and that kind of explained why he would never talk about his combat experiences.

I called my wife at her work, told her what had happened. Now the guy ended up living, but at that time if anybody would've bet me that

that guy was going to live, I'd have lost a year's wages. In fact, everybody who was at that scene would have lost a lot of money 'cause we all figured he wouldn't make it.

So I told her, "I shot this guy in the head; he's probably gonna die."

And she goes, "Well, what's gonna happen next?"

I replied, "Well, you know, I'll probably be home late, but they're gonna give me five days off for it," the standard five-day administrative leave.

My wife, the understanding individual she is, said, "Oh, good, I'll have a list of stuff for you to do." Now my lieutenant was standing right behind me when I was talking to my wife, so I turned around and told him what she had just said. He about wet his pants laughing.

—◈—

I fired as the guy swung his gun toward me. I knew I hit him because I saw him flinch as I was firing. He flinched up and back. With my experience hunting, I know that that's what happens when something—an animal or whatever—has been hit by a bullet. So when I saw that flinch, I knew that I had hit him. Then he took off down the stairway where the shooting took place and made it outside where some other officers caught him. The second robber got away, so I went downstairs to where the suspect I shot was. He was lying on the ground in handcuffs. I asked the guy who was watching the suspect, "Is he OK?" He said, "No, he's been hit." I reached down, pulled the suspect's shirt back, and saw that there was a hole in his right side. It wasn't anything like you would picture; it was just a small hole with no exit. I didn't know it at the time, but I had also shot him in the leg and in the back. All I saw was the hole in his side.

After that point, it kind of started cycling through my head that my wife was seven months pregnant with our first child. That got to me. I knelt down, and I got beside the suspect, and I told him, "You and that other son of a bitch aren't going to keep me from seeing my child. You're lucky to be alive." I was angry at this guy for coming at me with a gun. What if he would have shot me, and I never would have seen my child, never would have seen my wife again? I was pissed.

After that discussion, I realized that the other guy was still on the loose, so I went to help look for him. I was helping the other guys look for about ten or fifteen minutes, when I realized, "Shit, I was just in a shooting. I need to call somebody." So I quit looking for the second suspect and called my wife. I explained everything to her, basically told her that I was involved in a shooting and that I was OK. The next thing I did was call my attorney and basically explained to him what happened.

As I was waiting for my attorney and the investigators to show up, I went through a stage of anger because of what this guy did. He would have shot me if I hadn't shot him first, so I was thinking about my kid. I was determined to see my family, but I was also angry that he put himself in this predicament. I thought, "What about his family?" Here he doesn't think about himself, but what about his family that's got to go through all this stuff? So I started thinking about that, but then I came to the conclusion that I should forget about that. If the table had been turned and he shot me and got away, would this guy be thinking about my family the way I was thinking about his?

I really didn't think so. Especially now, knowing what I know about his extensive criminal background, I don't think that he would have. I guess maybe I had those thoughts because my religious faith made me more concerned about the other people involved. On top of all that, I was also pissed at this guy for making me shoot him. I could have gone through my whole career without having to shoot somebody, and that would have been great. But I didn't have any other recourse but to shoot him.

The emotions really hit me when I was done giving my statement and I went home to my wife. Just seeing her pregnant with my child, I broke down and cried. We discussed the situation and what happened and that I was pissed. Even at that time, I was still pissed that that guy had placed me in this situation. What in the hell over? Freaking money? He was willing to lose his life over that money and risk the things that that would do to his family? We talked about all that. I ran the whole situation down with my wife, told her everything about it and what I was feeling. Later that day, I talked about the shooting with friends on the PD. After that, I didn't experience anything like waking up in the middle of the night, crying, or being real depressed. Nothing like that. So I guess I just felt better after getting the story out to my wife and my friends. It helped me out.

Right after the shooting, my wife was worried about me. She was wondering how it was gonna affect me. Matter of fact, she told me about a year after it happened that I really changed, but she never would tell me how or why. I know that I did to a point, but I don't know to what extent, and she never would tell me. Still, to this day, nine years later, she won't tell me, and we've been married for seventeen years.

—∿∿—

I got in two shootings within five months of each other my first year on the job, and my family started to worry about me. In fact, my mom's younger sister to this day is just deathly afraid of me being a policeman. She just goes nuts whenever we talk about my job. She doesn't want me hurt. She and I are about probably twelve or thirteen years apart. We're the closest kids in age in my entire family, so as we grew up, I was almost her younger brother rather than her nephew, and she just didn't want to see her nephew go through that stuff. And then my mom and my grandma would say stuff like, "Oh, please be careful. I worry about you." So it's like your typical sheltered family that really wants to hold on to memories of Frank the altar boy, and Frank singing in the choir, and Frank the Boy Scout, not Frank the policeman who's having to cap these people coming after him with guns.

—∿∿—

The shooting went down around three in the morning, and the detectives released me about eight or nine. I hadn't had a chance to talk to my husband, but another officer called and told him what happened. He passed the information on to our twelve-year-old son, who was home because it was summertime. Then he went to work. When I pulled into our driveway, my son came running out to the car. He was crying. He's really sensitive at times, and as soon as he saw me, he just lost it.

I calmed him down and told him I was OK. I told him that everything was fine, that Mama's not hurt, that I did what I was supposed to do, and that I didn't kill the guy. I knew that beyond my safety, he was a little concerned that I maybe killed somebody. I said, "No, I didn't kill him, but if I had killed him, it would've been because he pointed a gun at me, but I didn't kill him. He's gonna be all right, so there's nothing for you to worry about." After that, he was fine.

My son loves to walk our dogs, so we got the pups, went for a walk, and when we came back, I let him pick what he wanted to eat for breakfast. That was a mistake, because he picked egg burritos and French fries. I thought, "Well. Whatever. That's fine," and we went out to get some breakfast. So I consciously spent a lot of time with my son that morning.

Deadly Dreams

Psychologists tell us that dreams are the place where we deal with emotions and conflicts that we have not worked out consciously and that nightmares are the expression of fears and anxieties about particular aspects of our waking lives that trouble us.[4] Given the traumatic nature of police shootings, it should come as no surprise that it is not at all unusual for officers to experience nightmares in the wake of shootings.

The stories in this section provide some insight into the sorts of bad dreams that officers have, the contexts in which these nightmares emerge, and what these episodes might mean. We will hear of dreams in which officers did not fire soon enough, could not get their guns to work, or watched assailants press their attacks despite a hail of accurate gunfire. If the psychologists are correct about the sources of nightmares, the fact that officers sometimes have such dreams indicates that shootings sometimes produce fear and anxiety about their safety that officers do not know how to process during their waking hours. Whatever the case, it is clear from the stories that follow that officers who shoot sometimes experience substantial horror during what is supposed to be the peaceful time of slumber.

The first day, everything was so pumped up that I couldn't get to sleep. I'd been up well over twenty-four hours when I finally got back home. I wanted to go to sleep, but I was just so pumped up that I couldn't. I was zombied into the TV, just clicking channels, not even thinking about it. The next few days were like that, too. I'd try to go to sleep, but then I'd start to think about the shooting, and boy, there went my adrenaline right back up to that spot where it was right after it happened. Then, when I finally did fall asleep, I'd wake up after about four hours, think about the shooting, and get charged up again, which made it hard to go back to sleep.

I was having some dreams too. I remember one night, I think it was about a week and a half after the shooting, a guy I grew up with came to visit. He brought some drinks over, so we just sat around, watching a game or a movie, talking and drinking some beers. We finally went to bed. He was sleeping on the couch, and I went in and fell asleep on my bed.

All of a sudden, I heard this "BOOM!" and I came sailing up out of my bed, grabbed my gun, and went over to the window.

He woke up, saw me stumbling around in the dark, knocking everything over, and asked me, "What's going on?"

I asked him if he heard that gunshot, and he replied, "No." So then I was thinking, "Shit, maybe I capped a round off in my sleep!" So I opened my gun up, saw six rounds in the cylinder, and knew the shot wasn't from me. I'd apparently been dreaming about the shooting and heard my gunshots go off. It just sent me straight up out of bed.

—∿∿—

I never had any dreams about the shooting incident—none that were even similar to it—but the dreams I do have have changed since the shooting. I used to get these recurring dreams where I'd either go to pull my trigger and it's so rusted that I can't pull it, or I'm pulling and the bullets are coming out in slow motion, or I'm pulling and I'm hitting the shit out of the suspect but he's just laughing at me. I had these dreams even before I was a cop, when I first started getting interested in law enforcement. Once I got hired, I had probably three or four of these dreams a month. Well, since the shooting, I don't have those dreams anymore. I haven't had them for two years, but I recently had two dreams where I got shot.

In all the dreams before the shooting where my equipment doesn't work, or I was shooting the suspect but he's laughing at me, or the rounds just aren't working, I was never shot. I guess the recent dreams about getting shot are because of all the cops that've been shot back East and up North. There's been so many incidents of officers shot and killed lately; one that really bugged me was where two deputy sheriffs were shot and killed. Both of my dreams happened since that incident.

In the first one, I got shot in the leg, and I remember going down on the ground, but I don't remember reacting before I woke up. I was pissed I didn't get a chance to respond, because I took a law enforcement survival class a long time ago where they told us that we can take control of our dreams and survive those bad ones. The second one was different. In the second dream, I got shot really bad. I got shot in the leg, and I remember the round burning really bad; then I took two hits to my chest. I got so fucking pissed, I started to wake up. But I told myself before I woke up, "Uh-uh, this shit ain't over. The son of a bitch is going with you." So I stayed in the dream and shot this guy probably eighteen times. When I woke up, I thought, "At least I survived this one. I got shot, but I didn't die." That's what I always tell myself in the field: "If you ever get shot, you're not gonna die. You're not gonna frickin' die. You're gonna get rounds back downrange." And that's what I did in that dream. Since that dream, that second dream about getting shot, I haven't had any more of 'em.

—∿∿—

It's been eight years since the last incident happened, but I still dream about my shootings. I don't think that stuff will ever go away. I also have dreams about shootings in general, like having to shoot somebody and my gun won't fire because I don't have the strength to squeeze my trigger. I'm in justifiable shooting situations, where there's absolutely no way that they could ever hold anything against me, and then, all of a sudden, I try to shoot, but I can't pull the trigger, or I squeeze and the gun just clicks, or my gun falls apart, or I shoot the person and it doesn't even phase 'em. I can tell I'm hitting 'em in the head because part of their head is blowing off, and I see their brains and all this stuff, but nothing happens. They're still talking normal; they're still coming toward me. I've had those dreams quite often. It's not something that happens every night, but it happens pretty regular, maybe a couple of times a month.

Nerves

The fear and anxiety that officers sometimes experience about dangerous encounters is not limited to the subconscious venue of their dreams. Conscious concerns about shooting situations, moreover, are not limited to fear and anxiety about their personal safety. Some officers become quite concerned about whether they will be able to pull the trigger again if circumstances call for them to do so, usually worrying that their potential inability to act could jeopardize their fellow officers or innocent citizens.

For most officers who experienced them, worries about their safety and their ability to shoot again arose during their time off following their shootings, manifested themselves most strongly when they first returned to duty, and then dissipated as they got back into their work routine. For other officers, however, such concerns lasted long after they went back to work and as a result became a persistent thorn in their side. The stories in this section address the fear and anxiety that officers who shoot sometimes experience during their waking hours, how these concerns affect their behavior, and how these problematic reactions play themselves out.

The shooting happened on a Friday, and I had the next three days off. During that time, I was pretty anxious about going back to work. In fact, I wanted to go back to work. I wanted to get with my partner and talk to him about it. I also knew that everybody else in the division was going to have been talking about it. I was still pretty new on the job, and I wanted to see how the veteran officers responded. The older guys don't know what to expect from the young guys like me, who haven't been tried and tested. I figured that because I showed I could do the ultimate thing if I needed to, that I was gonna be accepted by a lot of the older guys.

As I recall, the other cops did offer a lot of support when I did get back to work. The thing I remember the most about the first shift back, though, is that I was what I call "holster happy." My partner and I both were. The guy I shot had kind of got the jump on us, so we were nervous about it happening again. Anytime anyone reached for their wallet, we had our hands on our guns. Anytime anyone did anything sudden or unexpected, we drew our guns. It was the longest night I ever had at work. I was physically and mentally exhausted at the end of the night. We stayed busy that night. We were answering calls, we were stopping cars, but anytime anybody did anything sudden—like reaching to pull up an emergency brake—we drew down on them. You know, "Let me see your hands." It was real intense the first night back to work.

I slowly got back to normal after a few weeks to where I'd see a movement and tell myself, "OK, he's reaching for his wallet," or whatever. I'd still keep a sharp eye out. I was still ready, I just wasn't drawing down on people all the time.

———

After my first shooting, I was worried about how I'd perform if I got involved in another one. The local newspapers had reamed me, saying that I'd shot too soon, so I wondered, Was I gonna hesitate and risk somebody else's life? Some other citizen's? Some other officer's? Then, a little while after the shooting, I had a rookie that I was training, and we came upon a guy that had a gun in his car. It was on the front passenger's seat, hidden underneath a sack of beer, and when he started to reach for it, I drew my gun, ready to start shooting if I had to. I wasn't even thinking about anything else. I said to myself, "As soon as he touches it, I'm going to cap him." We were yelling at him, "Don't touch the gun! Don't touch the gun!" He finally quit reaching before his fingers touched the gun, and we got him under control.

After we took the guy into custody, I thought, "I didn't even think about my other shooting. That's good. I'm not going to hesitate." That really helped alleviate my fears that I might hesitate to shoot again because of all the crap that had happened in the media with the first one. Once I realized I wasn't going to hesitate, I was fine.

———

The shooting happened on my Friday, and I started back to work on my Monday. So I didn't miss a single day of work. My regular partner took that day off, so I was with another officer, a newer officer, that first day back after the shooting. Our very first call out of the barn was just a "preserve the peace" call. It turned out to involve three guys that were living together, with some type of love triangle that involved some type of DV. We met one of the guys outside, and he told us what was going on and that he wanted to get some stuff from inside the place. We said, "OK, we'll go see if they'll let you get your property, and if they do, great, we'll just stay back and make sure no one causes any problems. Otherwise, you'll have to take it to court, because it's a civil issue."

We went inside, and the guy in there was being real nice, letting the other guy get his stuff. We were standing against this wall near the front entry, just watching this going on, when all of a sudden what looked like maybe the feminine partner of the other two came out of a bedroom. He had long, long stringy hair, long fingernails, was very skinny, and he was screaming like a banshee, saying stuff like, "Get him out of here! He hurt me!"

I said, "Hold on a second. It's OK, he's not gonna hurt you. We're right here. Your friend let him get his stuff. He's just gonna get his stuff and go."

The guy replied, "No, I want him out of here."

I said, "He's gonna get out of here shortly. We're just getting his stuff and then we're leaving."

He said, "No, he hurt me. I'm gonna kill him," and took off running toward the kitchen. I ran after him because everybody knows what's in kitchens, and sure enough, right when I turned the corner into the kitchen, here was this guy—I mean he was just totally pathetic looking—holding this big ole butcher knife up in the air.

I drew my gun and said, "Drop the knife!" He said, "No, he hurt me." Legally and technically and everything else, I could've shot him if I wanted to, but I just kept telling him, "Drop the knife! Drop the knife! Put the knife down!" Finally, he dropped the knife and he started crying. I went into the kitchen, put the handcuffs on him, and gave him to my partner. I said, "You take care of this guy," leaned against a wall, and started taking some deep breaths. I was thinking, "I can't believe this. First call out of the barn, first day back from the shooting, and here I am, almost getting in another shooting." I was also thinking, "The press would have a field day with this." You know, here's this guy with an itchy trigger finger.

As I was against the wall, thinking, "God, I can't believe this!" the guy who was being very cooperative said, "Officer, can you come here for a second?" and motioned me into the bedroom. When I started walking into the room, he was on the other side of this small, maybe ten-by-twelve-foot, room facing away from me. He started to turn toward me, and as he did, I saw that he had a Smith & Wesson semi-auto in his hands. I said, "No!" That's all I could do. I couldn't react to pull my gun again, and the guy said, "No, no. I want to give it to you, I want to give it to you." He didn't want this skinny guy to have it in the house. I took it from him, and I was so pissed that I started lecturing to this guy, "Don't you ever . . . !"

When my partner saw what happened, he called for a supervisor. When the sarge got there, he asked me, "Billy, you want to go home today?" I should've, but I was thinking that I handled what happened properly. Even though my heart was going a mile a minute, I figured I could handle it. Since then, I've always been able to handle dangerous situations properly. It's just the aftereffects. It takes me a little while to calm down after something like that happens. It just takes some time.

—◊◊◊—

I was scared to death to go back to work. Absolutely terrified. I did not want to go back. The administration hadn't given me the prosecutor's statement saying that they weren't going to file charges on me. I knew that that had happened on all the other shootings involving our officers since I came on the job, but I still had this situation pending on me. I was worried that I'd get in trouble if I had another shooting before the prosecutor cleared the first one, so I questioned my ability to pull the trigger again. Then, one of my first days back in the field, a call came out that there was a man with a shotgun in the cemetery threatening to commit suicide. All the other units got on the air. "Unit 24 en route. Unit 21 en route. Blah, blah, en route." But I didn't respond. I was thinking, "I'm just happy right here." The guy I'd shot was suicidal, and I was scared, absolutely terrified, that the same thing would happen again, and I didn't know if I could shoot if I had to.

Before I'd gone back to work, the department sent me to a psychologist for a mental-fitness evaluation, but I kept my feelings bottled up, didn't tell him the truth of what I was feeling. He went ahead and signed me off for duty, and I thought, "You stupid fool. You don't have a clue." I didn't tell him because I didn't trust the fact that he was working for the department. I was afraid that if I'd sat there and told him all my emotions, all my fears, all of what I was going through, that he would say, "You're not fit to go back to duty," and I'd lose my job. So I didn't tell him I was still having an emotional time dealing with it, that I was afraid to go on calls. That fear lasted for a very long time, even after I was cleared by the prosecutor.

Tough Adjustments

Even though the stories presented thus far have focused on specific aspects of officers' post-shooting responses, some of them also make the point that officers can experience more than one reaction in the wake of shootings. Some officers who experience several difficulties resolve them in rather short order, whereas other officers are not so fortunate.

The stories in this section focus on the tough times that officers have when troubling reactions gang up on them. They include stories from officers who managed to put the difficulties they experienced behind them rather quickly, officers who took considerably longer to work things out, and officers who were still suffering quite a bit at the time they shared their stories with me.

All of the stories in this section illustrate just how deeply disturbing shootings can be for officers who pull the trigger. Those from the officers who fell into the latter two adjustment categories show that shootings can even bring some officers to points of anger, guilt, and despair that quite literally place their careers, their peace of mind, and even their lives in substantial jeopardy.

—◊◊◊—

My second shooting hit me a lot harder than my first. About an hour after it happened, I felt like I was going to vomit. I don't know why. Maybe it was something I ate for dinner, but I don't think it was, because I felt lousy for about three days—lost my appetite and got diarrhea. I was pretty bad off. I don't know what happened to me. I suppose it could have been that I was going to get sick anyway, but about an hour after I killed the guy, I told the investigators, "Somebody get me a bag because I feel like I'm going to puke."

Then, after I got home, I was really tired. The shooting happened at 10:00 P.M. I got home at about 7:00 the next morning, and I slept like a rock until about 2:00 P.M. Then I got up to go to my daughter's softball picnic, came back home, went back to bed about 9:00 P.M., and slept till about 7:00 the next morning. I probably could have slept even more that first day, but the phone was ringing constantly, and my pager kept going off between 2:00 P.M. and when we left for the picnic. Seemed like everybody I knew wanted to check up on me and find out what happened.

The picnic didn't go real well. I was sitting there with all the other parents, feeling real pensive, thinking about the night before. My wife asked me a few questions, and I responded with real short answers.

She didn't like that, so she said, "What's the matter with you?"

I lost it right then. I stood up and said, "Goddamn it, Sally, I just fucking killed somebody last night. You think that might be weighing on my mind a little bit?" Then I just started walking to the car, and as I was walking, I started crying a little bit. I couldn't believe my wife's attitude. I'd been married to her for all these years. She's a cop's wife, and she asked me what's wrong with me the night after I shoot somebody? I couldn't believe it.

Sally caught up to me just as I got to the car. I was still crying. I wiped away the tears and said to her, "You, of all people! I thought you would understand. I can't believe you said something stupid like that."

Her response surprised me. She told me that she didn't know how to deal with what I was going through, that she didn't know what to say. Then she said, "I'm sorry. I shouldn't have said that. It was the stupidest thing I have ever said in my life. I don't know why I said it. I'm sorry. Forgive me." I told her that I did, and that's all there was to the crying.

The upset stomach and whatnot lasted for another couple of days. Then some other stuff came along. The biggest thing was that I started to become more concerned about my safety. I had gotten into a bad habit over the years of sometimes not taking my gun with me when I went out. I'd always bring it with me if I went downtown or some place like that, but I'd leave it at the house if I was just gonna run to the store to get some milk or return a videotape, short trips like that. A few days after I killed this guy, I noticed that I no longer felt comfortable if I went someplace without my gun. I don't know what it was, but something prompted me to start carrying my gun wherever I went. I guess I just want to be sure that I'm ready. Something can go wrong anyplace, and I don't want to be caught with my pants down, so now I don't leave my house without my gun.

I wasn't the only one who got more concerned for my safety. My oldest daughter was eight when the second shooting went down, so she was old enough to understand what it was all about. She started getting scared. I'd been on the SWAT team since before she was born, and my work never bothered her before, but she started going through a phase where she got scared when I was home and the pager went off to call me to work. I talked to her about it, and she told me that she was afraid that I was going to die, that some bad guy was going to shoot me. So I had to deal with that for a while.

Maybe that was the difference between the two shootings. I had kids now.

—◊—

I think the toughest thing that happened after the shooting was seeing a picture of the guy I shot on TV about a day or so after I killed him. He was a real bad guy, wanted for all sorts of stuff, including escaping from prison, cooking crystal meth, and attempted murder on both citizens and police officers. We got called out when the U.S. marshals caught up to him at his condo and he refused to surrender. We tried everything to get the guy to give up: negotiations, gas, even did an explosive breach on his front door to get a better view of the inside of the place. I was posted up near some of the other guys watching through the front doorway when all of a sudden the guy came running toward the doorway pointing a handgun at me.

Things started slowing down for me, and my eyes focused on the gun. I could see it real clearly, the squareness of the barrel and the gloss of it, stuff like that, but for some reason I didn't see the guy's face. I fired two short bursts on full auto, and when I started shooting, things got real weird. I never heard any of my shots going off, but I did hear a "clack, clack, clack" sound from my gun, maybe the spring action of the bolt in the carrier moving back and forth. I could also feel the gun. It was kind of shaking and vibrating while I was shooting. I was aware that other officers were also firing, and I saw some rounds hitting the door frame, which sent wood chips flying off, but I still didn't see the guy's face. The whole time I was firing, it was like I was watching from a few steps behind where I was, just standing there watching me shoot, the bullets hit, and so on. In fact, it took a few seconds after I stopped firing for me to realize exactly what had just happened. By then, the guy had fallen down, and it was basically all over.

He fell face first, so when we went into the condo a few minutes later to clear it, all I could see was the back of his head. That was fine with me because I didn't want to see his face. In fact, I didn't want to know anything about this guy, didn't want to see what he looked like, didn't want to know his name. I didn't want to know what kind of husband he was, what kind of a dad, any of that. I just wanted to know the things that I had seen, that this guy was an asshole who was out to hurt people and didn't give a shit about the police or anybody else. So

I was glad that I didn't see his face out at the scene. In fact, I was hoping that I'd never see the guy's picture, and I was hoping I'd never hear his name. For some reason, I wanted to keep a sense of distance from the guy, but it didn't work out that way.

I had been feeling kind of sad since the shooting. I didn't feel sorry for the guy, because he wasn't a decent person. I just felt that it was a shame that his life had to end the way it did. I also had a sense of sadness that I wasn't able to make it through my career without killing someone. Shooting situations weren't something I sought out, and after fifteen years on the job with none, I figured I'd never have any, 'cause they tend to happen to younger guys. I also felt sorry for everybody else that was involved with the guy, like his wife and the people that owned the condo, because it was so messed up. Overall, I just had a sense that it was too bad that it happened.

I didn't realize how much it was bugging me till I saw the guy on TV.

It was either the day after the shooting or the day after that when I was just sitting on the sofa casually watching the TV. All of a sudden, they flashed a picture of the guy up on the screen and said his name. It wasn't the type of picture you'd expect for some guy who just got killed by the police, like a prison picture or maybe a driver's license photo. It was a family picture. There was this happy-looking guy with a smile on his face up on my TV screen. It really upset me a lot because the picture that they put up there portrayed him as if he was a kind of a regular happy-go-lucky guy. He didn't look like a biker or anything like that. He just looked like a regular guy, and I thought, "Shit, I didn't want to see that picture." Then I started crying. A few seconds later, my wife came in the room. When she saw me crying, it kind of upset her. I'm not some macho-type guy, I'm pretty easy going, but I'm almost always in control of my emotions. So crying felt strange because it was a loss of control on my part. I wasn't embarrassed or anything like that. In fact, it felt kind of good to let it out, but it sure bothered my wife. I don't think she ever would have expected to see me crying, and she just didn't know how to handle it.

—◊—

The guy fell right after I fired my fourth round. He went down face first with his hands up underneath him. I remember thinking that he wasn't hit, that he was trying to get me to move close to him so he could bring the knife out and stab me, so I stayed about three or four yards away. One of the other two officers on the scene came running up on my shoulder and asked me what happened. I told him that the guy pulled a knife. Then I told him that I thought he had it underneath him and not to get too close. Then we started moving up on the guy, real slow. I kind of went around to his feet, where I could see a large pool of blood starting to form up by his head. I looked to see where it was coming from, and I could see he had a large mass of blood in his hair, in the back of his head. He looked lifeless, so I was pretty sure he was dead.

At that point, I kind of went numb.

Then things started happening. The third officer who was there from the start began to secure the scene. A corporal arrived soon after that, and he took my gun immediately from me. He said, "You know your rights, right?" I said "Yeah." He asked me what happened, and I told him. He said, "OK, why don't you go stand over there," pointing to the car of this other officer who had just arrived. From that point on, everything that happened out at the scene I experienced as if I was watching it from above. I was looking down from across the street, seeing me standing at the police car next to this other officer. I saw some other officers put the crime scene tape up. Then the paramedics got there, they checked the guy, and said he was dead.

A little while later, I remembered that I needed to get something out of my patrol car. It was still parked in the street, just outside the crime scene tape. When I walked to my car, there was a couple standing by it. The girl was crying. The guy was holding her. I remember thinking that that was his family, that they were going to see that I didn't have a gun in my holster and know that I was the guy that did it. After I got the stuff from my car, I went back to the officer I'd been standing with. Then, very shortly after that, they had him take me to the station. It was probably three in the morning by then.

After they got done with me out at the scene, I was real antsy. I felt like I had to talk to somebody who'd know what I was going through. I wanted to talk to a buddy of mine named Mitch Barnes. He and I went through the academy together and he's my best friend. I wanted to talk to him because he'd been in a shooting at the first agency he worked, and I figured he'd know what I was feeling. So after I called my wife and told her what happened, I called Mitch and woke him up. I just had to talk to somebody who knew what I was going through. I don't know why I felt that way. I just had this overwhelming desire and urge to talk to somebody who knew what I was feeling. I think that I figured that was the only way I could calm down. I was really keyed up, walking around, not able to sit still. I figured I needed to do something to occupy myself, and I thought that when I talked to Mitch that I could calm down, that he was the only person that was going to know what I was thinking.

So I called him up, told him what happened, and he came right down to the station. We hadn't had a whole lot of officer-involved shootings in my agency, so it was mass chaos at the PD. Nobody knew how to handle it. Commanders came in, but they didn't know what to do, so I spent several hours just hanging around. After this went on for a while, Mitch said to them, "Hey, Ted's been at this thing for a while. He was supposed to get off at three o'clock this morning and it's now nine o'clock. He hasn't had anything to eat. Let me take him out to breakfast. We'll come back and you can finish up with him, but he needs some food." They said, "OK," and we started to get ready to head for breakfast.

Now, like I said, they had taken my gun away early on in the investigation, but I was still in uniform. I mentioned the fact that I didn't have a gun to this one particular captain, but he said I would just have to do without one for right now. Mitch pulled me aside and told me he had something I could use. So we went over to his desk, he fished around in it and brought out a model 60. I put it in my holster. It fit, it didn't flop out, so off we went to breakfast with this little gun in my holster.

We talked about the shooting a little bit there, just general stuff. He told me not to turn in the report that I was going to have to write when we went back to the PD until he read it. He said that I might write some weird stuff in there and that I needed to be logical, that I needed to write with clear-cut thoughts in mind. I said, "OK." We went back to IA and I sat down and wrote my report. Mitch reviewed it, I made a couple of changes, and we turned in the final product.

I finally went home about two o'clock in the afternoon, maybe later. Incredibly, I couldn't go to sleep. I'd been up all night, stayed up all day, but I couldn't go to sleep. I was glued to the news. Five o'clock, six o'clock, ten o'clock news, glued to it. Everybody told me before I left the station, "Don't watch the news, don't read the papers." I didn't want to read the papers because I hated our newspaper. We called it the "News and Slander." But I was glued to the television. Flipping back and forth between the different networks. I slept that night. I don't remember how well, but after I woke up the next day, Mitch called and asked me how I was doing. I told him I was OK but that I had this weird tightness in my chest. Mitch said that they were going to send some guys over to sit in my driveway and watch my place because someone had phoned in some threats to the department. He said the threats were nothing serious, that nobody knew where I lived, but they wanted me to be able to sleep. Nothing ever came of the threats, but I had guys sitting in my driveway and in my garage twenty-four hours a day for about three days.

The tightness in my chest lasted for the next few days. It was always there. It just never went away for those first few days. I felt really anxious. I don't know what about—nothing in particular, just a general feeling. I was constantly replaying the shooting in my mind, thinking, "Did I do the right thing? Was I justified?" That kind of thing. I also felt real numb the first few days—maybe the whole week—after the shooting. It was almost a detached feeling, like what was going on wasn't really happening. On top of all that, I had trouble sleeping the first few nights. I'd go to bed and I'd fall asleep OK, but then I'd wake up and I'd toss and turn, then go back to bed. Then I'd get up and get a drink, maybe turn on TV for a little bit, and then go back to bed. That kind of thing.

Then, about ten days after the shooting, I had this weird dream where my wife and I were going for a walk in the neighborhood. We went to the next street over on the block. As we were walking down there, we ran into a group of guys. It was the cousin and other family members of the guy I shot. Now I never go anywhere without my off-duty gun, but in the dream, I forgot my off-duty gun. I left it at home. The guys start chasing me. My wife can't run as fast as me, and I looked over as we're running and she falls down. Then I woke up. I had the dream just one time, but boy, was it weird.

After that, things smoothed out, and I was functioning fine up until about three months after the shooting. My wife and I basically quit communicating; we started having problems. Things deteriorated so bad that about eight months after the shooting my wife and I separated and I went to live with my folks. When I was living with my folks, I started going through a bout of depression. I didn't know what it was at the time, but it was real bad. I would stay up to two or three o'clock in the morning trying to get tired, so I could get a good night's sleep. I'd sleep for a couple of hours and dream of the separation with my wife, dream of my kids, that kind of thing. Then I'd wake up with my stomach tied in knots, sweating. The bedsheet would be completely wet with sweat. Then I couldn't get back to sleep. After a couple of nights like that, I asked my mom if she had anything to make me sleep a good sleep, and she had some Valium. So I started taking Valium before I'd go to bed, trying to sleep, but it wasn't doing a thing. It was like I couldn't even feel it. On top of all that, I started dropping weight like you wouldn't believe—I think I lost like ten pounds in a week. So I was pretty bad off.

A week or so after the depression hit, my wife and I went for some counseling with my pastor at church because of the problems we were having. I just started bawling, crying my eyes out, saying my wife didn't love me anymore, that the only reason she married me was that she wanted kids, and now she's got the kids. We'd just had our second daughter. She was born in June, and the shooting went down the previous December, so my daughter wasn't a month old, and I was wailing that my wife didn't love me anymore, that she wanted kids, that she had them now, so she didn't need me, blah, blah, blah. As I was crying, my pastor said, "Ted, I think your shooting is bothering you more than you realize." I said, "The shooting? That was six months ago. I'm not bothered by that. My wife doesn't love me anymore. That's my problem now." He gave me the name and number of a psychiatrist and told me that he wanted me to go see her. I took the number from him, thinking, "OK. I'm not gonna insult him. I'll take it, but I ain't gonna see nobody. This isn't a psychiatrist issue." I put the number in my wallet just to be polite and we left.

It wasn't two or three days later when a detective asked me if I had time to run down to Mercy Hospital for him and pick up a rape kit that had been done on a rape that had occurred the night before. I was working a plainclothes assignment up in investigations, so I said, "Yeah, no problem." Driving to the hospital, I was thinking about the shooting and everything else. About two miles from the hospital, I started to cry. I pulled over, bawling like a baby, thinking, "What can I do to make my life like it was before?" My life had been a bed of roses up until that point. Nothing had ever gone wrong in my life. Everything that I had ever tried for I had gotten. Tried to get on the police department, got it on the first time, the only department I had ever tried for. Never been rejected or turned down for anything I'd ever really wanted and tried to get, and now I'm separated from my wife. I couldn't believe the crap that was going on in my life and how bad I was feeling. I didn't know why I was feeling so bad. I was just bawling like a baby, trying to figure out what to do, and I said to myself, "Well, you can kill yourself." Then I thought, "Holy shit, I need some help."

I regained my composure, got the rape kit, went back to the station, gave the kit to the detective, went back into the office, shut the door, locked it, and pulled out the phone number my pastor had given me. I called her and told her that I had been having problems with my marriage and my pastor had given me her number. She asked me if anything else had happened. I told her that I was a police officer and that I'd been involved in a shooting about six months ago, but that that wasn't the problem. I told her the problem was my marriage. She asked me a couple of questions I can't remember; then she asked me if I had had any thoughts about harming myself. I got quiet for a few seconds; then I said, "Well, I thought about it, but I'm not gonna do it. I mean, the thought crossed my mind, but I know that I don't need to do that. I have some sanity left."

She asked me, "When can you be here?"

I said, "I'm not doing anything right now."

She said, "I want you to come down here now." Half an hour later, I was in her office.

I basically spent the first hour with her doing nothing but crying. Then I saw her about twice a week for three or four weeks. The first four or five times I was there, she'd asked me a couple of questions and the entire time I tried to answer her, it'd be through bouts of crying. Eventually, I got to where we could talk and I didn't just break out crying all the time. When I finally made it through a whole hour without crying at all, we went down to one session a week. I did that for a couple or three weeks, and then she brought my wife in privately. She met with her alone for a couple or three visits. Then my wife and I went to see her together either once or twice, and then we didn't see her anymore. I moved back in with my wife, and things gradually got better after that.

The biggest thing I learned through the counseling was what had happened between my wife and me over the shooting. I didn't see it when it was happening, but she was doing what she thought I wanted to deal with the shooting. My wife knew that I really didn't like to talk about it. Everybody was asking me questions about the shooting, and I would tell them about it. I felt like I needed to tell them, but as soon as I started to talk, I felt like, "What an idiot, you are going to sound like you are bragging. Everybody's going to think that you think that this is a really neat deal," crap like that. So as I was talking, I was thinking, "Shut your mouth and quit. You sound like an idiot."

My wife was the only person I felt comfortable talking to, but I'd told her that I felt really bad when I told people about these things, that I thought they were gonna feel that I was bragging about it or that I felt good about it. So she knew I didn't like to talk about it. I never told her that I felt comfortable talking to her, so she just figured I didn't want to talk about it at all and quit talking about it with me.

Then we basically quit talking about everything. She just quit communicating. When we went in to see the psychiatrist, she said, "I'll tell you what your problem is—you guys are not talking to each other. You're not talking to her. You're not talking to him. When was the last time you actually sat down and talked about something involving the kids or outside of the fact that you're separated and arguing about your problems with the separation? When was the last time you sat down and talked about anything to do with going and doing something, or the kids growing up, or something else about your family life?" We couldn't remember, and she said, "You gotta start talking." So we left and went home and talked. It was either that night or the next night that I moved back in. And it was really good. My wife sat down with me and made me talk about the shooting, about how I was feeling, that kind of stuff.

So the counseling got us back on track, but I still had some tough times. Prior to the shooting, I wasn't a moody person. I was always in a good mood, always, but after the shooting I was real moody. I'd be sitting there watching TV—I could be watching a comedy—a commercial would come on, and for no reason I would get pissed off. Then I would be pissed off because I had no reason to be pissed off. It was like a vicious circle. That type of stuff happened all the time for about three and a half years, until the civil suit finally ended.

The single thing that bothered me the most about the whole lawsuit was the plaintiff's attorney. He tried to make me out to be the bad guy. I mean, the guy I shot was a parolee living in a halfway house, working at a job at a commercial laundry. He didn't show up for work and his boss reported him. That violated his parole, so he was a felony absconder. He had gone back to his workplace looking for his boss, pulled a knife, and started threatening people, demanding to know where the boss was. At one point, he took a swipe at this guy through the window of his car, so he was wanted for felony absconding and ADW. As I was chasing him, he pulled the knife on me, so I shot him.

In my deposition, when we got to the question of the shooting and my bullet hitting the guy in the head, the attorney got all indignant. He asked me, "Did you think about shooting him in the legs?" I said, "No. We're trained to shoot center mass because that's the biggest target." So he goes, "Well, you don't think you can hit him in the thigh, but you can hit him in the back of his head. You think that the head is about the same width as the thigh? If you can hit one, why can't you hit the other?" He was being real accusatory, insinuating in his questions that I was an idiot. When I answered him, I said, "You're assuming that I was aiming at his head, but I wasn't. I was running, he was running, but I was shooting center mass. I wasn't aiming at his head. I just happened to hit him there." The manner that he asked things pissed me off. It was all I could do to keep my cool in that deposition and answer those questions. He was just a typical attorney, not caring about what really happened, just spouting off with righteous indignation.

The suit went all the way up to the Supreme Court. The Supreme Court rejected it. They wouldn't even review it. They upheld the appellate court's decision that the shooting was justified. When that happened, the periods of me getting pissed off for no reason started declining. I still have them, and it pisses me off when it happens, because I sit there and for no reason I'll just get mad. Pissed off at the world. It's one of those things that still bothers me. I'll still blow up at my kids for no reason, but it happens a lot less than it did when the lawsuit was going on.

Another thing that came from the shooting is that I completely quit hunting. I used to love to hunt. I hunted almost religiously all through college and even after I became an officer, but since the shooting, I don't want to hunt anymore. I don't know why; it's just that I don't have any desire to hunt. I still fish, fly-fish, the quiet sport. That's what I want. I want that quiet solitude, just to get away from things.

The guy I shot was barricaded up near a fence between two houses. It started out as a pursuit where he'd tried to run several cars off the road. We'd chased him all over the county until he tried to make a U-turn and one of the other units smashed his car and knocked him into a ditch. The guy bailed out of the car. And when he did, he put a pistol to his head. He walked backwards from the car, telling us to stay back or he'd shoot us or he'd shoot himself; then he took off running, still holding the gun to his head. When we finally caught up with him between the houses, he sat down against the fence, kept the gun against his head, and told us that he was gonna off himself and that he'd kill us if we came near him. Then it was a standoff.

I stayed about twenty-five feet away back at the corner of the first house and covered him with my gun while some other officers negotiated with him for several hours. They even brought his girl-friend to the scene to talk to him. After a while, he put the gun down, and a couple of the guys got close to him and tried to grab him before he could get to his gun. The guy slipped from their grasp, picked up the gun, and started to swing it toward them. That's when I started firing.

I could actually see his body taking the rounds. It was kind of like a *Rocky* movie when Rocky's punched in the face and you see his head snap back. I saw his chest and his arm and his body moving like some-body was kicking him or hitting him or something. So I knew I hit him. I quit shooting when the guy totally collapsed to the ground. His body just went completely limp. In my mind, that was the cutoff switch. He wasn't gonna harm anybody anymore, so I started advanc-ing on him. As I came up on him, I could see blood spurting out of the side of his chest.

The negotiator was asking for a knife to cut the guy's shirt off, so we could start CPR and cover his wounds. I gave him my pocketknife, and he ripped the guy's shirt open. I looked over, and I could really see the blood pumping out. The only wound I could see was a sucking chest wound underneath his right arm. There was blood everywhere. Blood was just pouring out of him like a faucet. He was looking up at me, and I could tell that he knew it was me that shot him. I remember looking at his face thinking, "Well, what do I do now?" I knew that if you hurt somebody, you gotta take 'em to the hospital, but that's all I could think of. I was freaking out. Not emotionally or anything, but just like, "Man I can't believe what's going on." It all happened real quick.

On top of that, the guy's girlfriend started screaming and holler-ing. No one had thought to get her out of there, and at one point she started hitting me in the back, so I had to fight with her while I was still dealing with this guy. I said to the other guys, "You all need to get this bitch out of here." For one, she was getting hysterical, and for two, I just shot her friend and that ain't looking good for us to be fighting. Someone took her away, and I turned back to the guy.

Now we're taught by watching videos and stuff that if you see a sucking chest wound that you need to put something over the wound to keep the chest from sucking in air. Blood going out is not as bad as the air coming in. So the negotiator asked for a cigarette wrapper, which is plastic. I got one for him, and he stuck the cigarette wrapper on the hole. At that point, the guy's body started to twitch and jerk. I knew he was going out. I didn't think he could survive, but still I thought we needed to get EMS up to where we were.

I said, "Somebody get EMS up here now!"

The negotiator said, "No, no. Disregard EMS. He's dead."

Well, the guy was still gasping for air. He was looking at me in the eyes. So I said, "You better get fucking EMS up here! Get them now!" I smoked this guy, I'm the one who shot him, and I wasn't gonna let them disregard EMS.

Right about the time I said, "Fuck you, get EMS over here," the guy's body stiffened out, and he stretched out in a flat position on his back. That's when I could kind of see the life going away from his eyes. At that point, my sergeant showed up, and he and my captain grabbed me, and we kind of walked away.

I told my buddy Artie afterwards that one of the things that bothers me the most about what happened was having to see the guy's face, because I saw every emotion he's ever had in that three-, four-, five-hour period we knew each other. I saw him hating everybody, trying to run people off the road. I saw him running down the road with a gun to his head in desperation. I saw fear in his eyes. I saw pain and agony, grouchiness. I saw a drunken stupor, and then, when I shot the guy, I saw the face of a two-year-old staring right at me in pain, pleading for help.

I work in a small town, but I'd seen a guy die before this guy. A guy who shot his ex-wife in a murder-suicide-type deal. I got there right after he had shot himself in the head and was taking his few last breaths. EMS was showing up, and he was doing the death gurgle, but he saw me. I looked over, and after I saw his ex-wife shot to hell, I said, "You better die, motherfucker," and he went out. It didn't bother me. I didn't shoot him, plus he was an asshole. He'd shot his wife, killed her. He looked in my eyes, but it didn't bother me. I had also seen a friend of mine's sister who got shot in the head. I heard her take her last breath on a police call. That didn't bother me, either. I knew it was my buddy's sister, but I didn't do it.

It was different with the guy I killed. When I had to see this guy's face, knowing the fact that I was the one that took his life away from him, that kind of disturbed me for a while. In fact, it's been a couple of years now, and it still kind of disturbs me. To this day, I feel really bad that I had to kill that guy. I mean, if it was the same situation, if it happened right now, somebody came in with a gun, I would react and take care of business. I don't have a problem with that. But I'm not a cold-blooded killer. I don't do that for kicks. A lot of people told me I was a hero for protecting those other officers, but I don't consider myself a hero. I mean, I'm a cop. I'm trained to help other people, and I'm also trained to react and I reacted. I did my job, to hell with it.

The fact that I killed a guy doesn't bother me. The fact that I had to look at him bothers me, and the fact that a life is gone because of something I had to do bothers me. I don't regret killing him, which I guess is kind of a contradiction of terms, but I do regret having to take a life. It's just the fact that I was raised in a Christian home. I was a good kid. I have pretty strong religious beliefs, and I believe in the death penalty, too. I think you deserve the punishment that fits the crime, and I believe if he intended to take our lives then he deserved to be shot. But you know, it just tears me up that I took a life.

My boyfriend was working the same shift, so after I gave my statement, I went home with him to my house. I remember him holding me and me crying. I was so mad at the guy I shot for putting me in that situation. So mad and I cried. He held me. I remember it being a hard cry. I remember it being a rip-out-your-guts-type cry, like when you were a kid and you just cry over something that has just devastated you. I mean devastated. It was like that. It was like a go-back-to-childhood-type thing. It was really nice to have my boyfriend there because he was able to comfort me. I don't remember ever being comforted like that other than when I was a child and going to my mom's arms when I was crying because I got hurt. That was the type of comfort he gave, and that's the type of cry it was.

I never wanted to shoot anybody, but I was also upset that he didn't die, because I thought that I didn't do my job. I shot the guy and he didn't die. I didn't do my job; my shots weren't good enough. Three out of six hit him, not all of 'em. On the other hand, the other part of me, the human part, the person who wants to do good for everybody and wants everything to be OK for everybody, is glad that he survived. I sometimes wonder if he had died if it would be harder on me emotionally. So I think that maybe the fact that he lived is a little bit of a saving grace, that it might have been harder on me if he died. Now, on the other hand, the guy is a mental, and if he goes off of his meds again and shoots and kills another person, I'll be devastated. Absolutely devastated.

I was in four shootings in my first two years on the job. The last two involved the same fourteen-year-old kid. In the first one, he pointed a .357 at me during a foot chase, but my shots missed him. Then, a few months later, he tried to run me and my partner down on this traffic stop. We shot the hell out of the car but didn't hit anybody.

I got to wishing I'd killed the kid that second time. I thought, "This is ridiculous, he did it to me once, then he turned around and did it to me again." What are the chances of something like that happening? I didn't want to get involved in anything like that again. It was terrible. I wouldn't want anybody to have to go through it. Just the idea of going in and doing the shooting and handling the paperwork and all the stuff that happened after the last one—I didn't want to deal with all that crap again. It's not like it is on *Cops,* where you get to see the chase and that's it. On TV, you don't get to see the reports, and you don't have to see the commander grilling the guy; you don't have to see the court testimony; you don't have to see the defense lawyer making his client out to be the best person in the world while you're just a big lump of shit that just likes to fire at people.

Coming back-to-back-to-back-to-back like that, I thought, "Man, what am I doing?" I wasn't quite sure that I wanted a job where people were always pointing guns at me and trying to kill me all the time. Plus, after the fourth shooting, it just got to the point where I was tired of being asked all the questions; I was tired of the Monday-morning quarterbacking; I was tired of the way that I was treated, the accusations that I was trigger-happy. I was out there trying to do my job; I had guns pointed at me; I had been run over by a car; I wasn't just looking to shoot.

I got tired of being in that position, and after a while I just finally thought, "Hey, there's got to be something better." I really started to think about being on the night watch, started to think about being up in the north end, started thinking about being a big-city policeman in general. I wanted to see if I could try to go with a federal agency, but I knew I needed at least three years on in the city before I could do that. That really started making me wonder if I'd made a bad decision on the career choice.

I knew that I needed at least almost two more years on the job before I could even attempt to go federal, and I knew that it would be beneficial if I had some type of investigative experience in order to do that, so I looked into getting into detectives. While I was waiting for a transfer, it was brought to my attention that since I had been in multiple shootings within a short amount of time, I was going to be watched a little bit more closely than the next guy. So I knew that I had to mind my p's and q's while I was on patrol.

I started to try to avoid situations where I might have to shoot. The last two shooting incidents started at Lacy Park and Washington when people flagged me down to tell me about something suspicious, so if I was at a busy intersection and somebody tried to flag me down, I'd tend to just wave and keep driving. I was very, very cautious on the calls that I went on. So I pretty much got lazy, but I was very, very safe when I did go out there. I always wore my vest. I usually would have a second gun. I was prepared to do what I had to do if faced with another situation like the others, but I would do things a lot more safely. I also decided that if another situation came up, I'd let the guy next to me do the shooting. I would be very hesitant to do the shooting again.

After I spent some time in detectives, I came over here to K-9. It turns out that I found a niche doing something that I really like over here with the dog, and luckily I'm still a policeman. I love being a policeman, but I don't enjoy a lot of the B.S. interactions that are involved with it. I haven't had a shooting in about ten years now, but my attitude about things so far as trying to avoid confrontations really hasn't changed.

—⁓—

I had my psych eval on Monday, and after that I had to go into work for a few hours here and there over the next few days, but the rest of that first week I spent most of my time with my friends and my family. I felt really good that whole time. I had this sense of elation, a happiness to be alive. Being around my father and my son and my wife and my friends, I was just elated to be alive because looking back at how close it was, I could have died. So I was just happier than shit.

Then, the Friday after my shooting, I was sitting with the rest of the guys, waiting to go do a warrant, when I got this page from communications, saying, "Your father's work called, and they're trying to get ahold of you. He didn't show up for work." I thought that something was wrong because my dad's a perfectionist who never missed a day of work in his life. That Sunday before, he had been over at my house talking to my wife about how depressed he was about my mom having died the year before from cancer. My wife had told me that he was really depressed about that, and it was hitting him really hard, so when

I got the page, I started thinking, "Shit, I hope he didn't kill himself." I really didn't think he would do that, but I thought it was possible because I knew he was really depressed about my mom's death. He had always said that when he dies, he hopes it's quick. Then, after seeing my mom suffer through eight months, dying slowing, he'd said, "When I go, I want it to be lights-out, and I'm gone. Quick and painless."

Because I was worried about him, I called down to the division where he lived and said, "Hey, go to the house. I give you permission to force entry. I know my dad wouldn't have a problem with that." He was the kind of guy that would always throw barbecues during Super Bowl and Thanksgiving, have a bunch of cops over there, so everybody pretty much knew him. So they forced entry into the house, and his car was there in the garage. His wallet was there. I said, "Go into the closet; there's a shotgun; I know he owns one shotgun. Make sure that shotgun's still there."

"Yeah the shotgun's in there with one box of rounds."

"OK, describe the house to me."

"Well, his jewelry's all here, rings are laying around and his watch and stuff."

I said, "Son of a bitch! He always takes that shit off when he runs," because my dad was a big runner. He ran all the time, ran circles around everybody. Then I said, "Shit! Shit!" and started thinking, "God, where could he be? Where could he be?"

He had a girlfriend at the time, but when we tracked her down, she didn't know where he was. So I called communications, and I said, "Hey I need you to do this for me. Did we have any John Does yesterday anywhere in Northern Division?" The operator started looking, and I was thinking, "God, please say no, please say no, please say no." Then she said, "Yeah we did. We had one on Coldwater"—which is the next street over from my dad's house—and I thought, "Oh, fuck! Here we go."

I said, "Give me a description," and she said, "Older white male. Graying, thinning hair. Early fifties." I was thinking, "Fuck, that's gotta be him." So I asked, "What was he wearing?" She said, "Jogging shorts, a shirt, and shoes." So I said, "Where did the body go?" And she said, "Well, he was transported for a heart attack, and they didn't revive him, so he's at the coroner's office now." I said, "All right, give me the number for the coroner's office."

I still didn't know it was him for sure, but I was already starting to get in a big panic, and then I went into that dreamscape again, like I did at the shooting, where I thought, "This isn't fucking happening. I'm gonna wake up any second now." So I started getting that fuzzy, dreamy feeling again, and then I called the coroner's office. I said, "Look, my dad didn't show up for work. He's missing. I checked with Northern Division, and they said they had a John Doe. Do you have the guy there?" The guy gave the description, and he gave it so distinctly I just knew it was my dad.

I was in the canine trailers at the time. I remember walking out, and when my lieutenant approached me, I just started bawling. I said, "I'm gonna have to leave. I can't do the mission, I'm gonna have to leave. My dad's missing, and I think he's at the coroner's office, and I've got to go to try to identify the body." Lieutenant Norris said, "Hey, fuck the mission. I ain't going either. I'll drive you over there." So he drove me over there. The coroner showed me the pictures, and sure enough, it was my dad.

We had a lot of close friends on the street where my dad lived, so I went over to his house and started letting everybody know what happened. As I was doing that, I started thinking, "Fuck! I killed somebody and this is my payback." That's what I thought. "I killed that guy last week and this is my payback. I took a life; now somebody's taking somebody I care about." I remember thinking that over and over and over again, even when I got home. I told my wife what I was thinking, and she said, "No, that's not the case." And I said, "Yeah, I know. But I just can't get the thought out of my mind." Then I started reverting back to the shooting again and getting pissed at this guy I killed again, saying in my mind to the guy, "You fucking put me in this situation, and now my dad's gone because of it."

The next day, I got a call from the counselor who handles the officer-involved shootings. She's a psychologist, a really sweet lady, and I told her what I was thinking and that it was really bothering me. She asked me, "Are you religious?" I said, "Yeah, I'm very religious. I'm a Christian. I'm not a Bible-thumper, but I have my beliefs." She said, "Well, if you have your belief in God, you know we don't have a vengeful God. God wouldn't do that. It just happened."

Then a couple of days after that, my wife and I were talking to this pastor about coming to this church near where we live. I told him about the shooting, my dad's death, about all that had been going on in our lives recently. He quoted something out of the Bible about how God makes allocations for police officers, and then he said, "You need to understand that there are those people out there that have to protect the flock, and that's what you do." Then he said, "Do you understand the difference between killing and murder? The Bible says 'Thou shall not kill,' but that's misinterpreted. What the Bible really means is 'Thou shall not murder.' Murder's premeditated. What you do as a police officer to survive and protect everybody else is not murder. Yes, you killed somebody, but it wasn't murder. There's a big difference in God's eyes."

As soon as he said that, holy shit, man, it was like it was gone. That was probably five days after my dad passed away, and as soon as that pastor deciphered the difference between killing and murder and pointed out that there are allocations in the Bible for people like soldiers and police officers and that there are people that have to do ugly things so the rest of us can lead normal lives, every stress from that shooting was gone. It was just an incredible rush of relief, especially with the religious words, because I believe in God; I believe in certain things and I believe you shouldn't kill. Then, when I heard the difference between killing and murdering and the interpretation of the Bible, that really was a big relief to me.

Then I started replaying everything about when my mom passed away and the way my dad led his life. He missed my mom so much, and he and I had no unfinished business. There was nothing we wanted to say but didn't, and I was at peace with that. He was a big drinker and he was a big partyer, always the life of the party. He loved to run, he wanted to go quick, and that's how he died. He went out for a run, he was in his cooldown, and he just totally blacked out.

After I broke it down, I said to myself, "You know what? He was fed up with what was going on at work. He was missing my mom so much. It was actually a good thing that it happened. He went exactly how he wanted to go." I was totally at peace with it after that, and I have been ever since. I think it's unfortunate that my dad's dead because my son is missing out on a great grandfather, but I'm at peace with it. I'm at peace with the shooting too. I didn't have any problems with the shooting at all those first few days, until that thing with my dad happened, and I started thinking, "Shit, I did this terrible thing and now my dad paid for it." That's what I was thinking at the time, but now I know that's not the case. It's just not the case.

Being involved in shootings was the main reason I left SWAT after almost ten years. It's kind of hard to explain, but every time I've been involved in a shooting—whether I fired the shots or one of the other guys did—I feel, for lack of a better term, like a machine. I don't mean to sound melodramatic, but it's just do the job, shoot the guy, get it over with.

When I'm involved in a situation where a decision about shooting has to be made, it's just perceive the threat and react. What's in his hand, what's not? Does he have a gun? It's just like a machine. I just go in there and do what I'm trained to do. I just do it, and if the guy's got a gun and he's threatening me or someone else, I'm going to shoot him. When I'm in those situations, I don't even think twice about it. If there is that threat, I'm going to cap 'em. And that's what bothers me: I can do it so easily. I just seem to myself to be too cold when it happens. That's it. I don't know how else to explain it. It just seems too cold, too calculating, too easy.

I was in two situations where I shot people. Then we had two others recently where I was the SWAT commander when other officers killed people. In the first of those other two, this barricaded suspect shot one of my guys, and one of my other officers killed him in the exchange of gunfire. It really pissed me off that the suspect had shot one of my guys, so that one didn't bother me too much, but a few months after that, I gave the order to one of our snipers to shoot this guy who was holding his kid hostage at knifepoint. He had a knife to his son's throat, threatening to kill him, so I told the sniper to take him out. I don't know why, but that one really bothered me.

I was just getting pretty tired of killing people and being around people getting killed and being responsible for shooting people and killing people. When I went home after we shot the guy holding the kid, I went to my wife and told her, "I don't want to do this anymore." I mean, I loved my job, but I hated what it made me do sometimes.

Then I started having dreams about my eleven-year-old boy dying, recurring nightmares with different scenarios. I'd have dreams about him falling off of things, getting hit by cars, just different stuff. They'd wake me up at two or three o'clock in the morning, and I couldn't go back to sleep.

About a year after we killed the guy who was holding his son hostage, I decided I needed to get out of SWAT. It was really hard because I helped start the team here and I loved the job. I loved the guys. I loved SWAT. But on top of the nightmares, I had basically gotten to the point where I had started hating the world. I needed to get back to where I liked people again. So I went back to patrol. Pretty soon after I left SWAT, my attitude about people started to improve, and the nightmares about my son started going away. I don't get them anymore, but I still miss SWAT. It's hard, because I know I could go back if I just said the word. In fact, not too long ago, I was at a meeting with the major, and he told me he wanted me to go back over to SWAT. We talked about it, but I turned him down. I really want to come back in, but I know I can't right now—not and maintain my sanity.

—∿∿—

Over the years, I've put on a lot of officer survival training where I talk about the situation where I got shot. The PD even made a training tape where we reenacted the shooting. So I can look at what happened with a sense of detachment, but I have also had times where I've been extremely upset about it.

The night I got shot, I was trying to kill the guy who was trying to kill me. I was doing everything possible to get an edge on him, and I've had some moments where the anger I felt that night comes back. Probably the biggest one came about ten years after the shooting when I was working as a sergeant in the Western Division. I was working a narcotics detail over there, teamed up with a guy named Vick Ancent, when we went to do an investigation over at the old St. Matthews Hotel. We were up on the roof, about ten stories up, looking around. There were needles up there, all kinds of other paraphernalia strewn around, and we were looking down into center-court windows of some of the rooms because we'd seen people shoot up right next to their windows before.

So I was standing on one side of the roof, and Vick was on the other, when he called me over. I walked around, and just three floors below us I could see somebody sitting at a table rolling what looked like a marijuana cigarette. Vick said, "Let's do an investigation," so we went downstairs, knocked on the door, and somebody opened it.

We went in and told everybody to turn around, get up against the wall, and put their hands up. I covered them while Vick searched them. They were all unarmed, so he had them sit down and started getting their IDs. I recognized the first guy he talked to, but I didn't know why. I was thinking, "Where do I know this guy from?" All of a sudden, it was like a mallet hit me over the head: "This is the guy who shot me. This is Oscar Smith, the suspect who shot me. He's supposed to be in prison. What's he doing here?" I couldn't believe it, because after he was convicted, the judge took me into his chambers and told me that this guy was going to spend the rest of his life in prison, that he was never going to see the light of day.

I was dumbfounded. Then I got very excited. I was in a rage that the suspect was in the same room with me. My face was probably redder than a beet. I was furious. This was somebody who tried to murder me.

I called Vick over and said, "Listen, I believe that's the guy that shot me. I'm going to throw him out of the window!"

He could tell that I wasn't kidding around, so he said, "Don't worry. He's going to jail. He's under the influence. I've already looked at the tracks on his arms. He's under the influence. Just keep it cool."

So there I was, wanting to throw this guy out the window. Then I started thinking about what Vick said, and about my family, my job, what I'd lose if I did throw him out a seventh-story window. I decided that it wasn't worth it, so I just played along with Vick and didn't let on that I knew this guy. He didn't act like he knew who I was, so I don't think it registered with him at all.

We hooked the suspects up, got them in the car, and drove to the station. On the way, Vick was prepping the guy with questions: "Do you know this officer?" Stuff like that. The guy kept saying that he didn't recognize me. Then, all of a sudden, he said, "I know."

And Vick asked, "What do you know?"

The suspect then said, "It's not something I'm proud of."

When we got to the station, Vick took him into the interrogation room while I waited outside. The suspect had a wallet that was taken in a street robbery just around the corner from the hotel where we'd arrested him. The victim couldn't ID him, but we booked him on the robbery of the wallet anyway. The suspect ended up doing some time for a misdemeanor out of that because he had used one of the victim's credit cards at a nearby gas station.

He did three or four months, and when he got out, I ran into him again. I'd responded to a call about a kidnapping at a motel to see what the officers had over there. There were several officers, and they had several suspects over to one side of the motel. One of the suspects was just walking around, so he caught my attention. When I looked at him, I realized it was Oscar Smith, and I drew down on him. All the other officers then drew down on the other suspects, not knowing what was up. After we got them all hooked up and searched, I explained to them who the guy was and that he was potentially very dangerous.

It turned out that the situation at the motel was a bag of worms, more of a narcotics thing than a kidnapping. The guys had a young female and a bunch of drugs, but it looked like the girl was a willing participant. So all the guy that shot me got booked on was another narcotics charge.

After he got out from that one, the guy came down to the station and told the officers on duty that he thought that I was after him and that he wanted to talk to me. I didn't want to talk to this guy, so I didn't. The captain up at Detective Assistance Division heard about this guy coming to the station and decided that it might be worth it to put a surveillance team on him, to see what he was up to. So they watched him for a while. The captain got back to me and told me that the suspect was nothing more than a penny-ante dope user, dope dealer, who wasn't worth anything.

That was good to know, but I was having some problems with the situation because he was supposed to still be in prison, and here I was running into him out on the streets. I was still real angry, so I went to talk with one of the department psychologists about what was going on. He was able to put my mind at ease.

He went over some of the same stuff I'd thought about when I was thinking about throwing the guy out the window. He asked me if this guy was worth everything that I'd worked for, my family, my job, and everything else. When I thought about that, it was easy to see that I needed to back off. On the one hand, I had this dope dealer who was probably going to be found dead in an alley with a needle hanging out of his arm someday, and on the other, I had my family and my career. That's what was important to me. Watching my kids play baseball on Saturday afternoon, going to the soccer games, stuff like that. When I looked at it that way, it was easy to put it in perspective and move on with my life.

Not a Problem

As hard as shootings are for some officers, they are a breeze for others. Some officers simply experience no notable negative reactions in the wake of shooting someone. They may have been a bit apprehensive about some aspect of their situation, such as how the investigation was going to proceed or how their family might react, but that's all. Some of the officers told me they had expected to have difficulties because they had received training that proclaimed that officers always experience substantial problems in the wake of shootings, and then they explained to me why they believed they didn't have any. Others left their lack of negative reactions unremarked upon, so I asked these officers why they supposed they were unaffected.

A common theme runs across what all the officers who did just fine told me: they were doing their job, shooting bad people who were doing bad things and who therefore deserved to be shot, so they had nothing to be concerned about. This section presents the stories of some of the officers who experienced no problems following their shootings, including their variation of the "it's my job and he deserved it" theme as an explanation for why they did so well.

I don't look at the shooting as an unpleasant experience. Now that may sound callous. When you kill somebody, how can that not be unpleasant? Well, if this had been an innocent person or somebody that I had accidentally killed, then I'd probably feel bad about it. But this guy was committing robberies, and he was trying to kill me, so I don't have the slightest bit of regret about shooting him.

I didn't really have any problems after the shooting. The shooting team came out to my house and interviewed me the next day. They had rolled out the night before and got all their physical evidence from the scene, took all their photos, interviewed all the witnesses, and whatnot. They saved me for last, I guess, just to make sure my story jibed with what everyone else said. I told them exactly what happened, ran them through it as they asked me questions, cleared up one or two points for them, and then they were done. I knew in my mind that what I'd done was right, and the detectives confirmed it just before they left: one of them told me that as shootings go, mine was as clean as a spring chicken.

I mean, it was pretty much cut-and-dried. He knifed me. I shot him. And that was that. I understood the gravity, and I understood the seriousness of what had happened, but it just didn't weigh on me any. After the detectives left, I thought everything through real carefully a couple of times. I kind of took myself down different paths. OK, what could I have done differently? What should I have done? There were probably a million other ways I could have handled it, but the bottom line was that I tried to keep some guy from hurting his wife, which I did. I sacrificed part of my arm in the process, but I can live with that. It sure could have been a whole lot worse, so I essentially resolved all that stuff within the first day or two, came to grips with it, and decided that it was OK.

Neither of the guys I shot died, and that's fine with me. If either or both of them would've died, that would've been fine also. When I talk to people about police shootings, I tell them it's not important to kill the person you shoot. You don't try to kill when you shoot; you try to stop. So if you stop what he's doing and you stop it right now, it's a successful shooting. You've done what you were supposed to do. You've accomplished your mission. If he dies, well, that's a consequence of his actions in trying to hurt someone. If he doesn't die, well, God just smiled on him that day. So to me, the injuries I inflicted are not material.

—◊◊◊—

The guy lived, even though I hit him six times. If he would've died, the only difference to me would've been that I would have gotten two weeks off instead of one day, because my department keeps officers out of the field for two weeks after a fatal. My intent was to stop the threat, and that's what I did, so what happened to him is totally immaterial to me. Fortunately for him, he lived. Unfortunately, someday we may have to go back and get him again because he's now out of prison. I think that's the bad end of it. If the guy isn't gonna hesitate to shoot a bunch of heavily armed policemen coming up to his house, he's sure not gonna hesitate to shoot a guy who pulls him over on traffic. For that reason, I would've probably felt better if he had died, because I'd hate to read the paper someday and find out that he was successful in killing either some civilian or another policeman.

I think he's definitely a threat. I don't think he is gonna change. While he was in the hospital, his friends were threatening to kill some police officers, and while he was out on bond awaiting his trial, he was supposedly back in business dealing. If a guy has that kind of mental attitude, then he's not gonna hesitate to shoot. I think he's a definite threat and that society needs to worry about the guy. But as far as my decision, once the threat has ended, the shooting stops. Once I stopped the threat, whether he lives or dies is irrelevant to me. So I wouldn't change a thing I did. Not a thing. But society would be better off if he was dead.

—◊◊◊—

We always do a critical debrief on all our incidents, so there was a lot of discussion among the team the next day. "Hey, what did you see? What did you do? How many rounds did you fire?" The guys who weren't involved asked, "Hey, what was it like? Did you use the sights?

Did you do this? Did you do that?" I think the debrief was a little bit more detailed on this because of all the things that happened. We want to decide whether we used the appropriate tactics. We want to know if we could have done it better. We ended up getting three people wounded, and of course the first thing we said was, "What could we have done to solve that problem? Could we have done it differently?"

I've been on the team for over fifteen years, so during the debrief some of the younger guys asked me, "Have you ever been on one like this before?" I said, "Man, what this reminds me of is Vietnam." This was the closest thing I'd ever been in to making contact since I was over there. The only thing different was we'd been in a building, and over there we were in a jungle. But it was a regular old Wild West shoot-out. There were bullets zinging everywhere, and that's the thing that got me reflecting back on what I did thirty-odd years ago. The shoot-out was the only thing that I've been involved in in police work that compared to Vietnam. We've had some other big shoot-outs here in the unit, but fortunately I haven't been involved in any of them.

Once the debrief was over, I thought about what I did. I figured there was nothing I could have done to contribute anything else besides what I did by shooting the guy. So I told myself, "You did a pretty good job," and left it at that. I'm not one to gnaw on things. I don't internalize things, so I don't have any problems with what I did.

I've shot six people, and three of them died. All of them had guns, and most of them fired some rounds at me or other officers. So I've been in some shoot-outs. But it never bothered me. In fact, after my fourth shooting I fell asleep on the psychologist's couch as I was waiting for my mandatory session with her. The shooting happened just before midnight, and after I got released from the investigation around nine the next morning, I went to see her because it's the policy of the PD for officers to see the psychologist as soon as possible after every shooting. I was so tired because I didn't sleep all night that I fell asleep on a couch in the waiting room outside her office. She came out, woke me up, and said, "I guess you don't have any problems sleeping." I said, "No." She let me go home, and I came back to work that night.

Now I've heard about officers getting in shootings, and they say, "Oh, my God, that was devastating." But that doesn't make sense to me because I look at shootings as something officers come on this job to do. In fact, it's the most exhilarating part of this job. It's why policemen rush to get to hot calls when they come out—not to shoot anybody, but to confront the bad guys. It's our job to go to the danger. Over the years, I confronted many armed suspects that I've taken into custody without using deadly force. But when someone shoots at me, I shoot back. If an armed suspect confronts you and you prevail in the shoot-out, you and your partner go home that night. What's devastating about that? I just don't understand why officers would have a problem with that. So to me, because the possibility of shooting people is part of the job, I've never had a problem after any of my shootings.

Validation

As previously noted, many men and women headed for law enforcement jobs wonder if they will be able to shoot someone if the need arises. This concern persists in the minds of some officers once they come on the job and emerges among some of those who had harbored no such doubts during their pre-police days. Similarly, because police officers must often count on one another for protection, many officers harbor the same question about fellow officers—particularly rookies—who have yet to prove themselves capable of shooting someone. An officer's first shooting, consequently, can have the immensely positive effects of striking the reservations they had harbored about their ability to pull the trigger and demonstrating to their peers that they can be counted on when danger comes a-callin'.

Some officers have the question about their own ability to take a life answered through situations in which they could have shot—the officer who actually had to stop pulling his trigger during his encounter with the newspaper-armed emotionally disturbed individual, for example. For many others, however, only a shooting can erase the doubts. In a similar vein, sometimes only a shooting can allay any doubts an officer's peers may have about his or her ability to shoot when the need arises. The three stories in this brief section address the validation issue in greater depth, showing more thoroughly how shootings can both settle the minds of the officers who pulled the trigger and demonstrate to their peers that they possess the ability to do the ultimate police task when called upon to do so. The final story also illuminates the particular burden that female officers often bear when it comes to peers' opinions.

—⁓—

I was a brand-new rookie when it happened. Some of the veteran guys at the station went and bought a little bottle of Jack Daniels while my partner and I were being interviewed. As we were leaving, they were like, "Here, kid. Have a drink, you did good." Because I was still in training—with the "Yes sir. No sir." stuff—I took some. One of the guys took me aside and told me that people were going to look at me different because you never know how someone is going to react in a shooting situation until it happens. He said that people around the station that haven't been in a shooting will look at me differently now because even if they would like to treat me like a trainee, they won't because if they haven't done it, they'll always have the question in their mind, "Will I be able to do it?" He was right. The veterans started treating me differently. They gave me a little more respect because they knew that when the shit hits the fan out here that I'll be able to handle myself.

What happened also changed the way I looked at myself a little bit. I had a sense of pride, a sense of relief almost, that, "Hey, I did it. I was able to survive. When they threw the worst at me, I survived." Like a lot of cops, I'd wondered how I'd perform if push came to shove. After the shooting, the doubts I'd had were gone.

—◊◊◊—

My first shooting changed some minds about me and settled my mind about some things. I was one of the few guys on SWAT that didn't have a military background, and after it happened one of my supervisors, who was a Vietnam vet, told me that he always had doubts about whether I would pull the trigger on somebody. The shooting put his mind to rest. It also reinforced a lot of thinking that I had about shootings. There is a lot of training about police shootings that says, "You'll feel stress. You won't be able to see your front sights. You'll wet your pants. You'll do this and that afterward." Before my shooting, I didn't think any of that would happen to me. I'd say, "No, I won't," but I wasn't sure, so I didn't challenge any of it. That's different now. Now I know I won't because none of that stuff happened to me.

Another thing that happened with the first shooting is that it put to rest whatever tiny doubt I had in my mind about how I'd do. I don't care who you are, no matter how good you think you are or how well you trained—until you've done it, there's always gonna be somewhere in the back of your brain, some doubt about how you will perform in a shooting. It might be tiny, tiny, tiny, but it'll be there. I've talked to my dad, who's a World War II combat veteran, and other guys who've been in shootings, and they all say the same thing. But the first one put all that to rest for me, so when the second one happened, my attitude was, "Been there, done that." I knew exactly what to do, and I knew how I was gonna do it because I'd already done it once before.

—◊◊◊—

Three of us—me, another female officer, and one of the SWAT offi-cers—had been chasing this guy through the grounds of this shopping mall early one morning, when he spun around with a gun in his hand. The SWAT officer and I were both pretty close to him at that point, maybe fifteen feet, and we both fired. After I fired my last round, the guy went down real hard onto his back, and he started screaming. I couldn't see where the gun went, but I saw that his hands were empty, so I moved up on his left side. I kept my gun trained on his chest the whole time and stopped up by his head.

The other female officer ran up behind the SWAT officer, and the two of them moved up on the suspect's right side. The SWAT officer then told the suspect to roll over onto his stomach so the other female officer could handcuff him. I didn't want to keep my gun pointed at his torso because that's where the other female was going to be when she moved in to cuff the guy, so I moved my aim point to the guy's head. As I did that, I spotted the gun on the ground, just above his head. I saw it had an orange trigger, which meant it was a toy gun, and I got pissed off. I was mad. I don't know if it's the mother instinct or what, but I just shouted at him, "You stupid idiot. What the hell did you make us shoot you for?" Then I kicked the gun away and said, "It's a toy," to the SWAT officer, because I knew he'd fired also. He said, "It's OK. It's all right. You did what you're supposed to do."

When he said that, I felt really great. I was very, very happy that I did what I was trained to do because that's always the unknown in police work. You can train for it and train for it, but it's an unknown if you'll pull the trigger until you actually do it. I had a big grin on my face; I was almost laughing. It was like I'd passed my own little test and maybe a test in the eyes of other people. Part of that was because I'm female. There are a lot of male officers who don't think females should be on the department, and I was thinking that I'd proved myself to them, so that was a big part of the elation I was feeling.

Other Consequences

Much of what happens to officers following a shooting does not fit neatly into any of the several categories that I used to organize the material I have presented thus far. This section includes a collection of stories that—in one way or another—shed addi-tional light on officers' post-shooting experiences.

—∿∿—

The team would go to elementary school classes, and the kids would always ask us, "Anybody ever shot anybody?"

Back then, I was the only one who had, so of course all the other guys would look at me. I'd say, "Well, yes, I have."

And I'd have kids saying, "Well, my mommy and daddy say that you're a bad person if you kill people."

And I'd say, "Well, they're right, they're absolutely right."

They'd say, "Well, aren't you a bad person?" What do you say to an eight-year-old?

I'd say, "But there are times that you try to defend somebody. When you want to help somebody, and it just turns out that someone doesn't want to be helped." So you try to explain it to them in eight-year-old terms, which is kind of hard sometimes.

—∿∿—

The guys investigating the shooting treated us pretty good, but it took an incredible amount of time for us to get any food. The shooting occurred before we got breakfast that morning, and we didn't get fed until way late that afternoon. I don't know if it was from that initial lack of food for so long or what, but I had an increased appetite for a month after this thing, and it started right then. I also became a little more sexually aggressive for a good long time. I don't know where that came from, but I was just horny more. I wanted sex more.

I'd almost been killed and I was pretty happy to be around. I wanted to do things that made me feel alive. I wanted to eat good food. I wanted to have good sex. I felt good about being alive. I enjoyed watching the butterflies. I went on vacation with my family. I spent more time with my kids. I found myself enjoying life a lot, really taking a moment to drink it all in. I wanted to try to gain new experiences. I wanted to go places I'd never been. I wanted to do things I'd never done. I wanted to do a lot more things before I died.

—∿∿—

The shooting taught me a lot about priorities. I used to work all the time, as much overtime as I could. It was a higher priority than my family obligations. I'm not married, I don't have kids, so it was easy for me to take all the overtime days and fill in when someone couldn't make it in. I'd do that at the drop of a hat. I worked because I basically had no life. After the shooting, I thought about all those days that I missed out of watching my nieces and nephews grow, watching their soccer games, having them over to spend the night, taking them to the park, going on hikes. I didn't do any of that stuff because I wanted to work.

But the shooting made me realize that work's not that important. It'll always be there, but how often is my nephew going to say, "Hey, Aunt Mary, can you come over and spend the night tonight?" He was going on twelve when the shooting happened, so pretty soon he wasn't going to want me there anymore. He's going to want to do other things, and I would have missed out on those chances if I would have kept on working like I used to. Now when the kids ask if I can come over, I jump at the chance. So the shooting helped me reprioritize, to realize what's really important.

—◊◊◊—

After my first shooting, I really felt like I was a hypocrite, so I quit going to church. The Bible says, "Thou shalt not kill," and here all the kids in church look at you, they almost idolize you when you walk in the door because you're a cop, you know. I knew that when I walked in the door after the first shooting that all these kids would be asking their moms and dads, "Hey, the Bible says, 'Thou shalt not kill.' How come Hal killed this guy?" I was having real hard trouble dealing with that, so I basically quit going to church altogether.

A little while after I quit going to church, this PD chaplain came out to me on an off-duty job to tell me that the prosecutor was about to make his announcement about whether to charge or clear me. After he told me that, he gave me this piece of paper with some scriptures on it and said, "When you get a chance, you might want to read these." So I did right there. One of the scriptures was from Romans, chapter thirteen: "Fear not the administrator"—and some versions actually say fear not the policeman—"for he is brought to you by God. You have no reason to fear him unless you do evil and if you do evil, then you have reason to fear him. For he does not bear the sword in vain." The other one was, "Above all else comes the law."

After I read them, the chaplain told me, "You know, a lot of people think the Bible says, 'Thou shalt not kill,' but it doesn't say that. It says, 'Thou shalt not commit murder.'" Then he said, "You know, there's a difference between killing and murder. Sometimes it's necessary to kill people, and you did not commit murder." When I heard that, I said, "He's right." And that really helped. I started going back to church, and by the time I got in my second shooting, I was involved in this Christian officers' organization we had.

—∿∿—

Overall, I was feeling pretty good. I was elated that the mission was successful, that I wasn't hurt, that none of my teammates were hurt, and that everything looked like it was a very good shooting. We went in with all of our officers; we came out with our officers. We had a violent situation, none of us got shot, and the suspect was down. The only remorse I had was that I had to shoot the dog. I was sad because the dog was just doing what he was supposed to do: protect his master. It wasn't the dog's fault that his owner happened to be a dope dealer with guns. It was a shame we had to shoot a good dog.

—∿∿—

I slept good that first night. I remember I put my son to bed. He was five at the time of the shooting. He's seven now. I sat in there for probably fifteen minutes after he fell asleep and listened to him breathe. That's like my favorite thing to do, hear him breathe. So I sat in there and listened to him breathe for about fifteen minutes. I had eaten good at the station, and I ate good again when I got home, so I had probably three or four beers after I put my son to bed, and then my wife and I went to bed. We actually made love that night and then I slept perfect. I didn't have any dreams. I slept really comfortably. I wasn't restless or anything. Slept eight, nine, ten hours. Woke up the next day, and the first thing I thought about was the shooting. Played it over in my mind a bunch of times. Then, probably an hour after I woke up, the phone started ringing off the hook.

I probably fielded fifty calls the first day, and I didn't have a problem with it, because it was mostly SWAT people who wanted to know what was going on, friends from work. And the first thing they asked was, "Do you have a problem talking about it?" I said, "No, I don't, I really don't." I said, "As far as I'm concerned, it was a righteous shooting. The guy caused the incident. We gave him every opportunity to give up, and he chose not to take them, so he pretty much forced the events to occur." So I didn't have any problem talking about it.

The only thing about that first day was that I felt really tired, a little burned out. I don't know if it was because I slept too long or what, but I just felt a little drained. I didn't feel like doing a whole heck of a lot, just hanging out with my kid and my wife. That's what I wanted to do. But I had to go into work for a debrief with the rest of the team. After it was over, Ralph—the other guy who fired—said, "Hey, let's go drinking downtown." I called my wife and asked her if that was OK with her. I told her that I felt like I should hang around with her, but she said, "Oh, no. Go hang out with Ralph. I'm sure he needs somebody to hang with."

We were drinking at the bar when the news came on, showing some footage from the scene that included some shots of Ralph and me. The waitress came up to us and said, "Hey, isn't that you guys?"

We were in street clothes, but she recognized us. So we said, "Yeah, that's us."

Then she asked, "Were you guys the shooters?"

And we replied, "Yeah, we were the shooters." We didn't know her, but she was really nice.

She said, "OK, I won't say anything out loud. I was just really curious because I saw your faces on the TV when you were walking through the scene, and you guys didn't have a whole lot of expression on your face, so I kind of thought you were the shooters."

I thought that was kind of funny that some civilian that doesn't really know about police work picked up on that.

—◆◆◆—

I called my wife—she was at work—and told her what happened. She was like, "Oh, my God! Are you all right?"

I said, "I'm fine," and told her, "I'll talk to you later about it, just wanted you to know that you're gonna hear it on the news." And then I didn't really feel like talking to anybody else but my teammates. I didn't want to talk to anybody else. The only people I wanted to be around were the guys I worked with, because they were the ones who were there. I didn't feel like telling the story ten or twelve times to everybody.

People had comments like, "God, you did a great job," but I didn't feel that way. I didn't feel like what I did was such a great job. I didn't feel like that at all. I don't feel like taking a life is doing a great job. Even though it may come with the territory, killing someone is not doing a great job. But you just have to suck it up and do it if you have to, because if you're gonna do this type of work, there's a possibility that something like this is gonna happen to you. You just have to take it.

—◆◆◆—

I don't think you can really understand what it's like to be in a shooting until you've been in one, because it's not like watching a Hollywood movie. Everybody's used to watching Hollywood, where cops take one shot and shoot the gun out of the bad guy's hand, or every shot they take is a perfect center mass hit. Plus, from movies, people don't know the fear of being shot at, the terror of gunfire coming at you. They don't know what it feels like to be hit, even by a fragment. Those things are missing from the movies. When I went through it, I felt everything. I utilized all five of my physical senses, but in the movie theater you don't have the cotton mouth, you don't smell the gunpowder, you don't feel the bullets hitting you.

The Pathos of Policing

The Not a Problem and Validation sections illustrate that shootings are not always detrimental for the involved officers and that they can even have positive repercussions. This does not mean, however, that officers who do fine after shooting people are immune from the stresses and strains of the violence they have confronted during their time on the job. Police work is widely regarded as one of the more stressful occupations in the world, at least partly because officers must regularly deal with the worst that humanity has to offer, the dead and broken bodies they produce, and the anguish they leave in their wake.

For some officers, it is a single atrocity that stands out in their minds. For others, it is the accumulation of horror and misery that gets them. The stories in this section relate how three officers whose shootings produced no remarkable problems for them still suffered from other sorts of encounters with human violence. They begin with the ruminations of the busy cop, who cannot forget a young woman whose life—despite his best efforts—he could not save from the murderous designs of her jealous ex-boyfriend.

—⁓—

I'd have to say that my three shootings didn't affect me too much. Even the fatals. But some other things on the job sure did. One of the biggest was a hostage situation that didn't work out. It was a domestic violence thing, a lovers' quarrel. It was one of those, "If I can't have you, then nobody can," deals. The guy went to the gal's place of business, grabbed her, took her into a conference room, and held her hostage for a while—I guess to say whatever he wanted to say—before he killed her and then killed himself.

When we got there, patrol had already determined the room they were in. The patrol cops had talked to him through the wall, so we were well aware of what was going on even before we got there. The negotiators got the guy on the phone, and my team got positioned right outside the room in order to do an emergency assault if we had to go in to rescue the girl. The door to the conference room was one of those that can't be locked, and we placed some fiber optics into the room, which showed that he hadn't barricaded the door. With that situation, we were almost guaranteed instant entry if we had to go in.

From the fiber optics, we knew exactly where he was, where she was, where the table and chairs were. He was holding her near the opposite end of the room from the door where we were stationed, lying down with her behind some chairs, partway under this long conference table. We knew everything about the room, so we felt real confident that we could rescue the girl if we were told to do so. There were no guarantees, but we felt confident. We assumed that it would be a simple matter of getting in as fast as we could and shooting him, unless, of course, he just threw his hands up and surrendered when we came in.

The plan I put together was to do a limited entry, where my point man was going to go to the end of the table that was near the door to try to get a shot straight down the table at him. If he didn't have a clear shot, he was going to continue on across the room until he could get a shot on him. The second man was going to go to a different spot in the room to try to draw the boyfriend's fire while the first guy moved to get a clear shot. I was going to go along the opposite wall to get a different firing angle. And the last guy was going to be my hands man. He was going to wait for my signal to come in, grab the hostage, and drag her out. So the plan was basically to draw the guy's fire toward us so that he didn't kill his girlfriend, shoot him, and get her out of there.

We told the commander we were ready to do it. The guy kept threatening to kill his girlfriend, but the commander told us not to go in unless the guy started shooting. Of course, I argued that if he started shooting, it was going to be too late to save the girl. But I didn't win that argument, and I did what I was told while the negotiators tried to get the guy to give up.

Sure enough, a little while after we were told to sit tight, we heard a shot go off. The girl let out a scream, and we started to go in. As we were turning the doorknob, we heard a second shot. As we were going through the door, a third shot rang out. Then my point man took a shot that hit the guy just as he stuck his gun in his mouth and blew his head off. The whole thing took about three or four seconds.

The investigation disclosed that the first two shots were the guy murdering his girlfriend and that the third shot was aimed at us; it lodged in the carpet just in front of the door we came through. It didn't bother me that he'd shot at us, and it sure didn't bother me that he killed himself, but I felt really bad, really angry, that the girl was dead. I was angry at the hostage taker, angry at the decision that was made not to go in earlier.

She was a pretty young girl, had her whole life ahead of her. If she had a chance of making it out of there, it would have been with us going in to rescue her. I was mad that we weren't allowed the chance to try and save her, but you know, I'm not the one who had to make that decision. So I didn't dwell on it, but it made me angry for several days, and to this day I still feel bad for the poor girl.

I thought about the shooting a lot in the first few days afterward. What could I have done better? How could I have done it safer? How can I improve? But then there was this surprise. When I was in the academy, they told us that shootings were very stressful events. That guys who get in shootings feel guilty, cry afterward, can't sleep, get divorced, and all sorts of other bad stuff. So during the academy, I got semiparanoid about getting into a shooting. I was worried about what a shooting would do to me, about these things that happen when you get in a shooting.

So after my shooting, I was waiting for all this stuff the academy teaches, all the shock and sleepless nights, the tears, and so on. I was waiting for it, but nada. Nothing ever came. Nothing at all. I'd told my wife what happened when I first saw her after the shooting and told her to get ready for the tough stuff. Told my other family and friends. Told the story till I got sick telling it because I wanted everybody to know what happened and how I was feeling, so they'd know what was going on when it hit. So I was braced, "OK, here it comes." But it never did. I was almost feeling guilty that I didn't have the guilty thoughts. But it wasn't there, it just wasn't there. I've never had any negative stuff about the shooting, and it's been a few years—no remorse or anything negative whatsoever.

Now maybe I repressed it, I don't know, but I don't think so, because some other stuff from the job does get to me. The biggest is that I keep getting this one nightmare from when I used to work patrol about twelve years ago. I got a call about these parents who beat up their child, a little baby. They were at the hospital, and Homicide had called me to detain the parents. I had to talk to the doctor first. I walked into the room and the baby was right there. He was dead. His eyes were wide open, big brown eyes, just like one of those Gerber babies. I could see this big impression of a fist on his stomach. The doctor was taking spinal fluid out of the child. I see all that in my dreams sometimes—the room, the kid, the fist mark. I mostly get them when I take a vacation. About the fourth or fifth night, I start getting these dreams. I don't get them day to day as long as I'm working, but when I go on an extended vacation, then they come back.

—◊—

I've always worked busy areas, so I've been involved in a lot of stuff in my six years on the street. I've been shot at several times, mostly sniper-type incidents, where we'd take rounds but couldn't identify where they were coming from. We didn't return fire in those cases because you can't just fire indiscriminately, even when the patrol car takes rounds. I've been in four shoot-outs with gang-bangers but only hit one of the guys I traded shots with. Then recently, I killed a sixteen-year-old kid who was holding his girlfriend hostage after he shot some deputies.

All these incidents had an impact on me, but it was other shootings where officers and deputies were killed that affected me the most. The first one happened when I was still in field training. Two officers from Reston, a neighboring city, were murdered when they made a traffic stop at this gas station. A couple of months after that happened, a deputy in my division was murdered at a man-with-a-gun call. About three years after that, I made the scene where a good friend of mine was shot and killed during a foot pursuit. And I just recently had a buddy who was killed in an off-duty deal, where a robber shot him in the head when he discovered my buddy was a deputy. I was at the hospital when he died. All of these deaths had a big impact on me, especially the two officers killed at the traffic stop when I was in training. I'll never forget what I saw when we responded to the assistance call.

When we got there, three one-man Reston cars had already responded. There was a fourth radio car with both the driver's-side door and the passenger's-side door wide open, parked in front of the gas station. The emergency lights were on, and there were two officers lying on their backs, basically parallel to each other, on either side of the radio car. The one on the driver's side was more toward the front of the car, and the other guy was more toward the back. They were both still alive. Two of the Reston officers were off to the side, not doing anything. They looked to be in shock, complete disbelief on their faces, just standing there. The other Reston officer was kneeling down next to the officer on the driver's side of the radio car.

So that's what I saw when we pulled up.

We found out later from the investigation what happened. The two officers, Dander and Johnston, made a regular vehicle stop on a blue sedan with just the driver in it. They got the suspect out of the car, and Officer Dander started to conduct a pat-down search. As he was searching, the guy pulled a gun out of his waistband. Apparently, Johnston didn't know the guy was going for a gun. He believed that it was just gonna be a fight, so he came running up to help Dander.

As Johnston was running up, rounds started going off. The first one hit Dander in the thigh. The second one caught him in his arm, his shooting arm, right at the elbow, incapacitating it. With his gun arm useless, he fell on his back. The suspect then fired several rounds at Johnston, who now had his back to the suspect because he had turned around and was trying to get to the other side of the car for cover. One of the rounds caught Johnston just above the vest and hit him in his neck area. He was bent over when he took the round; that's why it was a fatal. If he'd been standing up a little more, it would have caught him in the vest. So Johnston went down, and the suspect turned again on Dander. Dander had his feet up in the air, I guess in a defensive position. The guy put a round in the bottom of Dander's foot and then fired several more, striking him twice in the head. He then went over to Johnston, straddled him, did a coup de grâce on Johnston, jumped back in his car, and took off. So the suspect was gone long before we got there.

When I got out of the car, I got one of the Reston officers to give me some information, and I put that out over the air real quick. Then I went over to Dander—I knew him from court—and looked at him. I yelled at him, "You're going to be all right, buddy, hang in there." But in my mind, I was saying, "Just die," because he was messed up. From the severity of the wounds, I knew that if he survived that he was going to be a vegetable. I mean, I could see that he'd taken one round that entered above his right eye and exited the back of his head. He was a mess.

Then I went over to Johnston. He was down on the ground, kind of shaking. There was what appeared to be brain matter off to the side of his head. It may have been, but it could have been food. Apparently, they had just finished eating. They'd each had a burrito, and they'd both been regurgitating, so there was like rice and stuff to the side of Johnston's head. That's why I'm not sure if the other stuff was brains or some other food.

Both officers' guns were still in their holsters, and I'll never forget that, seeing both guns in their holsters. Another thing that stuck in my mind is that Dander was wearing his black gloves because it was nighttime in March, and it was still kind of cold. I was standing there in just complete disbelief, just in shock, looking at both of them and knowing they were going to die, thinking that we'll do whatever we can for them, but knowing that they were going to die. I played that picture constantly back in my mind for a long time. It just was an incredible scene to see two guys down like that. Periodically, after all these years, when I think about it, that picture of them lying there dying still comes back.

The Last Word

The final voice we hear from is that of a veteran officer who shot two people, one fatally, during the first of his two decades in police work. Over the years, he has struggled mightily with both shootings, spending considerable time researching the consequences of killing and discussing with other officers how their shootings affected them. Given his informed perspective on the topic, he has the last word.

—∿∿—

I've gone through some really tough times after my shootings, and I've talked to a lot of other officers who've been in shootings about how they handled it. Some have had some tough times like me, and some it hasn't really bothered much at all. I teach shootings up at the academy, and one of the biggest things I tell those recruits is that everybody handles things different. I tell them about Hank Rickly on our department. He killed a guy who jumped through the window of his car armed with a knife.

The guy had come up to his window, being real genial and just talking to him very nice and polite and calling him "sir," when all of a sudden, he just pulled out this huge knife, said, "You son of a bitch!" and started trying to stab Hank through the open window. Hank just leaned away, pulled his gun, and shot the guy four times. Hank was fine about everything. He knew about the difficulties I had after my shootings, and he told me that he woke up three days after the incident and said to himself, "Why don't I feel bad?" So he and I are on opposite ends of the spectrum.

But I think that shooting someone changes just about every cop who does it. If you haven't been in a shooting, you can't really understand it, and I don't really know how to explain it, but after you shoot someone, things will never be the same. It's almost like there's a loss of innocence involved. You'll just never look at life the same way.

Epilogue

However their shootings affected them, the eighty men and women I interviewed have pressed on with their lives. Many of them still worked the same assignments they held when we spoke, some have been promoted or otherwise moved on to different jobs with their departments, some have taken positions with other law enforcement agencies, and several have left police work entirely.

Among these officers, one resigned to start a small business, one quit to train horses, one went back to graduate school after retiring with twenty years of police service, one was forced to retire due to injuries he suffered during a scuffle with a resisting suspect, and one received a disability pension from the injuries he sustained in the incident described in the Officer Down section of the fourth chapter.

Several of the officers who stayed in law enforcement have been in additional shootings since the time they sat for interviews. These include a pair of patrol officers who each killed gunmen in separate early-morning shoot-outs, another patrol officer who killed a young man who was holding his girlfriend hostage, three SWAT officers who shot armed murder suspects who were trying to evade capture, a SWAT sniper who killed a suspect who pointed a gun at his teammates, and a SWAT officer who shot two people in separate incidents during the summer of 2001.

Finally, and tragically, one of the officers I interviewed did not survive a return visit to the kill zone. He was murdered late one February evening in 2001 when he caught up with a thief he'd been chasing through one of the housing projects that dot his inner-city patrol beat. In the bland parlance that is often used by both the press and the police to describe knock-down-drag-out fights between cops and crooks, "a struggle ensued," and the thief somehow managed to wrest the officer's gun from his holster, place the barrel against his forehead, and pull the trigger. This brave officer was thirty-seven when he was murdered. His youngest child was just seven weeks old.

—∿∿—

I have lived with the kill zone for a quarter century now: contemplating the possibility that I might have to shoot someone prior to joining the LAPD, preparing for this prospect during my academy and field training, taking a life while I was still wet behind the ears, living with the consequences, holding my fire during numerous close calls, grieving the loss of friends and colleagues who were gunned down, studying how other officers deal with their time in the kill zone, and teaching both college students and police officers around the country about the role that deadly force plays in our society and how using it affects the men and women who pull the trigger. As I reflect back on all this experience, two things stand out in my mind—one social, the other personal.

On the social front, I believe that the profound effect that shooting someone can have on officers reflects the deep ambivalence that our freedom-loving society has about granting representatives of the state the power over life and death. We demand protection from the criminals and others in our society who might harm us, so we've given the police the power to use lethal force on our behalf. But we also fear for our freedoms, so we want our men and women in blue to use the awesome power they possess judiciously, perhaps even grudgingly.

Thus, in some ways, it's comforting to know that officers often have some difficulty in the wake of shootings. Their pain and reflection show us that our police are cut from the same cloth as we are, that they share our values, that they do not take lightly the power we've given them. And this assures us, at some deep level, that the men and women we empower to protect us are not likely to turn against us.

On the personal front, I am struck by the honor of the men and women who willingly go into harm's way every day to protect the rest of us. By and large, they understand the social compact that binds us; they understand that the awesome power they hold is not to be taken lightly; they understand that we expect them to be restrained. And so they are, even when—as the stories in the third chapter indicate—it exposes them and fellow officers to considerable danger.

But officers also understand that there are times when they must exercise their ultimate power on our behalf. And when they believe they must, they do so, despite the fact that they know they will be criticized and second-guessed; that they may be sued or even prosecuted; and that there is a good chance their hearts, minds, or souls will suffer for what they have done.

And so I tip my hat to all the good cops throughout our nation who risk their lives and strive to do the right thing when facing split-second decisions about life and death every day in the kill zone.

Glossary

00-buck: A type of shotgun shell that holds several (usually nine or twelve) .32-caliber pellets. Often carried in police shotguns. (00 is pronounced "double ott.")

12-gauge: A large-bore shotgun.

20-gauge: A medium-bore shotgun.

.22: A small-caliber handgun.

.25 auto: A small-caliber semiautomatic handgun.

.223: A high-velocity, small-caliber bullet that is typically used in assault rifles such as AR-15s, M-16s, and similar weapons (see definitions later in this section).

.38: A medium-caliber revolver.

.308: A medium-bore, high-velocity rifle bullet.

.357 Magnum: A revolver that fires a medium-caliber, high-velocity bullet.

.40-cal H&K: A medium-caliber semiautomatic pistol manufactured by Heckler & Koch Inc.

.45: A large-caliber semiautomatic handgun.

417: California Penal Code section that covers brandishing weapons.

Adios, mi hijo: Spanish for "good-bye, my little one."

ADW: Assault with a deadly weapon.

AK-47: A fully automatic assault rifle that was the standard-issue shoulder weapon in Soviet-bloc armies.

AR-15: A semiautomatic assault rifle that fires .223-caliber ammunition. The law enforcement and civilian version of the M-16 fully automatic assault rifle that was standard issue to U.S. infantry units for many years (see M-16).

Bail, Bailed, Bailing: Getting out of a vehicle, usually used to refer to a suspect exiting a vehicle to flee.

Bang, Banger: Short for flash-bang (see also noise flash diversionary device).

BDU: Short for battle dress uniform, the military fatigue-like utility clothes that SWAT team members usually wear during operations.

Benelli: Short for the semiautomatic .12-gauge shotgun made by the Benelli corporation that is carried by many SWAT teams.

Beretta 92F: A 9-millimeter semiautomatic handgun made by the Beretta corporation.

Black Talons: A brand of hollow-point ammunition that is designed to mushroom upon impact, creating a larger wound channel in the body than would a standard round.

Blue steel: A type of handgun finish.

Body bunker: A type of handheld ballistic shield that is used to protect officers from gunfire.

Brass: Bullet casings.

Breacher: A police officer (usually a member of a SWAT or narcotics raid team) assigned to force open doors so that the rest of his or her teammates can enter a location unimpeded.

Break and rake: A tactical procedure in which police officers standing outside a building shatter a window with a pole (the break) and then move the pole around the inside of the window frame to remove whatever glass or window treatments might remain (the rake). This tactic is usually used to distract suspects inside houses during the service of narcotics search warrants but is sometimes used to gain access to rooms during other sorts of SWAT operations.

Bust caps, Busting caps: To fire one's gun. As in, "I was busting some caps as the guy was shooting at me."

Buy-bust: A tactic used by plainclothes narcotics officers in which an officer (or officers) purchase illegal drugs from a suspect (or suspects), then another officer arrests the suspect(s).

Cap: Bullet.

Caper: An incident, usually involving some sort of criminal undertaking.

Capped: Fired one's weapon. As in, "I just capped someone."

CAR-16: A fully automatic assault rifle that fires .223-caliber bullets and is smaller than a standard M-16 (see M-16).

Carotid: Short for carotid neck restraint, a self-defense technique used to control combative suspects in which the officer—from behind—places an arm around the neck of the suspect, takes the suspect to the ground, and then applies pressure to the sides of the suspect's neck in order to restrict the flow of blood and render the suspect unconscious.

Center mass: The middle of one's torso. The primary aim point for police gunfire.

Chrome: A type of handgun finish.

Clear: To search a location to ensure that no suspects or victims are present. As in, "Clear the objective."

Cleared leather: Drew one's gun.

Colt .45: A large-caliber, semiautomatic handgun manufactured by the
Colt Firearms Company.

Contact shot: A shot fired when the barrel of the gun is against the clothes
or skin of the person being shot.

Cord cuff: A length of cord used to secure the legs of combative suspects.

Cover: Any sort of object or material that will stop bullets (for example,
large trees, motor vehicle engines, armored vehicles). Also, being
behind any such object.

Covered, Covered down on: Pointing one's weapon at an individual
or area. As in, "I covered down on the suspect while my partner
cuffed him."

CP: Command post.

Cracked-up: High on crack cocaine.

Drill: Shoot. As in, "I drilled him right between the eyes."

Dry firing: A firearms training technique in which one pulls the trigger of
an empty gun. Often done to familiarize novices with the mechanics
of firing a gun.

DV: Domestic violence.

Entry stick: The single-file formation that SWAT team members or other
officers form as they prepare to enter a dwelling, typically when
serving a search warrant (see also stick and stack).

FATS: Short for firearms training simulator. A computer-controlled system that projects scenes of potentially violent encounters on a screen
to test officers' decision-making and shooting skills.

Fiber optics: A pinhole-type video camera attached to the end of a fiber-
optics cable, essentially the same technology used by M.D.s in ortho-
scopic surgery. In police work, typically used by SWAT teams to view
the interior of locations in which suspects are believed or known to
be hiding.

Flash-bang: (see noise flash diversionary device).

Flier: A bullet that misses its intended target by passing or striking above it.

FTO: Field training officer.

Full auto: Short for fully automatic gunfire, a mode of gunfire in which a
single pull of the trigger fires multiple rounds. When a weapon is
operating on full-auto mode, bullets continue to fire as long as the
trigger is depressed and there are bullets in the magazine or chamber.

Go out on: To get out of one's patrol car to investigate something or
someone.

Hallagan tool: A heavy-duty L-shaped breaching tool that is approximately two-and-one-half-feet long. Used primarily to pry open
doors.

Hammer: Shoot. As in, "I was going to hammer him again if he kept coming at me."

HK-53: A fully automatic assault rifle that fires .223-caliber bullets.

HK-91: A semiautomatic assault rifle that fires .223-caliber bullets.

Homicide: The unit of detectives that investigates homicides and other serious incidents, including police shootings.

Hooked up: Handcuffed.

Hot stop: A type of vehicle stop in which officers draw their weapons, stay behind their patrol car, and order the occupant(s) of the vehicle they have stopped out at gunpoint because they suspect the occupant(s) may be armed or dangerous.

IA, IAD: Short for Internal Affairs or Internal Affairs Division, the unit of detectives that investigates allegations of police misconduct and (in some police agencies) officer-involved shootings.

Index one's finger: To keep one's finger outside the trigger well by placing it against the frame of the gun that one is holding.

Jersey wall: A type of concrete retaining wall often used to separate lanes of traffic on highways.

Kevlar: High-tensile-strength fiber that is the bullet-stopping material used in the soft body armor many police officers wear.

Long gun: A rifle or shotgun. The term is generally used when one is not sure whether the weapon in question is the former or the later.

M-14: A semiautomatic rifle.

M-16: A fully automatic assault rifle that fires .223-caliber bullets. The standard-issue rifle in U.S. military infantry units and a weapon carried by many SWAT officers.

Mace: A nonlethal chemical irritant.

Magazine: The part of semiautomatic and fully automatic weapons in which bullets are stored.

Mandrix: A narcotic.

MAST suit: Short for military anti-shock trousers, inflatable pants that medics place on severely injured people to keep their blood pressure from falling to fatal lows.

Meth-head: A chronic methamphetamine user.

MO: Short for modus operandi, the way a crook capers.

MOBY: Term used by some SWAT teams when referring to large, heavy, handheld rams that are used to smash doors open, usually during the service of high-risk warrants. Named after the great white whale in the Herman Melville novel *Moby-Dick*. The MOBY man is the SWAT officer assigned to carry the ram during a given operation.

Model 60: A small, five-shot .38-caliber revolver with a two-inch barrel.

MOS: Short for military occupational specialty, one's assignment in the military.

MP-5: A compact submachine gun that many SWAT officers carry. Comes in 9-millimeter and .40-caliber models.

No billed: A verdict from a grand jury that a shooting was justified, that they will not issue a bill of indictment against the officer.

Noise flash diversionary device: A small, handheld canister that contains a small amount of extremely fast-burning material that emits a brilliant light and thunderous noise when detonated. Typically used by SWAT teams to distract suspects during operations such as high-risk warrants and hostage rescues.

North Hollywood bank robbery: A 1997 bank robbery in the North Hollywood area of Los Angeles that led to a nationally televised shoot-out between two heavily armed suspects who were wearing body armor and dozens of LAPD officers. Several officers and citizens were wounded. Both suspects were killed.

OC: Short for oleoresin capsicum, a nonlethal chemical irritant. Also known as pepper spray, because the irritant is derived from a pepper plant.

Optical sights: An "after-market" tubular device that attaches to the top of firearms that officers look through to aim the weapon. Most optical sights present crosshairs as the aim point, but some project electronic images inside the tube (usually a red dot) as the aim point.

Overpenetration: When a bullet travels all the way through its intended target, which raises the possibility that it could strike an unintended object or person.

Point: The lead officer in a tactical formation.

Probation: The first year to eighteen months that a new police officer is on the job.

Put out, Putting it out: Broadcasting a message over the police radio. As in, "I put out that we just capped somebody."

Q-beam: A high-intensity spotlight.

RA unit: Short for rescue ambulance.

Rabbiting: To flee from the police.

Rape kit: A packet of materials for collecting physical evidence in sexual-assault investigations.

React team: A small group of SWAT officers who stand by in the immediate vicinity of a barricaded suspect and in hostage incidents in order to take immediate action if the situation calls for it.

Red dot: The electronic image inside some optical aiming devices that indicates the aim point.

Red-handle training: Training with replica firearms that are made of a
solid red hard-rubber composite material.

Remington 1100: A type of 12-gauge shotgun manufactured by the
Remington corporation.

Riding the dot: Shooting a weapon multiple times while making sure
that the red dot of one's optical sights is on target before pulling the
trigger each time.

Running code: Driving with the police vehicle's emergency lights and siren
turned on.

Sap pocket: A long, narrow pocket that is sewn into the side of many
police trousers. Originally used to hold a sap, a lead-filled leather
striking implement. Now used primarily to hold police flashlights.

Shooting team: A group of detectives in some big law enforcement agencies whose primary job is to investigate officer-involved shootings.

Sighted in for room distance: Setting the sights on one's gun so that the
aim point corresponds to where a fired bullet will strike when the
shooter and suspect are approximately twelve to fifteen feet apart,
the typical length of a room in a standard house. This is how many
SWAT team members set the sights on their submachine guns and
assault rifles because they often confront suspects inside houses at
room distance.

SKS: An assault rifle similar to an AK-47.

Smith: Short for Smith & Wesson.

Smith & Wesson: A gun manufacturer.

Stack: (see entry stick).

Stainless: A type of handgun finish.

Stick: (see entry stick).

Sting ball: A noise flash diversionary device that contains numerous small
rubber balls that are expelled when the device goes off.

Sub-gun: Short for submachine gun. Primarily used in reference to an
MP-5 or similar submachine guns often carried by SWAT officers.

SWAT-cam: A pole-mounted camera system.

Tac vest: Heavy ballistic body armor worn on the outside of one's shirt
(and sometimes underneath one's raid jacket).

Tap, rack, and shoot: A drill designed to clear a malfunction in a semiautomatic handgun in which the operator slams the gun's magazine
into the palm of his or her opposite hand (the tap), pulls the slide of
the gun back (the rack), and then reengages the target (the shoot).

TASER: A handheld electronic stun gun that fires two small darts that are connected by wires to the gun. Used to disable potentially dangerous people by delivering a fifty-thousand-volt shock (with very low amperage) without killing them. TASER is short for Thomas A. Swift Electric Rifle.

Ten-ring: The middle of one's chest. From the fact that the paper targets used in many police firearms qualification courses award ten points for each bullet that strikes the middle portion of the target.

Terminal wound: A wound that causes death.

Tweakerish: Having the appearance of a meth-head, sometimes called a tweaker.

UC: Short for Undercover.

Uwara handle: The short handle on the side-handle batons that many police officers carry.

Walther PPK: A semiautomatic handgun manufactured by the Walther Firearms company.

Watch commander: The police officer in charge of a patrol shift, or watch. Usually a sergeant or higher in rank.

Notes

Introduction

1. Examples of research on officers' reactions following shootings include "Post-Traumatic Stress: Study of Police Officers Involved in Shootings," by John G. Stratton, David Parker, and John R. Snibbe, *Psychological Reports* 55 (1984): 127–131; "Patterns of PTSD Among Police Officers Following Shooting Incidents: A Two-Dimensional Model and Treatment Implications," by Berthold P. R. Gersons, *Journal of Traumatic Stress* 2 (1989): 247–257; and "A Comparative Analysis of the Effects of Post-Shooting Trauma on the Special Agents of the Federal Bureau of Investigation," by John Henry Campbell, unpublished doctoral dissertation (Department of Educational Administration, Michigan State University, 1992).

2. Examples of the research on officers' reactions during shootings include *Deadly Force Encounters: What Cops Need to Know to Mentally and Physically Prepare for and Survive a Gunfight,* by Alexis Artwohl and Loren W. Christensen (Boulder, Colo.: Paladin Press, 1997); and "A Comparative Analysis of the Effects of Post-Shooting Trauma on the Special Agents of the Federal Bureau of Investigation," by John Henry Campbell, unpublished doctoral dissertation (Department of Educational Administration, Michigan State University, 1992).

    It should be noted here that police officers who are involved in shootings are not alone when it comes to experiencing unusual reactions during and after stressful events. Research has established that people involved in a wide variety of traumatic events—including combat, criminal victimization, and mass disasters—can experience the sorts of things that cops deal with during and after shootings. For a good overview of the research on how humans react to traumatic incidents, see *Stress and Trauma,* by Patricia A. Resick (Philadelphia: Taylor and Francis, 2001).

3. Readers interested in learning more about the research project can do so by reading the final report that I submitted to the Department of Justice. This report can be accessed on the Internet via a link at www.killzonevoices.com.

4. The basis for the psychological claim that humans are naturally both drawn to and repulsed by violence lies in Freud's work on Eros and Thanatos. See, for example, *Civilisation, War, and Death,* by Sigmund Freud, edited by John Rickman (London: Hogarth Press, 1968; originally published 1939). A more recent treatment of this line of thinking can be found in *On Killing: The Psychological Cost of Killing in War and Society,* by Dave Grossman (Boston: Little, Brown, 1995).

5. For a general discussion of how the tension between order and liberty is manifest in the American criminal justice system, see *The Limits of the Criminal Sanction,* by Herbert Packer (Stanford, Calif.: Stanford University Press, 1968). Discussions of the issue where the police in particular are concerned can be found in *The Functions of the Police in Modern Society,* by Egon Bittner (Rockville, Md.: National Institute of Mental Health, 1970); and *Justice Without Trial: Law Enforcement in a Democratic Society,* 3rd ed., by Jerome Skolnick (Old Tappan, N.J.: Macmillan, 1994).

6. A brief history of the riots in the early and mid-1960s can be found in the official report of the federal commission convened to investigate them— commonly called the Kerner Commission (after its chair, Otto Kerner, then governor of Illinois)—*The Kerner Commission Report of the National Advisory Commission on Civil Disorders* (New York: Bantam Books, 1968).

7. A succinct discussion of the historical tension between blacks and the police can be found in "The Evolving Strategy of Police: A Minority View," in *Perspectives on Policing,* no. 13, by Hubert Williams and Patrick V. Murphy (Washington, D.C.: U.S. Department of Justice and Kennedy School of Government, Harvard University, 1990). For a somewhat longer discussion of black-police tensions regarding the use of force in particular, see "The Color of Law and the Issue of Color: Race and the Abuse of Police Power," by Hubert G. Locke, in William A. Geller and Hans Toch (eds.) *Police Violence: Understanding and Controlling Police Abuse of Force* (New Haven, Conn.: Yale University Press, 1996).

8. On black involvement in police shootings, see, for example, *Policing and Homicide, 1976–1998: Justifiable Homicide by Police, Police Officers Murdered by Felons,* by Jody M. Brown and Patrick A. Langdon (U.S. Department of Justice, Bureau of Justice Statistics, NCJ 180987, 2001); *A Balance of Forces,* by Kenneth J. Matulia (Gaithersberg, Md.: International Association of Chiefs of Police, 1982); and *Deadly Force: What We Know,* by William A. Geller and Michael S. Scott (Washington, D.C.: Police Executive Research Forum, 1992).

9. On differential black involvement in crime, including as victims, see, for example, *When Work Disappears: The World of the New Urban Poor,* by

William Julius Wilson (New York: Knopf, 1996) and *The Color of Justice: Race, Ethnicity, and Crime in America* (3rd ed.), by Samuel Walker, Cassia Sphon, and Miriam DeLone (Belmont, Calif.: Wadsworth/Thomson Learning, 2004).

On racial disparities in police shootings being comparable to disparities in serious crime, see *Police Use of Deadly Force,* by Catherine H. Milton, Jeanne W. Halleck, James Lardner, and Gary L. Albrecht (Washington, D.C.: Police Foundation, 1977); *Use of Deadly Force by Police Officers: Final Report,* by Arnold Binder, Peter Scharf, and Raymond Galvin (Washington, D.C.: National Institute of Justice, 1982); "Race and Extreme Police-Citizen Violence," by James J. Fyfe, in R. L. McNeely and Carl E. Pope (eds.) *Race, Crime, and Criminal Justice* (Thousand Oaks, Calif.: Sage, 1981); and *Deadly Force: What We Know,* by William A. Geller and Michael S. Scott (Washington, D.C.: Police Executive Research Forum, 1992).

10. See "Four Miami Police Officers Convicted of Conspiracy in Shootings," *New York Times,* Apr. 10, 2003, p. A18; and "The Rampart Scandal: LAPD Probe Fades into Oblivion," *Los Angeles Times,* Aug. 11, 2003, main news, part 1, p. 1.

11. The FBI tracks fatal police shootings through a program known as the Supplemental Homicide Reports (SHR), but the SHR records of fatal shootings are incomplete because police departments are not required to report to the FBI when their officers kill someone. Nobody keeps any sort of official national count of nonfatal shootings. See *Policing and Homicide: 1976–1998: Justifiable Homicide by Police, Police Officers Murdered by Felons,* by Jody M. Brown and Patrick A. Langdon (U.S. Department of Justice, Bureau of Justice Statistics, NCJ 180987, 2001) for an overview of the SHR program as it relates to police shootings. See "Too Many Missing Cases: Holes in Our Knowledge About Police Use of Force," by James J. Fyfe, *Justice Research and Policy* 4 (2002): 87–102, for a critique of the SHR program and a call for better data collection on police shootings.

12. The estimate of a thousand fatal shootings can be found in "Police Use of Deadly Force: Research and Reform," by James J. Fyfe, *Justice Quarterly* 5 (1988): 165–205. The lower estimate comes from *Crime File Deadly Force: A Study Guide,* by William A. Geller (Washington, D.C.: National Institute of Justice, U.S. Department of Justice, 1986).

13. The data on NYPD shootings can be found on p. 94 of "Too Many Missing Cases: Holes in Our Knowledge About Police Use of Force," by James J. Fyfe, *Justice Research and Policy* 4 (2002): 87–102.

14. Information on attacks on police officers comes from "Law Enforcement Officers Killed and Assaulted," 2000, which is developed from data collected

by the FBI as part of their Uniform Crime Reports Program. This publication can be located by clicking on the Library and Reference section of the FBI's Web page at www.fbi.gov.

Chapter One

1. The argument that humans have an innate aversion to killing their fellows has been most prominently made in recent years in *On Killing: The Psychological Cost of Killing in War and Society,* by Dave Grossman (Boston: Little, Brown, 1995).

Chapter Two

1. The full citation for the Garner decision is *Tennessee* v. *Garner,* 105 S. Ct. 1694 (1985).
2. A discussion of the effect of Garner on state laws governing the use of deadly force can be found in "Garner Plus Five Years: An Examination of Supreme Court Intervention into Police Discretion and Legislative Prerogatives," by James J. Fyfe and Jeffery T. Walker, *American Journal of Criminal Justice* 14 (1990): 167–188.
3. Discussions of shooting policies, as well as sample and model policies, can be found in *Deadly Force: What We Know,* by William A. Geller and Michael S. Scott (Washington, D.C.: Police Executive Research Forum, 1992).

Chapter Three

1. Discussions of the limitations of law and policy to direct police use of their firearms, the discretionary nature of police firearms usage, and how officers' personal shooting policies are often more restrictive than law and policy can be found in *Deadly Force: What We Know,* by William A. Geller and Michael S. Scott (Washington, D.C.: Police Executive Research Forum, 1992); and *The Badge and the Bullet,* by Peter Scharf and Arnold Binder (New York: Praeger, 1983).
2. The federal study that documented police restraint is *Use of Deadly Force by Police Officers: Final Report,* by Arnold Binder, Peter Scharf, and Raymond Galvin (Washington, D.C.: National Institute of Justice, 1982). The findings of this study are also reported in *The Badge and the Bullet,* by Peter Scharf and Arnold Binder (New York: Praeger, 1983).
3. A discussion of the advent and development of SWAT teams can be found in *The Management of Police Specialized Tactical Units,* by Tomas C. Mijares, Ronald M. McCarthy, and David B. Perkins (Springfield, Ill.: Thomas, 2000).

Chapter Four

1. The study reporting that 10 percent of police shootings involve troubled individuals seeking to end their own lives is "Suicide by Cop," by H. Range Hutson and others, *Annals of Emergency Medicine* 32, no. 6 (1998): 665–669. This article also includes a general discussion of the suicide-by-cop phenomenon. A broader discussion of the phenomenon can be found in "Suicidal Intent in Victim-Precipitated Homicide: Insights from the Study of Suicide-by-Cop," by David A. Klinger, *Homicide Studies* 5, no. 3 (2001): 206–226.
2. Information on distances between officers and suspects, the number of rounds fired per shooting, and the speed at which officers discharge their weapons can be found in *Deadly Force: What We Know,* by William A. Geller and Michael S. Scott (Washington, D.C.: Police Executive Research Forum, 1992).
3. The count of officers killed with their own guns comes from the FBI's "Law Enforcement Officers Killed and Assaulted," 2000, which can be found under the Library and Reference section of the FBI Web page at www.fbi.gov.
4. The assertion that officers may use force that appears to be necessary even when no actual threat exists is based on the *objective reasonableness standard* as articulated by the U.S. Supreme Court in *Graham* v. *Connor,* 490 U.S. 386 (1989). See also *The Badge and the Bullet,* by Peter Scharf and Arnold Binder (New York: Praeger, 1983); and *Deadly Force: What We Know,* by William A. Geller and Michael S. Scott (Washington, D.C.: Police Executive Research Forum, 1992).

Chapter Five

1. General information about the investigations into police shootings, the inquiries that follow, and their outcomes can be found in *Deadly Force: What We Know,* by William A. Geller and Michael S. Scott (Washington, D.C.: Police Executive Research Forum, 1992). A case study of the investigation process in one jurisdiction can be found in *Police Shootings and the Prosecutor in Los Angeles County: An Evaluation of Operation Rollout,* by Craig D. Uchida, Lawrence Sherman, and James J. Fyfe (Washington, D.C.: Police Foundation, 1981).
2. A discussion of civil litigation against the police can be found in *Critical Issues in Police Civil Liability,* by Victor E. Kappeler (Prospect Heights, Ill.: Waveland Press, 1993).
3. Discussions of police officers' tendency to be insular and suspicious of both those outside law enforcement and their superiors in the department can

be found in *Violence and the Police,* by William Westley (Cambridge, Mass.: MIT Press, 1970); *Working the Street: Police Discretion and the Dilemmas of Reform,* by Michael Brown (New York: Russell Sage Foundation, 1981); and *Justice Without Trial: Law Enforcement in a Democratic Society,* 3rd ed., by Jerome Skolnick (Old Tappan, N.J.: Macmillan, 1994).

4. Perhaps the most influential treatise on dreams is *The Interpretation of Dreams,* by Sigmund Freud, authorized translation of 3rd ed., with introduction by A. A. Brill (Old Tappan, N.J.: Macmillan, 1913). For a more recent discussion of nightmares, see, for example, *The Nightmare: The Psychology and Biology of Terrifying Dreams,* by Ernest Hartman (New York: Basic Books, 1984).

About the Author

David A. Klinger is associate professor of criminology and criminal justice at the University of Missouri-St. Louis. He holds a master's degree in justice from American University in Washington, D.C., and a doctorate in sociology from the University of Washington in Seattle. Prior to pursuing his graduate degrees, Klinger worked for three and a half years as a patrol officer for the Los Angeles and Redmond (Washington) Police Departments. He has held research positions at the Police Foundation in Washington, D.C.; the University of Washington, Seattle; the Washington State's Attorney's Office; and the Seattle Police Department.

In 1997, Klinger was the recipient of the American Society of Criminology's inaugural Ruth Cavan Young Scholar Award for outstanding early-career contributions to the discipline of criminology. He has recently completed service as a member of the National Academy of Sciences Committee on Police Policy and Practices and has written more than twenty scholarly articles, book chapters, and encyclopedia entries that address topics such as arrest practices, the use of force, how features of communities affect the actions of patrol officers, and terrorism. He currently serves on the Police Foundation's Research Advisory Board and on the Training Advisory Committee of the Texas Tactical Police Officers Association (TTPOA).